Practicing the Promise

Other titles by Bruce Taylor

The Word in the Wind
No Business as Usual
Looking Up at Love
Life Woven into God
Between Advents
Christ's New Address
Love Walks on Wounded Feet
God at Work
What Happens Next?
Truth Be Told

Practicing the Promise

More Sermons for the Lectionary,
Year C, Advent through Eastertide

BRUCE L. TAYLOR

WIPF & STOCK · Eugene, Oregon

PRACTICING THE PROMISE
More Sermons for the Lectionary, Year C, Advent through Eastertide

Copyright © 2024 Bruce L. Taylor. All rights reserved. Except for brief quotations in critical publications or reviews, no part of this book may be reproduced in any manner without prior written permission from the publisher. Write: Permissions, Wipf and Stock Publishers, 199 W. 8th Ave., Suite 3, Eugene, OR 97401.

Wipf & Stock
An Imprint of Wipf and Stock Publishers
199 W. 8th Ave., Suite 3
Eugene, OR 97401

www.wipfandstock.com

PAPERBACK ISBN: 979-8-3852-0745-9
HARDCOVER ISBN: 979-8-3852-0746-6
EBOOK ISBN: 979-8-3852-0747-3

VERSION NUMBER 022624

Unless otherwise noted, scripture quotations are from the Common Bible: New Revised Standard Version Bible, copyright © 1989 National Council of the Churches of Christ in the United States of America. Used by permission. All rights reserved worldwide. Emphasis added.

Scripture quotations marked (RSV) are from the Revised Standard Version of the Bible, copyright © 1946, 1952, and 1971 National Council of the Churches of Christ in the United States of America. Used by permission. All rights reserved. Emphasis added.

In memory of
Duncan and Eleanor Spining

Contents

Introduction   xiii

FIRST SUNDAY OF ADVENT
Spanish Springs Presbyterian Church, Sparks, Nevada—November 30, 2003
Jeremiah 33:14–16, 1 Thessalonians 3:9–13, Luke 21:25–36
"Hope Alongside the Ruins"   1

SECOND SUNDAY OF ADVENT
Spanish Springs Presbyterian Church, Sparks, Nevada—December 10, 2006
Malachi 3:1–4, Philippians 1:3–11, Luke 3:1–6
"God's Construction Zone"   6

THIRD SUNDAY OF ADVENT
First Presbyterian Church, Dodge City, Kansas—December 14, 1997
Zephaniah 3:14–20, Philippians 4:4–7, Luke 3:7–18
"The Good News Crisis"   11

FOURTH SUNDAY OF ADVENT
Spanish Springs Presbyterian Church, Sparks, Nevada—December 24, 2006
Micah 5:2–5a, Hebrews 10:5–10, Luke 1:39–55
"He Shall Be Our Peace"   17

CHRISTMAS EVE
Spanish Springs Presbyterian Church, Sparks, Nevada—December 24, 2009
Isaiah 9:2–7, Titus 2:11–14, Luke 2:1–20
"Looking for the Manger"   22

CHRISTMAS EVE (MIDNIGHT)
Spanish Springs Presbyterian Church, Sparks, Nevada—December 24, 2003
Isaiah 9:2–7, Titus 2:11–14, Luke 2:1–20
"No Longer a Wish"   27

CHRISTMAS DAY
Isaiah 52:7–10, Hebrews 1:1–4, John 1:1–14
"Eyes of Faith"   32

FIRST SUNDAY AFTER CHRISTMAS DAY
First Presbyterian Church, Dodge City, Kansas—December 28, 1997
1 Samuel 2:18–20, 26, Colossians 3:12–17, Luke 2:41–52
"Dedicated to God" 36

SECOND SUNDAY AFTER CHRISTMAS DAY
First Presbyterian Church, Dodge City, Kansas—January 5, 1992
Jeremiah 31:7–14, Ephesians 1:3–14, John 1:1–18
"Does the Light Still Shine?" 41

EPIPHANY OF THE LORD
Isaiah 60:1–6, Ephesians 3:1–12, Matthew 2:1–12
"Two-Way Evangelism" 46

BAPTISM OF THE LORD
Spanish Springs Presbyterian Church, Sparks, Nevada—January 10, 2010
Isaiah 43:1–7, Acts 8:14–17, Luke 3:15–17, 21–22
"What Do You Expect?" 52

SECOND SUNDAY IN ORDINARY TIME
First Presbyterian Church, Ponca City, Oklahoma—January 20, 2013
Isaiah 62:1–5, 1 Corinthians 12:1–11, John 2:1–11
"Not Just Another Wedding" 57

THIRD SUNDAY IN ORDINARY TIME
First Presbyterian Church, Dodge City, Kansas—January 18, 1998
Nehemiah 8:1–3, 5–6, 8–10, 1 Corinthians 12:12–31a, Luke 4:14–21
"Job Description" 62

FOURTH SUNDAY IN ORDINARY TIME
Spanish Springs Presbyterian Church, Sparks, Nevada—January 31, 2010
Jeremiah 1:4–10, 1 Corinthians 13:1–13, Luke 4:21–30
"Pride *Is* a Deadly Sin" 67

FIFTH SUNDAY IN ORDINARY TIME
Spanish Springs Presbyterian Church, Sparks, Nevada—February 8, 2004
Isaiah 6:1–8, 1 Corinthians 15:1–11, Luke 5:1–11
"Truth in Advertising" 72

SIXTH SUNDAY IN ORDINARY TIME
First Presbyterian Church, Dodge City, Kansas—February 15, 1998
Jeremiah 17:5–10, 1 Corinthians 15:12–20, Luke 6:17–26
"The Guarantee" 77

SEVENTH SUNDAY IN ORDINARY TIME
First Presbyterian Church, Dodge City, Kansas—February 23, 1992
Genesis 45:3–11, 15, 1 Corinthians 15:35–38, 42–50, Luke 6:27–38
"Picture the Spirit"   82

EIGHTH SUNDAY IN ORDINARY TIME
Isaiah 55:10–13, 1 Corinthians 15:51–58, Luke 6:39–49
"The Resurrection Hope"   87

TRANSFIGURATION OF THE LORD
Spanish Springs Presbyterian Church, Sparks, Nevada—February 14, 2010
Exodus 34:29–35, 2 Corinthians 3:12—4:2, Luke 9:28–43
"The Greatness of God"   92

ASH WEDNESDAY
Spanish Springs Presbyterian Church, Sparks, Nevada—February 21, 2007
Joel 2:1–2, 12–17, 2 Corinthians 5:20b—6:10, Matthew 6:1–6, 16–21
"Perhaps God Will Relent"   97

FIRST SUNDAY IN LENT
Spanish Springs Presbyterian Church, Sparks, Nevada—February 21, 2010
Deuteronomy 26:1–11, Romans 10:8b–13, Luke 4:1–13
"Jesus Is Lord"   102

SECOND SUNDAY IN LENT
Grace Episcopal Church, Ponca City, Oklahoma—February 21, 2016
Genesis 15:1–12, 17–18, Philippians 3:17—4:1, Luke 13:31–35
"Practicing the Promise"   107

THIRD SUNDAY IN LENT
Spanish Springs Presbyterian Church, Sparks, Nevada—March 7, 2010
Isaiah 55:1–9, 1 Corinthians 10:1–13, Luke 13:1–9
"Invitation to Salvation"   112

FOURTH SUNDAY IN LENT
First Presbyterian Church, Dodge City, Kansas—March 22, 1998
Joshua 5:9–12, 2 Corinthians 5:16–21, Luke 15:1–3, 11–32
"Learning to Say 'Brother'"   117

FIFTH SUNDAY IN LENT
Spanish Springs Presbyterian Church, Sparks, Nevada—March 28, 2004
Isaiah 43:16–21, Philippians 3:4b–14, John 12:1–8
"Through the Eyes of Faith"   122

PALM/PASSION SUNDAY
Spanish Springs Presbyterian Church, Sparks, Nevada—March 28, 2010
Isaiah 50:4–9a, Philippians 2:5–11, Luke 19:28–40
"What Was Jesus Thinking?" 127

MAUNDY THURSDAY
Spanish Springs Presbyterian Church, Sparks, Nevada—April 8, 2004
Exodus 12:1–4, 11–14, 1 Corinthians 11:23–26, John 13:1–17, 31b–35
"The Center of Life" 132

GOOD FRIDAY
Spanish Springs Presbyterian Church, Sparks, Nevada—April 2, 2010
Isaiah 52:13—53:12, Hebrews 10:16–25, John 18:1—19:42
"One Particular Cross" 137

THE RESURRECTION OF THE LORD
Spanish Springs Presbyterian Church, Sparks, Nevada—April 8, 2007
Acts 10:34–43, 1 Corinthians 15:19–26, Luke 24:1–12
"The Great Easter Adventure" 141

SECOND SUNDAY OF EASTER
First Presbyterian Church, Dodge City, Kansas—April 23, 1995
Acts 5:27–32, Revelation 1:4–8, John 20:19–31
"Closing Argument" 146

THIRD SUNDAY OF EASTER
Spanish Springs Presbyterian Church, Sparks, Nevada—April 25, 2004
Acts 9:1–20, Revelation 5:11–14, John 21:1–19
"Godparents All" 151

FOURTH SUNDAY OF EASTER
Spanish Springs Presbyterian Church, Sparks, Nevada—April 25, 2010
Acts 9:36–43, Revelation 7:9–17, John 10:22–30
"The Subversive Gospel" 157

FIFTH SUNDAY OF EASTER
First Presbyterian Church, Dodge City, Kansas—May 17, 1992
Acts 14:8–18, Revelation 21:1–6, John 13:31–35
"The Miracle People" 162

SIXTH SUNDAY OF EASTER
Spanish Springs Presbyterian Church, Sparks, Nevada—May 20, 2001
Acts 15:1–2, 22–29, Revelation 21:10, 22–27, John 14:23–29
"Open Gates for the Spirit"   167

ASCENSION OF THE LORD
Spanish Springs Presbyterian Church, Sparks, Nevada—May 20, 2004
Acts 1:1–11, Ephesians 1:15–23, Luke 24:46–53
"Ours Is the Power"   173

SEVENTH SUNDAY OF EASTER
Spanish Springs Presbyterian Church, Sparks, Nevada—May 20, 2007
Acts 16:16–34, Revelation 22:12–14, 16–17, 20–21, John 17:20–26
"'As We Are One'"   178

Appendix   183

CHRISTMAS EVE (EARLY)
Grace Presbyterian Church, Plano, Texas—December 24, 1988
Isaiah 9:2–7, Titus 2:11–14, Luke 2:1–20
"Mary's Donkey"   185

SPARKS HIGH SCHOOLS BACCALAUREATE
John Ascuaga's Nugget, Sparks, Nevada—May 20, 2012
Ezekiel 37:1–14, Hebrews 11:1–3   190

WEEK OF PRAYER FOR CHRISTIAN UNITY
Spanish Springs Presbyterian Church, Sparks, Nevada—January 23, 2004
Isaiah 57:19–21; 60:17–22, Ephesians 2:13–18, John 14:23–31
"The Peace of Christ"   195

WEEK OF PRAYER FOR CHRISTIAN UNITY
Spanish Springs Presbyterian Church, Sparks, Nevada—January 22, 2010
Isaiah 61:1–4, Acts 10:34–48a, Luke 24:44–49a
"To What Do We Witness?"   200

FIFTH SUNDAY IN ORDINARY TIME
Spanish Springs Presbyterian Church, Sparks, Nevada—February 4, 2001
Isaiah 6:1–8, 1 Corinthians 15:1–11, Luke 5:1–11
"Salvation Doesn't End with Me"   205

List of Sources Cited   211

Introduction

This volume takes its title from one of the sermons contained herein, but which expresses a theme that is shared by many of the sets of scripture readings for Advent through Eastertide of Year C of the Common Lectionary (Revised)—to live *in* and live *into* the promises of God. Jesus' proclamation of the kingdom was a summons to place confidence in, and give witness by one's daily living to, the reality and reliability of a realm that exists beyond today's often ungodly headlines, and to embrace a heavenly hope with our very breath and being. Believers' failure to abide in the brightness of God's promises and act upon them might well be the chief obstacle to the full redemption of creation. It is not that our own efforts determine whether God's will shall be done, but throughout the history of salvation, the Bible testifies, God has called upon human agents to live and work in trust that God's promises are true. Surely, beyond any question of human instrumentality, faith in God must mean that believers *believe*, rather than thinking and behaving in reliance upon some vision that is contrary to the gospel.

The Gospel of Luke, which is the featured source for the story of Jesus' life and ministry, death, and resurrection in Year C of the lectionary, is a testimony to the reliability of God's promises. Over the centuries, most scholars, in concert with the testimony of the patristic writers Irenaeus and Tertullian, have been of the opinion that the anonymous book was written by Luke, the apostolic colleague of Paul who is mentioned, in passing, in three Pauline epistles, at least one of which was penned or dictated by Paul himself. The Gospel's particular interest in ministry to and inclusion of Gentiles suggests the likelihood of a Gentile author, and the book of Acts, styled as a sequel to the story told in the Gospel and ostensibly addressed to an influential Gentile reader, relating the story of Christianity's spread into the Gentile world and filled with parallels to the Gospel of Luke, all render plausible a close association between its author and the great apostle to the Gentiles. "Nothing in the writing [viz., the book of Acts, purportedly written by the same hand as the Gospel of Luke] prohibits composition by a companion of Paul who was eyewitness to some events he narrates."[1] Some scholars point to discrepancies between events spoken of in Paul's letters

---

1. Johnson, *Luke*, 2. For a brief expression of the contrary view, see Schweizer, *Luke*, 7.

and various details chronicled in the book of Acts as arguments against the author of Luke-Acts as being the "Luke" referenced in Colossians, Second Timothy, and Philemon. But there are also variances between the reports of events at the end of the Gospel of Luke and the beginning of the book of Acts, and yet very few scholars regard *those* differences as evidence against the common consensus that the two books were written by the same author. I am unpersuaded that Irenaeus and Tertullian were credulous, or that the perceived discrepancies between Acts and the epistles disqualify the Gospel as having been written by the "Luke" mentioned by Paul, while I quickly admit that the references to medical matters in the Gospel hardly require the conclusion that the book was written by a "beloved physician" (Col 4:14).

As I worked at compiling this collection, however, I frequently pondered the contrast between the Gospel and the writings of Paul. The Gospel of Luke is well known for its lengthy birth narrative, its many engaging parables, and, like the other canonical Gospels, its obvious interest in Jesus' ministry of healing and teaching and forgiveness carried out for and among specific individuals at specific times and in specific places as well as the details of Jesus' arrest, crucifixion, and (in Matthew and John, anyway) the events in the days immediately following discovery of the empty tomb. Paul's letters make no reference to Jesus' birth or the events of Jesus' earthly ministry or instances of his teachings, either in sermon, discourse, or parable, nor to his healings or exorcisms or restoration of the dead. The only event of Jesus' incarnated life that receives Paul's epistolary attention, and laser-focused at that, is the crucifixion. Paul's testimony that he preached only Christ "and him crucified" (1 Cor 2:2), at least among the Corinthians, seems a startling contrast with the abundant witness of Luke's Gospel, which provides such a treasure trove of seemingly vital words and deeds of the pre-crucifixion Jesus. Given their putative close association, and the resultant likelihood that Paul would have been the source of much of what the evangelist knew about Jesus, how do we account for the absence of biographical material in the one and the rich detail of origins and ministry in the other? Granted the differences between the two literary genres, and the decades that passed between the writing of the epistles and the writing of the Gospel, shouldn't we nevertheless expect clear evidence of influence between the epistles and the Gospel written, respectively, by teacher and pupil, tutor and protégé?

In forty years of sermon preparation, I have never come across a scholarly investigation or exposition of a biblio-theological relationship between the Gospel of Luke and the canonical writings of Paul. Yet, if the writer of the Gospel was indeed the close associate of the great apostle, the one would surely have been strongly influenced by the other in his understanding of

Introduction

the Christian faith. Perhaps Luke learned about Christ first and primarily from Paul, and, thus, presumably much of what we read in the Gospel was known to Paul. If it were all so important to Luke, why is there no clear evidence of Jesus' specific teachings and ministry in the epistles of Paul? The traditional conjecture that the author of the Gospel is the "Luke" mentioned in Colossians, Second Timothy, and Philemon is reported in virtually every commentary on Luke, but other than the evangelist's "Gentile-ness," the historical observation receives little further discussion. We are left with a bit of biblical trivia, unaccompanied by theological elaboration. If the author of the Gospel was indeed an associate of Paul, where is the textual nexus that would demonstrate conclusively that the apostle and the evangelist were inspired by and operating on a common fund of information convincing both of them that the crucified one was the Christ, the same incarnate Son of God who taught, healed, and forgave with God's own authority?

Perhaps Paul distilled all of the story eventually told by Luke into one of the most famous and frequently quoted passages in scripture, the thirteenth chapter of that same letter to the Corinthian believers in which the apostle reminded Christians acting so contrary to their namesake that he "did not come proclaiming the mystery of God to you in lofty words or wisdom. For I decided to know nothing among you except Jesus Christ, and him crucified" (2:1b-2). Especially verses 4-7 of First Corinthians chapter 13,

> Love is patient; love is kind; love is not envious or boastful or arrogant or rude. It does not insist on its own way; it is not irritable or resentful; it does not rejoice in wrongdoing, but rejoices in the truth. It bears all things, believes all things, hopes all things, endures all things,

which with the rest of the chapter comprises the epistle reading for the fourth Sunday in Ordinary Time and is paired in the lectionary with the hostile response to Jesus' announcement of his messianic mission at the synagogue in Nazareth, express Paul's reflection on everything that he knew about the earthly ways and wonders of the Christ who, as Luke's Gospel testifies, was born in a cattle stall and fed thousands of hungry people and forgave a notoriously sinful woman and calmed a raging storm and brought back from the dead a desperate man's daughter and stood submissively before a murderous tyrant. Do not all these details revealed in the evangelist's beloved Gospel illustrate perfectly Paul's definition of love? And Paul promises that *our* doing all these things is the *practice* of love—the love that demonstrates faith in Jesus Christ and demonstrates the presence of the kingdom of God.

First Sunday of Advent

Spanish Springs Presbyterian Church, Sparks, Nevada

November 30, 2003

Jeremiah 33:14–16
1 Thessalonians 3:9–13
Luke 21:25–36

"Hope Alongside the Ruins"

In many ways, the Bible is not an easy book to read. By faith, we perceive that its words are timeless and its truth is vital for modern day. But, clearly, it was written in an ancient time, and it refers to events and circumstances of which our knowledge is imperfect, at best. It tells its story with reference to the prevailing worldview and common understandings of science and nature that existed at the time, and yet if we treat it as a science textbook or an almanac of historical facts, we risk trivializing its meaning and devaluing God's gift of intellect. It is sometimes repetitious and even tedious in detail, and yet to ignore its nuances is often to distort its message. And the message itself is sometimes harsh, as when it foretells times of destruction and disaster, which seems incongruous alongside its promises of peace and prosperity.

Something else that makes the Bible difficult to read is the fact that some of it is made up of letters, only one half of an exchange of correspondence and information that frequently leaves us, and even the best biblical scholars, scratching our heads and, frankly, guessing at what it was that was being talked about. So, for instance, in what is probably the earliest letter preserved in the New Testament, First Thessalonians, Paul writes to one of the first congregations that he established in Greece, and then had to leave prematurely because of persecution. "You yourselves know, brothers and sisters, that our coming to you was not in vain, but though we had already suffered and been shamefully mistreated at Philippi, as you know, we had courage in our God to declare to you the gospel of God in spite of great opposition" (1 Thess 2:1–2)—opposition from both Greeks and Jews living in Thessalonica. The occasion of Paul's letter, First Thessalonians, seems to be the report from his associate Timothy, who had just returned from a visit to the city, that the congregation was demonstrating its faith and love, but Paul said that he longed to travel to Thessalonica himself, "that we may see you face to face and restore whatever is lacking in your faith" (3:10). Timothy's report, Paul just said, was good news about their love and faith. But Timothy seems to have reported also that something was not right, not mature, not complete—something that Paul thought he could provide by way of personal witness or face-to-face instruction. But then he dropped the subject, not referring to it again (explicitly, at least), and we are left to wonder what it was that the Thessalonian Christians still needed to work on.

Some scholars have pointed out that Timothy brought Paul a good report of the Thessalonians' faith and love, but that faith and love are only two parts of Paul's customary triad of "faith, *hope*, and love." The Thessalonian church had continued to undergo severe persecution. Paul encouraged the Thessalonian Christians to continue standing firm in their faith. But was the constant threat of persecution, the continuing experience of opposition, wearing them down, causing them to lose hope that God would protect their bodies and safeguard their souls? "May [the Lord] so strengthen your hearts in holiness," Paul prayed, "that you may be blameless before our God and Father at the coming of our Lord Jesus with all his saints" (3:13).

We wish we knew what was going on. We wish we understood what Paul meant about supplying the Thessalonian Christians with whatever they were lacking. Our curiosity is at least partly practical—might *we* be missing the same thing, too? And if, as many scholars suggest, what was *imperfect* about their Christian belief was their lack of hope in the *future*—that is, lack of hope in what *God* was going to *do* in the future—we might have real sympathy for people who wondered if and when their persecution would cease, if and when the good news would defeat their illnesses and heal their broken homes and alleviate their fear of arrest and imprisonment and execution, and banish the universal menace of death, whatever its cause. For believers in Jesus Christ were still getting sick; their faith was putting strains on marriages to non-Christian spouses, strains on relations with non-Christian employers, strains on long-time friendships, strains on personal finances, probably, as their allegiance to Christ was causing many of them to be routed out and abused by mobs, and some among their number were dying before Christ's promised return, and that raised the question of whether they and their loved ones would be included in the blessings of the kingdom of heaven. Their faith was strong—their loyalty to Jesus Christ, even through their persecutions, had become known well beyond their own congregation, throughout the rest of Macedonia and even far down south in Achaia, where Corinth was located. The Thessalonians were not spiritual weaklings by any means. But was what was happening to them and around them causing them to despair?

When you're in the midst of catastrophe, when it seems like Armageddon has broken out on the landscape of your life and turned it into a hellish nightmare, all may seem like a lost cause. Hope may seem silly, may even seem like being disloyal to your allegiances and your affections. I was haunted this week, moved to tears, by the tape recording of the 911 telephone call of a man in the Virginia suburbs of Washington whose wife had just been shot outside a Home Depot store, allegedly one of the victims of the Washington-area snipers. "My wife," he sobbed. "She's shot in the head." The man's world had just been shattered, his dreams, his expectations, his hope. Insanity and a rifle had just plunged him into a personal chaos quite as deep as the cosmic chaos from which, Genesis testifies, God created the world and called it good. For the rest of us, even for people thousands of miles away from the carnage, we may wonder, when we reflect on such incidents, whether a corner of God's good creation has come unsnapped to reveal the boiling cauldron of chaos that God once tamed but not completely, chaos that still threatens and has the power to undo the world. Already, September 11, 2001, is beginning to fit into historical perspective just like December 7, 1941, did. But, at the time, the families of the victims, and the whole nation, thought perhaps the world was coming to an end. On both occasions, terrorists came out of the skies like falling sun and moon and stars, and we *were* terrified.

But the fact that the earth continues to spin and the lives of most of us continue as normal until the next disaster, personal or national, disrupts our routine and threatens our hopes, renders *other* parts of the Bible difficult to understand—like the sayings of Jesus about the nearness of the promised kingdom. "Truly I tell you, this generation will not pass away until all things have taken place" (Luke 21:32). Well, the *whole generation* of Jesus' *first* disciples passed away before he returned, at least in the way that was expected. And the first generation of believers in *Thessalonica* was beginning to pass away without Jesus having returned. And, so, their hope very likely was being tested, if not shaken, by the appearance of things only getting *worse*, not *better*; of suffering *increasing*, not *abating*; of *death* still the winner, not *life*.

Jesus told his disciples to be alert and observant—to read through the present distress the fact that God's promised redemption was one day closer, whatever the date of its arrival might be. He did not hand out platitudes on a bumper sticker, recited nothing clever or cutesy, nothing insulting or ridiculing. He didn't tell people that their ailments were insignificant or that their worries were unimportant. He took them seriously, and Paul, after him, took seriously the severe and bewildering afflictions of the Thessalonian Christians. It *does* help to know that Luke was quoting Jesus fifty years or so *after* Jesus had said, "Now when these things begin to take place, stand up and raise your heads, because your redemption is drawing near.... Truly I tell you, this generation will not pass away until all things have taken place" (21:28, 32). By the time Luke wrote it down, obviously, most of Jesus' *original* audience were no longer living. Believers *had* died. The first generation of Christians *was* passing away.

But the *church* was alive. The *church* was *growing*. The *church* was *enduring*. The *church* was *witnessing* that the petty kings and emperors with their gruesome jealousies were *no match* for the *risen Christ*—the company of the faithful was outlasting every one of them. The church was penetrating walls and borders even as laws were being passed against it and its martyrs were being thrown to wild beasts and burned as live torches. And a profound new sense of life and all of history as meaningful, not just a sorry span of time between cradle and grave, between a big bang and a cold cinder, was placing each person, each event, on the stage of God's great drama of mercy and redemption. And, so, every natural disaster, every human cruelty, did not augur the *undoing* of God's good creation, but was an indication of the last death throes of a natural chaos and human evil that God decisively triumphed over when he raised Jesus from the tomb, crucified and dead, to glory and life everlasting in the kingdom of heaven, whose advent the world is resisting but cannot halt. War, starvation, disease, cruelty, death—these are the desperate tactics of an old order in nature and in human affairs that will and must pass away before the advancing triumph of God's kingdom of peace and fullness and joy. They are painful. They are wicked. They are designed to shake our confidence and destroy our hope. And the Bible suggests that the worse they get, the closer is the final accomplishment of God's complete victory, which is already assured by the fact that only *God is God*. And scripture bears witness to the living Word of God, who is our guarantee that God's ways are love and harmony and compassion and mercy and peace. *Chaos* will not rule God's creation. *God* will. *Death* will not define our life. *God* will. *Satan* will not write history. *God* will.

"Then Jesus told them a parable: 'Look at the fig tree and all the trees; as soon as they sprout leaves you can see for yourselves and know that summer is already near. So also, when you see these things taking place, you know that the kingdom of God is near'" (21:29–31). In spite of the December 7s and the September 11s, despite the heartbreaks of disease and divorce, despite the losses of jobs and loved ones, there has remained in the world a testimony to hope, a generation that has *not* passed away—the generation, the race, the community of faithful believers whose hope emerges from suffering and affliction more *sure*, whose confidence rises from the rubble of disappointments and trials more *mature*, who daily look forward more eagerly to the fulfillment of the kingdom of God. And that generation that has not passed away is the church of Jesus Christ—the saints who have come before us, we ourselves, and the saints who will come after us—God's planting of hope alongside the ruins of evil's painful but vain attempts to obstruct God's purpose of redemption and to prevent the full and inevitable flowering of God's kingdom.

Long years before Paul wrote to the Thessalonians, a prophet's voice pronounced hope alongside the ruins of destroyed Jerusalem and scattered Israel. "The days are surely coming, says the Lord, when I will fulfill the promise I made to the house of Israel and the house of Judah. In those days and at that time I will cause a righteous Branch to spring up for David; and he shall execute justice and righteousness in the land. In those days Judah will be saved and Jerusalem will live in safety. And this is the name by which it will be called: 'The Lord is our righteousness'" (Jer 33:114–16). And God was faithful to the promise, and sent Jesus the Christ. And to every disaster, natural or of human making, to every disease, to every famine, to every indignity, to every bereavement, the generation of the faithful that is still in the world testifies: "Christ has died. Christ is risen. Christ will come again." Hope alongside the ruins.

Second Sunday of Advent
Spanish Springs Presbyterian Church, Sparks, Nevada
December 10, 2006

Malachi 3:1–4
Philippians 1:3–11
Luke 3:1–6

"God's Construction Zone"

Like many of you, the Taylor family has been contending for about two years now with the inconvenience of construction on Sparks Boulevard. First there was the widening project along the half mile or so on the west side of the Reed High School football stadium and Shadow Mountain Sports Complex. Then there was the widening project along the half mile or so *between* but not all the way *to* Disc Drive and Los Altos Parkway. And now, for the past six months, the one that affects the *Taylors* the most—the one-mile-long widening project between Shadow Lane and Disc Drive. Some days we can turn left out of our subdivision; some days we can't. Some days we've had a four-inch ledge to maneuver; some days we haven't been able to come out onto Sparks Boulevard at all. I have been having a personal test of wills with one of the flaggers whose assigned post is at the intersection of Sparks Boulevard and Whitney Circle. And it was not very many years ago that we went through the same experience on *Vista* Boulevard. That is one of the "benefits" of population growth, of course, and something with which all of us have been faced from time to time and from place to place, and it doesn't seem any good for us to have a better idea of how it could be done.

One of the byproducts of the current widening project has been to make more shallow what used to be a wide curve on Sparks Boulevard as it comes through the Satellite Hills. Some of you may have noticed that there is now a retaining wall, already adorned with graffiti, where power shovels and front-end loaders bit away at the slope, so that when the construction project is completed, the curve will not be as sharp and visibility along the thoroughfare will be better. I rather wish that, for the sake of visibility for cars turning out of our area, the engineers had called for lowering the roadway over the crest of the hill, but nobody consulted me about that. Still, it is a far easier task *we* have going from point A to point B than, say, wagoners had driving teams of horses up the Geiger Grade to Virginia City. But imagine what an improvement it was to have the Geiger Grade over whatever trails existed before *that*. When I started taking Latin in junior high school, I remember a unit in our textbook about the tremendous engineering feats of the ancient Roman roadbuilders, constructing roads up over the Alps, even, that *still* provide the roadbed for highways there today, taking advantage of the shallow grades and gentle curves over which horses and foot soldiers once crossed the mountain passes. But the Roman road builders were also capable of removing hillsides when they had to—I once visited a little town on the Italian seacoast where, two thousand years before, a cliff had been chiseled away to provide a roadway along the water, and carved into the vertical rock face were Roman numerals, marking off the number of feet of rock that had been excavated.

Sometimes, in Nevada, it seems that every developer's dream is expressed in verse 5 of chapter 3 of Luke:

> "'Every valley shall be filled,
>   and every mountain and hill shall be made low,
> and the crooked shall be made straight,
>   and the rough ways made smooth.'" (Luke 3:5)

It was a much more daunting prospect in biblical times—there was no dynamite back then, and the task usually fell to slaves. But the image was clear *enough* for ancient Israelites and the Mediterranean peoples generally, who did not have automobiles and trucks to get them from here to there, but only the power of horses and donkeys and oxen and, of course, their own feet. How blessed it would be to have *any* impediment removed, *any* obstacle, *any* hill that the road had to go *up*, and *any* valley that the road had to go *down*. And people were familiar with the marching from one place to another of generals and their armies—the need to move troops quickly to restore order here and to confront invaders there. That same need to move soldiers and equipment was one of the rationales for launching, in the early days of the Cold War, our own American interstate highway system, officially named the "National System of Interstate and Defense Highways"—the largest construction project in our nation's history, spreading twin ribbons of pavement back and forth from ocean to ocean and border to border to ease the task of getting from here to there.

In each of the Gospels, John, reported by Luke to be an older relative of Jesus, is identified with Isaiah's call to prepare a way for the Lord. John's prophetic ministry of calling for repentance, his liturgical ministry of baptizing those who *were* repentant, was seen by each of the evangelists as fulfilling Isaiah's prophecy about the voice of one crying in the wilderness. And, so, John is commonly interpreted as preparing a way for the ministry of Christ, even baptizing Jesus himself when *he* came to the Jordan. But of course, the message of the one crying out in *Isaiah* was that his *audience* should prepare the way of the Lord by clearing his path, raising the valleys and lowering the mountains and making the way straight and smooth for God's entry into the world so that his salvation might be witnessed by all. John, the evangelists testified, *did* prepare the way of the Lord Jesus Christ, and faithfully so, as John's father, Zechariah, had prophesied when he was filled with the Holy Spirit when John was born:

> "And you, child, will be called the prophet of the Most High;
>   for you will go before the Lord to prepare his ways,
> to give knowledge of salvation to his people
>   by the forgiveness of their sins." (Luke 1:76–77)

But preparing the way for God's salvation is a task for *all* of God's people. So it was, for instance, that the apostle Paul gave thanks for the active involvement of the Christians at Philippi in his ministry of spreading and defending the gospel in the various places he traveled, often encountering opposition and even imprisonment, as he had at Philippi itself. In the case of the Philippians, preparing the way for God's salvation included their prayers for Paul and, apparently, their providing materially for his work in other parts of the Roman Empire, and, undoubtedly, their continuing to evangelize in their own town. In countless ways—prayers, offerings, words of forgiveness, deeds of kindness, acts of courage, demonstrations of hope,—they were daily filling the valleys and lowering the mountains that were obstacles to the gospel of salvation. Ultimately, after generations of such faithful Christian witness in *many* towns and in spite of *much* suffering, Christianity was legalized and found advocates in the highest levels of society.

But the work of making a way for the Lord was a continuing one. Jesus himself said that he came to bring good news to the poor, to proclaim release to the captives, to restore sight to the blind, to bring about the conditions of jubilee. Yet there continued, there *continue*, poverty and hunger and homelessness, and people remained, *remain*, imprisoned behind bars of iron and within walls less obvious. There were and still are people suffering from blindness both physical and intellectual, and whole populations as well as individuals continued and continue to be oppressed, and the burden of debt continued to crush and *still* crushes individuals and societies and keeps them from enjoying the fruits of freedom and the fullness of life that God intends for everyone and *to* which Christ invites *all* people. John explained just what each person can and must do to repent—next Sunday's Gospel reading is very specific about it, as we shall see. The point for us to understand today is that the call to get out the shovels and steamrollers is a call that is issued to *all* believers, and the *benefit* is intended for *all* people. In the phrase "Prepare the way of the Lord," the word "prepare" is an *imperative* and it is *plural*—it is a command to everyone who hears it. In the phrase "make the paths straight," the word "make" is an *imperative* and it is *plural*—it is a command to everyone who hears it. It is not just a command to and about John, preaching and baptizing along the Jordan River twenty centuries ago. It is a command to and about *us*, faithfully taking up the task of filling life's potholes and tamping down life's bumps so that not a single person fails to know and experience the salvation of God—salvation from sin, but also salvation from the cold, salvation from hunger, salvation from illness, salvation from oppression, salvation from imprisonment, salvation from injustice, salvation from indignity, salvation from any condition that makes life less than what God intends it to be for *every* person.

God's construction zone is wherever there are obstacles or impediments to salvation, and wherever salvation is not yet known, not yet experienced, not yet complete. And *we* are God's construction crew—each and every one of us and all of us together are called to be engaged in the process of making a straight way for the Lord's entry into the world so that all flesh—*all* flesh—shall see the salvation of God. Surely that means that the ministry that you and I are to be about is for the ultimate purpose that all people will *experience* the salvation of God *themselves*. That requires *repentance*—changing direction, turning around, going a different way from the one that the person has *been* going. But it also involves, *requires*, removing the barriers, filling in the ruts, providing a manageable grade, not going about being Christ's followers in a way that excludes or disqualifies the very people who are most in need of experiencing the merciful love of God, whether it be class or race or language or nationality or anything else, but giving testimony to the *truth* of God, chipping away at walls of prejudice, exposing dishonesty, preaching a gospel that is truly good news to the poor and the afflicted and the outcast. It may require our going out into some wilderness that we would rather not visit, encountering some people with whom we usually do not associate. But it is just as possible that it may *also* require making an uncomfortable witness in places that are very *well* known to us, confronting even people to whom we feel *obligated*. It is certain that making the way straight for God will include our *own* repentance, discarding and changing the attitudes and behaviors that put up or perpetuate barriers to God in our *own* souls and that make *us* less than effective workers in God's construction zone.

As he wrote about John's fulfilling of Isaiah's call to make straight the way of the Lord so that all flesh would see God's salvation, Luke surely had in mind the radical notion that even *Gentiles* would be included, as well as tax collectors and other characters considered disreputable in good Jewish society. Who are the people that we mentally or physically exclude from the benefits of God's merciful love by our notions of what sort of person is and isn't worthy of our time, our friendship, our welcome into the household of faith? Over its history, the Christian church has had a part in *creating* potholes that obstruct God's approach to people, not just filling them *in*; has had a hand in putting hills and mountains in the way of people when they weren't there before, and deep valleys nearly impossible of being crossed. Some of Paul's fellow apostles wanted at least to keep *some* obstacles in *place*—circumcision, the Jewish dietary laws. Consider how women were barred from official leadership in the Presbyterian Church until less than a century ago, and African Americans from membership in some congregations in the Presbyterian Church until less than *fifty* years ago. Are there still places in need of being made smoother and straighter in order that *all* people, *whatever* their condition, *whatever* their history, may see the salvation of God? Those are the places where you and I need to don a hardhat and roll up our sleeves and put ourselves to work, removing obstacles, smoothing out the bumps, and filling in the ruts that prevent God and people in need of God's love from meeting in reconciling embrace. For God came into the world in Jesus Christ not to destroy, but to build up; not to devour, but to refine; not to condemn, but to save. God came into the world in Jesus Christ not to make the way even *more* difficult for anyone who is weighed down with burdens either *self*-imposed or imposed by *others*, but to lift those burdens and lighten the load.

I trust that sometime in the next couple of months, all of the construction along Sparks Boulevard will be completed, and the cones and the barrels and the flashing signs will be gone, and the flagger. But John's call to repentance and the task of preparing the way of the Lord remains—until every dark valley is filled, and every forbidding mountain and hill shall be made low, and the crooked is made straight and the rough ways are made smooth for *everyone*—until, in other words, all flesh shall see, and experience as good news for *them*, the salvation of God.

Third Sunday of Advent

First Presbyterian Church, Dodge City, Kansas

December 14, 1997

Zephaniah 3:14–20
Philippians 4:4–7
Luke 3:7–18

"The Good News Crisis"

Annas, by the grace of God appointed high priest in Jerusalem, to Pontius Pilate, procurator of Judea in the service of Tiberius Caesar and the senate and people of Rome, greetings. I give thanks that you are in good health and pray that you will continue to be blessed with good fortune. Your diligence in your administration of Judea is spoken of far and wide, and has produced inestimable advantages among us, which redound to the honor of Caesar. We are fortunate indeed to have the benefit of your wise and benevolent governance in our land, and offer you every assistance that it is within our power to provide for the peaceful and just administration that is your purpose, we know, as well as our desire.

There has been little opportunity for us to correspond since you so wisely chose to grant me retirement and appoint Caiaphas, my son-in-law, as high priest, graciously permitting me to retain my honorable title though unburdened by the duties of the office that I held for ten years and sought faithfully and diligently to discharge. However, I hope that I may now bring to your attention a particular incident of which I believe you should be aware. It has come to my notice, through various agencies, that some of our people are being aroused to inappropriate expectations by the words of a vagrant preacher. By making certain identifications with our prophets of old, and reviving fantasies best left dormant, he is exciting among the ignorant and unwise rash desires that, I fear, may have unpleasant results both for your administration and for our religion.

I would be most pleased to have audience with you at your convenience to set forth more explicitly the evidences that this man is prejudicing the interests of good order and allegiance to Caesar. May you continue in good health and good fortune.

Annas, by appointment high priest of the people Israel, to the most excellent Pontius Pilate, procurator of Judea in the service of Tiberius Caesar, greetings. I rejoice in what I hear from *others*—that you are in good health and that you are experiencing good fortune—and I pray that you may continue to be so blessed.

As I have not yet received a reply to my letter of last week, I fear that my courier did not reach you, or perhaps your attention to more evidently pressing matters has kept you from reading it fully. Please be assured that my concern about the vagrant preacher is genuine, and that it is through *my long experience* in such matters that I am prompted to bring it to your attention. I do not wish to weary you with a repetition of the particulars, in the event that other business has understandably prevented you from yet replying to my letter. If, however, my letter did *not* reach you, please advise me, and I will be pleased to repeat my concerns.

May you continue to prosper, as we indeed prosper from your wise and just governance.

Annas, by appointment of the governor high priest of the people Israel, to the most excellent Pontius Pilate, procurator of Judea in the service of Tiberius Caesar, greetings. For your welfare and good health I give thanks daily, and pray that you will continue to be so blessed.

I thank you for the favor of your letter, which arrived today and which answered quite concisely my communications of the last two weeks. I can well appreciate your reluctance to enter into a matter that appears at first blush trivial and perhaps unworthy of your attention. I fear that I may have stated the case badly. May I humbly take this opportunity to put the matter more fully before you, that you may understand the significance of the claims being made by the man in question and the dangers of his receiving a hearing among the idle and restless?

I beg your indulgence for repeating any information that you already have of such things, but I would first point out that we have in Israel and Judah a long history of charlatans coming forward now and then to deliver what *they* say is a communication from God. Unfortunately, the claims of *true* prophets cannot always be immediately verified. In our far history, there were indeed bold and mighty prophets who truly stated the will of God for our people. We revere them. We thank God for them. We read and honor their writings even to this very day. But we also have experience with *false* prophets, who would lead our people toward ruin. The age of genuine prophets is clearly past. There has not been a real prophet among us for many centuries, but false prophets continue to seek a hearing among us for their foolish and blasphemous teachings. As high priest, when my duties matched my title, I regarded it as my responsibility to expose such impostors and their falsehoods, and I did so, if I may say so without sounding unduly boastful, effectively and with dispatch. Though you have graciously relieved me of such obligations, I feel yet compelled to be vigilant against all corruptions of our faith and dangers to our society.

Specifically, I am greatly alarmed by a man named John. I am reliably informed that this man suggests that ancient prophecies of a great savior who will rise among us to rule our nation are about to come true. This John calls upon his audience to do whatever is necessary to remove all obstacles to the rule of this one whom he says is coming. You can easily understand, I am sure, that this constitutes a threat to the order that you have established and maintained among us—an order that does credit to great Caesar and must also bring pleasure to our God. This man John preaches in the south, now here and now there. He is obviously a man of no honorable connections or wholesome livelihood. If I may be so bold as to suggest, is this not a situation worthy of your scrutiny, so that Caesar might not be caught unawares by unpleasantries in a land that you have so ably administered thus far?

May you continue to govern in peace and wisdom, and may you personally continue in good health and fortune.

Annas, high priest of the Jews, to the esteemed Pontius Pilate, procurator of Judea by the appointment of Tiberius Caesar, greetings. I am gratified to hear by your own hand of your continued good health and good fortune.

I have been daily hopeful of your reply to my last letter, for every day there come to my attention fresh reports of this false prophet named John, stirring the minds and hearts of the people to anticipate a new king, a rival to great Caesar. I thank you for your letter, which arrived within the hour.

I regret that you may find tiresome further communications on this matter, burdened as you are with matters critical both to Rome and to the inhabitants of this land. However, my sense of obligation will not allow me to remain silent, though my poor explanations are apparently unable to convey my true sense of urgency concerning this situation. Great numbers of people are thronging to this vagrant preacher from the desert. The danger of his preaching is demonstrated perhaps most clearly in this fact: though he insults them with insinuations about their sinfulness (it is reported that he has even called them a "brood of vipers"—while yet, of course, many of them certainly *are* sinners, and are sick and deformed and unemployed and the like), still they come to hear him preach. And what he preaches is sedition and encouragement to indolence. For instance, he not only does not *condemn* the poor for their *laziness*, but says that the *rich* must share their own hard-earned *wealth*. He stabs at the heart of the system of collecting taxes and tolls, which has been so efficient from Rome's point of view, and he discourages our people from even *being* tax collectors, which of course will have implications for Caesar. I fear that his teachings will soon be taken so to heart that there may be open talk of revolt against the authority of Rome. He quotes our sacred writings and yet twists their meaning in ways that incite his audience to unrest. He suggests that *all* peoples shall witness the salvation of Israel's God. This is a sacrilege to our very notion of righteousness, a clear threat to the laws that our people have regarded holy for hundreds of years.

The religious laws of our people may seem of little concern to Rome, yet the profane teaching that *all* classes, *all* races, *all* nationalities are regarded equally and shall benefit alike from our God, even though they be the rankest sinners, is obviously a threat to the constituted authority and civil order. This John has bewitching powers. He mesmerizes even many otherwise level-headed and right-thinking people to bizarre conclusions and revolutionary fervor. You must not imagine, Procurator, that an attack upon the religious foundations of our people will be without effect on the civil order that Caesar rightly values. Even some of your own soldiers have been seen seeking John out and listening to his words. Surely an attack upon constituted authority in one place is a threat to constituted authority everywhere. The interests of Palestine are tied directly to the interests of Rome.

I beseech you, Procurator, to have this man arrested at once, lest he turn the heads of even more people from their proper duties and allegiances to unprofitable hopes—hopes that might fix themselves on one of your ambitious generals, perhaps, or any country tradesman who happens to represent himself as the Messiah.

I eagerly await your reply, as I continue to pray for your health and happiness.

Annas, appointed high priest, to Pontius Pilate, procurator, etc. Greetings.

The blasphemies of John continue, unabated and augmented. It is obvious from your reply just now to my last letter, for which I waited several days, that you feel wearied by my correspondence, and perhaps you think me a foolish alarmist. And yet, I have reports this very day of this John promising his hearers that the poor, the sick, even the most vile sinners, can *repent* of their sins and be assured of God's favor. Surely you can appreciate what this means, if it goes unchecked. Our entire social fabric would be unraveled if such teaching were to be believed. Who will not suppose that he may rise above his proper social station? Where will be the incentive for people to be righteous and to obey the law? What will be the motive for making sacrifice in the temple? Common sense tells us that poverty is a sign of divine displeasure and that sickness is a judgment upon sin and that lameness is proof of God's rejection; what if people begin to think otherwise? Hundreds of years of our religious tradition are in danger. The very underpinnings of order are at stake here, Procurator—the very foundations upon which Caesar's authority rests.

You suggest in your letter that it is *we*, the priests of the Jews, who are threatened by John's preaching, that it is jealousy of John and the one whose coming he has announced that motivates my appeals to you. Do not allow yourself to be deceived! If this man is believed, if the people begin to think that a Messiah is coming who will overturn the established order by declaring that sins are forgiven and that God's approval is available to all, what is now the peaceful order you have striven for in Judea will be all chaos. Holiness will be ridiculed. Righteousness will be mocked. Every person will think of himself as equal before God. And Caesar will be ignored. All that we have depended upon will be dismantled, root and branch, unless we cut this monster down now. "Revolution" is not too harsh a word, Procurator. And when has revolution ever benefited those who are in authority?

I pray for your continued good health and prosperity.

Annas, high priest, to Pontius Pilate, Procurator. Good health and happiness.

It is happening. John's followers are at fever pitch. They were ready to hail *him* as Messiah, but he tells them that *he* is just a *forerunner*—someone is coming who is more powerful. Fire, he says—fire and destruction. That is what he will bring. They call it "good news," Procurator—*good news* that he will separate the grain from the chaff! But everyone knows that *they* are the chaff—*they* are the *real* dregs of society. *They* are the *sinners*. And now, these sinners say that it is *good news* that a more powerful one is coming? Surely, Procurator, that is a call for *revolution*, for disrupting everything we have known and know to be reliable, every certainty that we have, and much that is important to Rome. Surely, by now, you have heard how they murmur against Herod the king, and his marriage. Treason! And that God has forgiven them their sins by washing in water. Blasphemy! Treason and blasphemy, Procurator! What sort of person they will hail as their Messiah, who can tell? But I tell you, he will be a danger unlike any we have ever faced—a danger to the authority of Caesar and a danger to the purity of our tradition. "Good news" for whom, Procurator? Surely not for Rome, and surely not for us.

Good health to you.

Annas to Pontius Pilate.

You cannot wash your hands of this matter, Procurator. Arrest him. Arrest him before it is too late. Arrest him before their "good news" becomes true. I confidently tell you, if you do not deal forcefully with this man John now, before his promised powerful one comes, before the people think that the Messiah is here, who knows what you may have to deal with later? Who knows what sort of power will be unleashed among our people? He says the Messiah is coming. He says he is coming soon.

Fourth Sunday of Advent

Spanish Springs Presbyterian Church, Sparks, Nevada

December 24, 2006

Micah 5:2–5a
Hebrews 10:5–10
Luke 1:39–55

"He Shall Be Our Peace"

"For a child has been born for us, a son given to us; authority rests upon his shoulders; and he is named Wonderful Counselor, Mighty God, Everlasting Father, Prince of Peace" (Isa 9:6). Those words form the beloved core of the promise in Isaiah that we read every Christmas Eve, and that we will hear again tonight as we make our annual liturgical pilgrimage to the stable to pay homage to the Christ-child. Originally, those words floated like a benediction over a nation whose future was ominously beclouded by the threat of war. For that original audience, the word "peace" would have meant something very tangible and precious—an absence of military battle, freedom from the horrors of armed conflict, a bright promise not only for the *current* generation, but for the *next*. It was not merely about an unspecific sense of calm in the individual soul. It was about putting away armor, and breaking weapons.

Peace was a common theme of *Israel's* prophets, who saw the threat of *Assyria* to the *north*, and of *Judah's* prophets, who saw the threat of *Babylon* to the *east*, and read in them an alarming inevitability that could not be avoided by raising armies and entering into alliances: a reality that was the inexorable consequence of the people's failure to live in obedience to God's commands, most notably by failing to trust in God's promises for their security and by embracing the attitudes and adopting the behaviors of the pagan empires that surrounded them, empires founded on lust for wealth and resting on military power. The more dangerous their horizon appeared—God's threat of punishment upon their unfaithful ways,—the more they turned to *ungodly* forms of security—strategies of destruction. And all the while, they continued to oppress the poor and the foreigner in their midst, continued to abuse the sick and the lame and the widowed and the orphaned within their borders, continued to pursue the habits that had gotten them into trouble with God in the first place, and continued, vainly, trying to *appease* God by sacrificing burnt offerings of bulls and goats to atone for their sins rather than turning away from their sinful greed and their sinful injustice and their sinful prejudice and their sinful pride. And, ultimately, the axe fell, first on the northern kingdom of *Israel* and *its* capital, Samaria, and then on the southern kingdom of *Judah* and *its* capital, Jerusalem.

How many died in those wars we don't know. But it was enough to make mothers and fathers and sisters and brothers mourn their losses and yearn for peace. And even after the people of *Judah* were carried off into exile in Babylon as punishment for *their* unfaithfulness, and then eventually were permitted to *return* to Palestine to piece their society back together from the ruins of war, *still* the lesson had not been learned. *Again*, they oppressed the poor and the foreigner in their midst, *again* they abused the sick and the lame and the widowed and the orphaned within their borders, *again* their sinful greed and sinful injustice and sinful prejudice and sinful pride reasserted themselves and kept their nation from ever returning to the greatness their ancestors had known under David. And *another* generation of prophets rose up, promising the people a reign of peace if they would but look to *God* for their security and obey God's commands to worship rightly and tend to the poor and the needy. Micah, like Isaiah, promised the coming of a ruler who would reign in majesty, but one who would come nevertheless from humble roots, one who would have the genuine welfare of his people at heart, one who would bless the people with peace.

Peace is an appropriate subject for prayer. But too often, when we pray for peace in our lives, in the life of our nation, in the world, we seem to expect it to come as if by magic. And I imagine the same was probably true for the people of ancient Israel. We frankly don't think, most of us, about what changes in our *own* attitudes and behaviors would be necessary for our lives and the lives of people around us to *be* more peaceful. And, to be honest, neither do *nations*. It is not popular for politicians to call upon their people to repent, to change their way of living—think of how President Carter was vilified for asking people to turn down their thermostats and drive slower, and how quickly America resumed its gas-guzzling habits within just a few years afterward, and that was all *before* dramatic evidence of global warming. If we as individuals have been following certain habits, if a nation has been pursuing certain behaviors, and the result has been not *peace* but *strife*, not *amity* but *hostility*, common sense would seem to indicate that a different course was called for, and a goodly dose of self-examination. To pray for *peace* and yet not make any changes in the ways that have led repeatedly to *war*, or to expect *others* to lay down *their* weapons while *we* continue to upgrade our *own* armaments, or to expect that the God who created the world for all to enjoy will bless with stability and prosperity any society in which the wealthy are interested only in getting wealthier, and at the expense of the poor, defies not only *human* logic but *divine* logic as well. And yet Israel and Judah were clearly not the *last* nations to be so heedless of God's will and so oblivious to God's purpose.

It is not just a matter of *worshiping* God. It is also a matter of *obeying* God. And the people of Israel and Judah could *not*, by multiplying their offerings or intensifying their prayers, overcome the hard facts of their disobedience to God's commands to treat the poor fairly, to share the wealth of the land equitably, to receive the foreigner with hospitality, and to care even at inconvenience and expense for the sick and the lonely. They periodically increased their *religiosity*. What they *needed* to do was to increase their *righteousness*. They needed not a great general to lead them into battle with a foreign foe. They needed a Savior who would preach and demonstrate the habits that make for *peace*.

Manifestly, the habits that make for *peace*—for wholeness, for well-being, for shalom in the world that God created good and intended for all people to share—are not the habits of greed and waste, the habits of prejudice and abuse. And when people—individuals or a society—adopt the habits that create and sustain empires, whether geographical or economic, the God who worked a great miracle to bring his people up out of empire's oppression will not long remain complacent about the situation, surely will not bless it. And if a nation has geared its economy so that it requires war to function, to maintain the perquisites of the elite, and taxes and spends in a way that sacrifices the needs of its poor and sick and aged and dispossessed, then it is far out of step with God's priorities, and it will always need to have an enemy, and it will undoubtedly always find one.

Judah spiraled into just such a situation. Oh, the enemies were real enough, had designs upon her wealth and her land, but by that time she had so forfeited God's favor that she had no moral high ground left from which to stave off the enemy's onslaught.

> But you, O Bethlehem of Ephrathah,
>   who are one of the little clans of Judah,

> from you shall come forth for me
> > one who is to rule in Israel,
> > whose origin is from of old,
> > > from ancient days. . . .
> > And he shall stand and feed his flock in the strength of the L<small>ORD</small>,
> > > in the majesty of the name of the L<small>ORD</small> his God.
> > And they shall live secure, for now he shall be great
> > > to the ends of the earth;
> > and he shall be the one of peace. (Mic 5:2, 4–5a)

But it is not *magic*. The peace will come *only* when this one is acknowledged as ruler, only when he is listened to, only when people obey his teachings and adopt his ways—not the *other* guy, but *me*, when *I* decide to allow this king to rule *my* life and govern *my* actions and shape *my* attitudes and guide *my* thoughts, meaning when *I* abandon lust for wealth and power, when *I* change *my* habits and curb *my* appetites, when *I give more* and *take less*; in other words, when *I* repent of the ways of death and destruction and adopt the habits of life and peace.

Mary knew what it meant that the Son of God was coming:

> "He has brought down the powerful from their thrones,
> > and lifted up the lowly;
> he has filled the hungry with good things,
> > and sent the rich away empty.
> He has helped his servant Israel,
> > in remembrance of his mercy,
> > according to the promise he made to our ancestors,
> > > to Abraham and to his descendants forever." (Luke 1:52–55)

And a few months later, in Bethlehem of Ephrathah, she gave birth to the one who said to his followers, to those who pledged to obey his teachings and copy his example, "Peace I leave with you, my peace I give to you. I do not give to you as the world gives. Do not let your hearts be troubled, and do not let them be afraid" (John 14:27).

Not with guns and bombs, not with soldiers and cavalry, not even with defensive alliances did Jesus bring peace to the people he met, but with forgiveness, with healing, with listening, with feeding, with befriending, with blessing. Not with gold and decree and threat was he mighty, but by living simply, and by telling stories, and by speaking the truth. Not in aloofness and robes and ceremony was he majestic, but by championing the wretched, muddying his hands, giving up his own body and blood. The prophets called on all Israel to look forward to such a one, to discern in him their salvation and their peace. But they would also have to submit to his *rule* if they *truly* wanted *salvation*, if they *truly* wanted *peace*—to obey him, to do as he taught, to follow his example. And it was not a matter of waiting first for the *rest* of the world to follow his example, nor even for the *neighbor* to change *his* or *her* habits, not waiting for one's *friends* to abandon the rush for the biggest, the brightest, the fastest, the most expensive, not waiting for one's *enemies* first to put down *their* weapons. When would Israel learn to put its trust in God? When would Israel learn to adopt the priorities of God? When would Israel accept the salvation to which God was constantly inviting her, and receive the peace that God was offering?

A person is not moral just because he or she doesn't shoot people, just because he or she doesn't break into houses and steal things. A nation is not righteous because it hangs the Ten Commandments in its courtrooms or has a manger scene on the steps of its city halls. And the world is not at peace merely because there are no wars going on at a particular instant—though surely that would be a good start. The scriptures we read at this time of year again confront us with the question of whether we are really expecting the one whom God has promised through the prophets, whether we truly *want* the Savior whom God is sending us in a manger, whether we genuinely understand what it is all *about*, this good news, whether we will repent, as individuals, as communities, as societies, and submit to the rule of the *only* one through whom we *can* have peace, wholeness, shalom.

Jesus, the boy-child of Mary. Not a general, but a shepherd. Not a celebrity, but a servant. Not a potentate, but a pauper. *He* shall be our peace.

Christmas Eve

Spanish Springs Presbyterian Church, Sparks, Nevada

December 24, 2009

Isaiah 9:2–7
Titus 2:11–14
Luke 2:1–20

"Looking for the Manger"

When I was a little boy not quite seven years old, my parents and I moved from Salt Lake City, Utah, to El Paso, Texas. Every Christmas that I could remember up until that time had been a holiday with snow on the ground and a thick evergreen in the living room. Each year in Salt Lake City, the holiday looked like the Christmas cards and matched the commercials. But the scene both inside and outside the window on our first Christmas in El Paso did not at all look like what I had come to expect. No brightly lit Temple Square. No pine-covered mountains blanketed with snow. Dry, cactus-covered mountains instead. Everything was brown. And inside, an extremely spindly tree. *All* of the Christmas trees in west Texas were spindly.

But we soon came to appreciate the Christmas customs of El Paso. Living there was our introduction to luminarios. The roof of our church on a hill overlooking downtown was outlined by hundreds of little candles in plain brown paper sacks, and, on the mesa above the church, all the homes along Rim Drive, including even Jewish households, had lined the street with luminarios, which were visible from much of El Paso and even from Juarez across the Rio Grande. In its own way, the soft flickering glow was every bit as impressive as the bright electric lights of Temple Square at Christmastime. We learned that the El Paso Natural Gas Company building, where my father worked, lit up certain east-facing windows at Christmastime, forming a sixteen-story-high cross that could be seen for many miles as you approached the city from across the desert. And then someone told us that we must go see the plaza at night—the central square in downtown El Paso,—which had colored lights strung in the trees and animated displays and, at its center, a manger scene.

So this, too, was Christmas—every bit as magical as mountains clad in snow-flocked pine trees and perhaps, stripped of the "White Christmas" imagery, even a bit more Christ-centered. For the luminarios were not just pretty; they were specifically meant to light the way for the Christ-child into our homes and into our hearts. The cross on the company building was not an advertisement; it was a reminder that Christmas celebrates the birth of the one who died for our salvation. And although many towns had public manger scenes in those days, and some still do today, El Paso's wasn't placed apologetically in some obscure corner of the park, but was prominently at its very center, a clear reminder to shoppers and businesspeople passing by day and night that the most important Christmas gift was given two thousand years ago, and it was wrapped in swaddling clothes. And I think, during the time that we lived in El Paso, where the predominant color even in the springtime is brown, and snow seldom falls, and no one had ever seen a horse-drawn sleigh, we came to look forward to the luminarios and the cross on the side of the company building and the festively lit plaza with its manger scene with keener anticipation than we had ever awaited the more popular images of Christmas farther north. And, at least for me, as a child, I think that it deepened my understanding of what Christmas is truly about.

It was into a world of barren prospect and thin expectations that Jesus was born. Emperors were rattling off decrees, kings were feasting in their palaces, generals were commanding their armies the night that a weary couple from the hill country of Galilee finally found humble shelter in a tiny town about eight miles south of Jerusalem, and the woman gave birth to a baby and laid him in a feeding trough. Far from the bright lights and shopping emporiums, beyond even the shadow of the temple, the salvation of the world was being inaugurated, and not a single reporter or even blogger knew about it, much less Caesar or Herod or anyone else whom the world honored as great—those who planned military conquest and strategized personal advantage and thought that life is all about power and profit and prestige. And it wasn't in the brightly lit banquet halls and throne rooms that the birth of the Son of God was announced, and it wasn't accompanied with the aroma of turkey and dressing or roast beef and Yorkshire pudding or the blast of recorded Christmas music that had already been playing in the stores and on our radios for a month or more, and it wasn't in a snowy New England village such as we see on so many Christmas cards. It was in a field out on a hillside that an angel of the Lord told some fellows who would never see the inside of a palace or sit at a banquet table that a Savior had been born who was the Messiah, the Lord, and that this wondrous event, so common in appearance but cosmic in importance, was for them.

> And suddenly there was with the angel a multitude of the heavenly host, praising God and saying,
> "Glory to God in the highest heaven,
> and on earth peace among those whom he favors!" (Luke 2:14)

—a class of people that, unlikely though it would have seemed to shepherds, who were commonly despised and excluded from genteel company, now clearly included *them*.

There were no festive lights on the hillside. There were no Christmas cards with snowscapes on the front. The aromas of that first Christmas were—well, you can imagine, since it involved sheep and then a cattle shed. But angels sang the invited visitors on toward their destination—the manger, simple, even crude—and when they got there, they found themselves the only guests, other than perhaps the animals of the stable. No orchestras. No choirs. No priests, even. And no emperors or kings or generals. Just the humblest of settings in a land that is also brown throughout the year, surely in the winter, and where, except for the nebulous hope of a Messiah as promised in ancient scriptures, there was little expectation that tomorrow would be any different from today, or that things would likely get any better.

Among the people walking enchantedly through the plaza in downtown El Paso each Christmastime, a high proportion were Mexican families of modest means. Some of them probably lived in Juarez. And some of them probably included maids who cleaned houses up on Rim Drive, where all the luminarios lined the street. They, too, had come looking for the manger, responding to the promise of the priests that *they* would be privileged to see the Christ-child—that they, too, contrary to all earthly evidence, were favored by God and would experience the peace that God bestows. And when they came to the place in the plaza where the manger scene was, many of them knelt, and some of them prayed. Not so, we Anglo Protestants, sophisticated and intellectual, reluctant to participate in any activity that might be construed as superstitious. We knew this was only a replica, a mere representation, and probably not very authentic at that. For *these* people, it was as if they had actually come to the baby Jesus. For *them*, it was as if they had been looking for the manger, like the shepherds of old, and had found it.

Ultimately, there is something very important to be learned from such simple devotion. Without ever opening a theological treatise, beyond the sound of the several hundred voices of a famous choir, without snow, even, or perfectly shaped and ornamented trees, these people had found their way to the manger. Of course, they, too, knew that it was not the original manger of Bethlehem, knew that the doll was not the real baby Jesus. But, rather like an Orthodox icon, through these replicas, I think they could actually see the newborn Savior lying in the straw of the cattle shed, surrounded by the gentle beasts and adored by the scruffy shepherds and smiled upon by an exhausted Mary and a somewhat befuddled but proud Joseph. And, as much as it was through the simple manger scene that they witnessed a two-thousand-year-old miracle, it was by way of their own simple pilgrimage through the streets of El Paso and the maze of sidewalks in the plaza that they searched in a way that God credited and rewarded with a deepened faith. Their path illuminated by the flickering candle of hope glowing softly in the most common of circumstances, what more was needed to make a real celebration of Christmas?

Many of us think we have found Christmas when we have come to the greeting card aisle with its snowy scenes, when we have put up a tree and the decorations, when we have listened to the musical recordings, when we have participated in the family gatherings, when we have given and opened the gifts. Why, it would hardly be Christmas, would it, if we didn't have those things! They have come to define the season for us, and we measure the success of our Christmas by them. The more cards we receive, the more we must be thought of, perhaps even loved. The more certain the forecast of snow on Christmas—just a few inches, mind you, not enough to hinder our routines,—the more we are sure it *is* Christmas. The more ornate the lighting displays, the more distinctive this holiday is from all the others. The more gifts we open, the more memorable it all becomes. But the person who *ponders* what the Bible has to say about what the Messiah would be like, and the sorts of people to whom his birth was announced, and what they found when they looked for the manger, will come to understand that none of the other things we habitually associate with Christmas are really of the least importance, after all. The most bejeweled of palaces is suddenly poor by comparison. The accumulation of things is suddenly vulgar in the extreme. The bigger and better lighting displays become a competition that blinds us to God's preference for humility. Nice as a white Christmas is, it tempts us to disregard the truth that Jesus came not just for North Americans and Europeans, but for Africans, and for Asians, and for Latin Americans, and for the peoples of the South Seas, as well, and for the poor, who dare not even aspire to wrapping paper and ribbons, and for the war-weary and the estranged, for whom "Peace on earth" is not just a nice sentiment but an urgent need. And no mountain of greeting cards can begin to compare with the birth of Jesus as the sign of the greatest love by far that anyone can ever know.

Are you looking for the manger this Christmas Eve? Are you amazed that messengers from God have brought glad tidings to *you*, even *you*? Has that news prompted you to leave all the responsibilities and cares and proprieties of your life and set out on a heart's journey to kneel before the newborn King, who looks remarkably like *us* when *we* were born, and bids us to grow up and grow into him more and more as he nears the cross? If so, chances are you won't be able to keep from glorifying and praising God for all you have heard and seen, just as the shepherds on that brown, snowless hillside long ago after the angels announced to them that they would find a child wrapped in bands of cloth and lying in a manger. And they said to one another, "Let us go now to Bethlehem and see this thing that has taken place" (2:15).

CHRISTMAS EVE (MIDNIGHT)

Spanish Springs Presbyterian Church, Sparks, Nevada

DECEMBER 24, 2003

Isaiah 9:2–7
Titus 2:11–14
Luke 2:1–20

"No Longer a Wish"

As a child, I remember the eager anticipation with which I drew up my Christmas wish list each year. We didn't do such things in school, because many of my elementary school classmates were Jewish. They would celebrate Hanukkah with gift-giving and even with Hanukkah bushes that looked a lot like Christmas trees, at least in El Paso, where, in the 1950s anyway, Hanukkah bushes and Christmas trees were equally scrawny. So maybe it was at Cub Scouts or even at church that, every December, we got to take out a piece of paper and a pencil and think about what we most wished we would receive as a gift or gifts at Christmas, and write the wishes down, and then they were collected, and, I assume, were secretly forwarded to our parents.

When I got older and was in various settings where I was asked what I was wishing for Christmas, a developing sense of important *social needs* beyond my own *personal wants* prompted me sometimes to respond with more altruistic goals, like "world peace" or "an end to disease" or "food enough for everybody." I'm sure that my friends and I at church youth group and around the school lunch table competed with each other to voice the most self-denying responses we could think of—not that we didn't really mean them, of course, but because our sense of values was momentarily on stage. And during adolescence, for most of us, our talk about ending wars and stamping out illness and combating hunger was purely wishful, waving-a-magic-wand sort of stuff. We didn't really have a clue how such things would ever be accomplished. It was the 1960s, a time when anything seemed possible. And, despite assassinations in our streets and war splattered on our television screens nightly and cities erupting in flames, we hadn't personally experienced the full intractability of human greed and fear and vengefulness and pride and self-interest, or the devilish stubbornness of disease and prejudice. Not one of us wouldn't have given up every Christmas present we had ever received for the elimination of war and sickness and starvation. Just the same, not one of us gave up our wish for something special just for us under the tree on Christmas morning.

According to the *world's* calendar, the season of wishing ends sometime on December 25, and then we're all supposed to go back to whatever it is we do the *rest* of the year. The Sears "wish book" becomes once again just the Sears "catalogue" about the time we discover that one or more of the items on our wish list *did* end up under the tree—some are already broken by Christmas night or need to be exchanged for a different size or color the day after Christmas,—but war and illness and hunger persist, along with all of the other imperfections of the world and habits of the culture and flaws of the human spirit. By December 26, peace and wholeness and fullness are relegated to dreams, while the headlines scream the harsh realities of a broken and sinful world.

The world was an even harsher place in Old Testament times. Warfare was yet more brutal, people died from diseases that are easily cured today, and famine could not be relieved by transporting boxed and canned food to the places of want. Needs were more fundamental, and deprivation was more often fatal. But when *they* spoke of such blessings as peace and wholeness and fullness, the prophets of the Bible did not talk about wishes and dreams. They spoke about hope and salvation. They did not believe in magic wands. But they did have faith in God's promise. And they bolstered human expectation of an *end* to human sin and the *effects* of human sin, and for an *end* to nature's chaos and the *renewal* of God's creation.

There is a difference between a wish and a hope, between a dream and a vision. A *wish* is something that is not based on any known dependable fact; it is the design solely of one's own personal desire. *Hope* is the reason for persisting in a course of action or a way of behaving, based on a certainty. A *dream* is something without any substance, purely a fantasy. A *vision* is all about seeing clearly, despite the clutter on history's landscape. *Wish* and *dream* have to do with mutable emotions and fickle human fancy. *Hope* and *vision* have to do with the trustworthiness and authority of God.

From ancient times, human hope against death and destruction, against despair and disarray, have involved a vision of the way things will be when God's promise of a Savior is fulfilled. One of the prophets put it this way:

> The people who walked in darkness
>   have seen a great light;
> those who lived in a land of deep darkness—
>   on them light has shined.
> You have multiplied the nation,
>   you have increased its joy;
> they rejoice before you
>   as with joy at the harvest,
>   as people exult when dividing plunder.
> For the yoke of their burden,
>   and the bar across their shoulders,
>   the rod of their oppressor,
>   you have broken as on the day of Midian.
> For all the boots of the tramping warriors
>   and all the garments rolled in blood
>   shall be burned as fuel for the fire.
> For a child has been born for us,
>   a son given to us;
> authority rests upon his shoulders;
>   and he is named
> Wonderful Counselor, Mighty God,
>   Everlasting Father, Prince of Peace.
> His authority shall grow continually,
>   and there shall be endless peace
> for the throne of David and his kingdom.
>   He will establish and uphold it
> with justice and with righteousness
>   from this time onward and forevermore.
> The zeal of the LORD of hosts will do this. (Isa 9:2–7)

It wasn't a *wish*—the prophet was aware of the many ways in which God had been faithful to keep the ancient covenant promises with the people Israel, and how Israel had the reciprocal duty to point the way to God and testify to God's purpose for *all* nations. It was a *hope*, based on the trustworthiness of God in leading Abraham and Sarah to a promised land, in preserving their family through drought and famine and protecting them against tyrannies and armies, including bringing them up out of slavery in Egypt through the standing waters of the sea and the desolate barrenness of the desert and into a fertile land, of making them prosperous and mighty, of bringing them back from exile after they had been chastised for their ungrateful disobedience. It wasn't a *dream*—the prophet knew full well the hardness of human hearts and the sordidness of human history. It was a *vision*, planted in the prophet's mind and heart by the Spirit of God to be told and retold so that people of faith could see *through* the present miseries and disappointments, *past* threatening headlines and daily hardships, to the way God wants the world to be; and because *God* wants it, it *will* be. And the guarantee that it is *not* simply a *wish*, *not* simply a *dream*, is what happened one night in the very midst of human cruelty—the Roman oppression of the Jews in Palestine—and in the midst of family crisis—the unexpected pregnancy of a young woman not yet married—and in the midst of the hardships of life—there wasn't even room for her to have a decent bed in the inn, but she was relegated to the barn, to the place the animals ate and did everything else—smelly, probably, chilly, certainly, out of sight to all but a few shepherd lads whose nightly monotony had suddenly entwined them in the pivotal event in all of human history: "For the grace of God has appeared, bringing salvation to all, training us to renounce impiety and worldly passions, and in the present age to live lives that are self-controlled, upright, and godly, while we wait for the blessed hope and the manifestation of the glory of our great God and Savior, Jesus Christ" (Titus 2:11–13).

At that very instant, in that stable at Bethlehem, all human *wishes* for peace and wholeness and fullness were transcended by the *hope* of salvation from human sin and salvation from the *effects* of human sin, and *dreams* of personal satisfaction were excelled by the *vision* of God's creation restored and made new, not by the coronation of an earthly king in an earthly palace, as Isaiah's partial vision had foretold, but by the gift of God himself in the person of Jesus Christ, Lord and Savior, born into the world not to *condemn* it but to *save* it, not to minister to a favored *few* but to judge and redeem all humankind, not a present under a *tree* but the giver of eternal life crucified *on* a tree so that we have a destiny beyond the grave. "He it is who gave himself for us that he might redeem us from all iniquity and purify for himself a people of his own who are zealous for good deeds" (2:14). Not with a wave of a wand does he grant *wishes*, but in a manger and on a cross he gives himself to turn the world back from its headlong rush to destruction, exchanging our little wishes for the grand hope sealed in the birth, death, and resurrection of Christ.

That hope is incomparable to anything for which we could wish, because that hope is based on what God has already done. An end to war, an end to suffering, an end to disease, an end to grief, an end to injustice, an end to oppression, an end to imprisonment, an end to indignity—these are no longer just *wishes*. They are the Christian *hope*, an abiding *trust* that they *will happen*, because *God* has *promised* it, and, in Jesus Christ, God has already *kept* the most *important* promise of all. Peace, dignity, fullness, wholeness, freedom from the power of sin and from the fear of death need not be just your *dream*, but a *vision* into which you live *daily*, a vision that shapes your attitudes and dictates your behavior, a vision that directs how you spend your time and your money and your affections, a vision that enlists you *already* into citizenship in the kingdom of God and gives you *already* the fullness of trust and confidence in God that turns you from the world's ways of selfishness and churlishness and vengefulness and suspicion and lust and fear and makes you generous and loving and forgiving and compassionate and hope-full, demonstrating daily and every moment that you are *already* experiencing eternal life with God.

Those shepherds who were visited by an angel that night—they had a lot of reasons to wish, had a lot of time to dream. But something more profoundly meaningful than anything they had ever wished for—food, warmth, riches—made them return to their accustomed station in the fields, still in the dark of night, still hungry, perhaps, still cold, probably, still poor, certainly, but glorifying and praising God. Now, they had hope. It started with a vision of angels.

> [An] angel said to them . . . "I am bringing you good news of great joy for all the people; to you is born this day in the city of David a Savior, who is the Messiah, the Lord. This will be a sign for you: you will find a child wrapped in bands of cloth and lying in a manger." And suddenly there was with the angel a multitude of the heavenly host, praising God and saying,
>
> "Glory to God in the highest heaven,
>   and on earth peace among those whom he favors!"
>
> When the angels had left them and gone into heaven, the shepherds said to one another, "Let us go now to Bethlehem and see this thing that has taken place, which the Lord has made known to us." So they went with haste and found Mary and Joseph, and the child lying in the manger. When they saw this, they made known what had been told them about this child; and all who heard it were amazed at what the shepherds had told them. But Mary treasured all these words and pondered them in her heart. The shepherds returned, glorifying and praising God for all they had heard and seen, as it had been told them. (Luke 2:10–20)

And all they had ever wished for was replaced with hope for everything that God had promised.

Christmas Day
Isaiah 52:7–10
Hebrews 1:1–4
John 1:1–14

"Eyes of Faith"

It would have been so easy to ignore, to overlook, the most loving, the most decisive, most complete manifestation of God in all of human history. For many generations, the prophets had imagined the fulfillment of the promise that God would come to be with his people, that God would right history's wrongs, that God would take control and have God's way of righteousness and justice and peace, the triumph of God's own grace and truth. When things seemed the most bleak, when the landscape was most desolate, when the facts pointing persistently to hopelessness and despair were the most stubborn and irrefutable, one prophet, seeing through dust and smoke and gloom, envisioned an exhausted runner breathlessly heralding the nearness of God, announcing victory not merely for human hopes but, much more important still, victory for God's will of eternal wholeness:

> How beautiful upon the mountains
>   are the feet of the messenger who announces peace,
> who brings good news,
>   who announces salvation,
>   who says to Zion, "Your God reigns." (Isa 52:7)

How could it be? The ruins of Jerusalem were all around. The devastation was everywhere. It would take an unprecedented degree of faith for anyone, even the most devout, to see God's hand at work to redeem a reality so manifestly God-forsaken. The walls crumbled, the temple in shambles, the people scattered and demoralized beyond recognition as a holy nation—the prophet looks at it all and says,

> The LORD has bared his holy arm
>   before the eyes of all the nations;

> and all the ends of the earth shall see
> the salvation of our God. (52:10)

Madness. Or the most cruel sort of hoax. A disgusting joke in the poorest of taste. Salt in a deep, deep wound. Or . . . faith.

And it would have taken faith indeed to perceive that anything extraordinary had happened in that little village a few miles from Jerusalem, on the edge of nowhere, not just on the fringe of the desert. It was totally insignificant, except for the unlikely accident of history that it happened to be the birthplace of David, the little shepherd boy who, against all odds, once upon a time became the king of Israel. Other than that, it was eminently forgettable, undeserving of notice. It would have taken faith indeed to believe that the birth of a modest couple's tiny son, just one of thousands of births that night in the world's undistinguished villages, soon forgotten amid the decrees of potentates and the marchings of armies, undignified by any gold-embossed birth announcements, uncelebrated by festive baby showers, unworthy of a short sentence on the evening news or even as a brief statistic in the newspaper, was reason to

> [b]reak forth together into singing,
> you ruins of Jerusalem;
> for the LORD has comforted his people,
> he has redeemed Jerusalem. (52:9)

Today, after waiting perhaps hours in a long line of pilgrims and just plain tourists, you can crouch on hands and knees under an altar in the ancient Church of the Nativity in Bethlehem and peer down through a hole in the stone pavement at the spot where, according to long tradition, Jesus was born at the time and place that propelled Bethlehem, in the eyes of the faithful, from virtually being no place at all to being the center of the universe, from being a locale history nearly forgot to being the pivot around which all of history turns, the chief and only hope of the world. Not far away is a chapel, built much more recently, commemorating the encounter between frightened shepherds and a messenger from heaven, announcing to them the birth of Christ, and the angel chorus singing praise to God. But, unless you happen to live there virtually a prisoner in the place your family has inhabited for centuries, access to Bethlehem today is restricted to a gate in the wall built by the modern nation of Israel that isolates the Palestinian people, that renders visits to the site of Jesus' birth a government-scrutinized, tightly restricted privilege. Guards. Rifles. Security cameras. Access sometimes denied entirely. It takes faith to believe that the one born there was the Prince of Peace, the final and perfect revelation of God.

It has always taken faith, looking at the few facts of what Luke and Matthew describe as a scandal-ridden birth in an ordinary little hamlet in an unremarkable corner of a renowned empire, far away from what everyone thought counted, to behold in the baby Jesus the Son of God, the truth of the ages, the salvation of the world. John didn't repeat the details of that singular night more than two thousand years ago, but he surely knew them, the beloved stories that Luke and Matthew report, when he wrote, as his faith convinced him, that Jesus was the very Word of God. "He was in the beginning with God. All things came into being through him, and without him not one thing came into being. . . . And the Word became flesh and lived among us, and we have seen his glory, the glory as of a father's only son, full of grace and truth" (John 1:2, 14).

Standing on the decrepit ramparts of a ruined city—what a pitiful scene that must have been—a few devoted sentinels faithfully scanning the horizon for the promised sign of hope see a speck in the far distance. Maybe they wonder at first whether their eyes are playing tricks on them—just a bird or cloud of dust whipped up by the wind, perhaps merely a mirage, which can seem so real in the desert. But no, as the minutes go by, the image grows larger and more distinct—a runner coming toward them, which must mean that there is vitally important news to be shared. Think of the swift and athletic Inca messengers on the ancient Andean highways, or the runner Pheidippedes racing the twenty-six miles from Marathon to Athens, so intent on his mission that he never stopped to rest, but even shed his clothes to disencumber himself of anything that might slow him down. Nothing was more important than to bring the news, to deliver the message, in the case prophesied in Isaiah, that the Lord was returning to Zion, that God's people would be restored, that redemption was nigh. "To you is born this day in the city of David a Savior, who is the Messiah, the Lord" (Luke 2:11), proclaimed the angel in a blaze of glory on a dark and lonely hillside where simple people were struggling against monotonous poverty and cruel oppression and the occupation of foreign soldiers on their soil. The messenger brought no armed troops, no military weapons, no warhorses—just the assurance that God was present, despite human obstacles and human assessments, that God's purpose was inevitable, that God remembered and was in charge of history, that God was the judge of what was true and what was false, what was eternal and what would pass away. Did the people have eyes of faith to perceive it? Did they trust in God? Do people today, amidst war and disease and dishonesty, all the world's disasters and all our personal heartbreak, believe in God's Son?

Most of the world has already, by this morning, gotten past the religious celebrations of last night in churches around the world, and in Manger

Square in Bethlehem, a great open plaza where thousands of pilgrims come annually, braving the soldiers' rifles at the gate in the wall, the scrutiny of the omnipresent security cameras, braving even the barking cries of the souvenir sellers and the hustling shouts of the tour guides. Most of the world has gotten to what it thinks is the real business of Christmas—the opening of presents, the calorie-packed feasting, even now the holiday agenda of sports and strategizing battle plans for tomorrow's sales. To perceive the good news that is lying in the manger of the gospel proclamation—*that* requires the eyes of faith. The proclamations in the biblical past, God speaking to our ancestors in many and various ways by the prophets, eclipsed now by God speaking to us by a Son, reflecting God's glory, the exact imprint of God's very being, sustaining all things by his powerful word—it still takes the eyes of faith to perceive that "[w]hat has come into being in him was life, and the life was the light of all people" (John 1:3b–4). But the darkness has never overcome that light—not human reversion to war, not family discord, not injury and disease and the inevitability of decline and death, not even the menacing darkness of police states and apartheids. In the midst of the very ordinariness of our need, our daily duty and our daily sin and our daily obedience, our struggles with doubt and our blessed comfort in forgiveness, the eyes of faith gaze upon the manger and open to the Bible's vision that we, too, can become children of God, born not of blood or the will of the flesh or really of any human will at all, but of God. And, through the eyes of faith, we believe that "the Word became flesh and lived among us, and we have seen his glory, the glory as of a father's only son" (1:14). And, through the eyes of faith, we know that life-giving, life-affirming Word to be "full of grace and truth."

First Sunday after Christmas Day
First Presbyterian Church, Dodge City, Kansas
December 28, 1997

1 Samuel 2:18–20, 26
Colossians 3:12–17
Luke 2:41–52

"Dedicated to God"

Now every year his parents went to Wichita for the festival of the shopping mall to fill out a few items on their Christmas list. And when he was six years old, they went up as usual for the shopping and a movie. When the movie ended, and they started to return to the hotel, the boy Jesse stayed behind in the video arcade, but his parents did not know it. Assuming that he was trailing right behind, they got as far as the parking lot, and discovered that he was not with them. Then they started to look for him among the huge crowd of shoppers going in and out. When they did not find him, they returned to the concourses and stores to search for him, for they were in a panic that he was wandering about the shopping center or, worse, that he had been kidnapped. After the better part of an hour, they found him, standing in front of the Galaxy Blaster, pushing the buttons and pulling the joystick—to no effect, of course, because he had no money to feed into the coin slot. When his parents saw him, they were astonished; and his mother said to him, "Child, why have you treated us like this? Look, your father and I have been searching for you in great anxiety"—or something like that. He said to them, "Why were you searching for me? Did you not know that I must be in Aladdin's Palace?" But they did not understand what he said to them or why he had gone in there in the first place. Then he went down with them and came to Dodge City, totally unfazed by the experience and probably having learned nothing from it. His mother chalked this up in her heart as the latest trial of parenthood.

I don't mean to be sacrilegious, but the one episode of Jesus' childhood that the Bible reports—after his presentation to the Lord in the temple—is one with which almost any parent can identify—the frustration, the anxiety, the panic at having a child wander off in a crowd, and the parent having no idea where to begin looking. We are always a little puzzled how it was that, in spite of the angels and the shepherds and the wise men, Mary and Joseph seemed so unprepared for Jesus' strong sense of dedication to God—dedication that meant, yes, of course, he *must* be in the temple. Just so, knowing *Jesse's* personality, his mother and I should have started our search for our boy by looking in the video arcade directly across the concourse from the movie theater that we were just coming out of. Knowing Jesse, *of course* that's where he would be—attracted by all the lights and sounds and gadgets and the throngs of adolescents. On the other hand, we didn't even see him come out of the theater. How he slipped past us as we were pushing our way up the aisle and out of the lobby, I still don't understand. In just some such way, the boy *Jesus* had become separated from *his* family, or had separated *himself* from them, to do what was most natural for him. "'Child, why have you treated us like this? Look, your father'"—with a small f—"'and I have been searching for you in great anxiety.' [Jesus] said to them, 'Why were you searching for me? Did you not know that I must be in my Father's'"—with a capital F—"'house?'" (Luke 2:48b-50). "Did you not know that I would be where I *must* be—taking care of God's interests, doing God's business?"

Luke tells this story—the only real glimpse into Jesus' childhood anywhere in the Bible—immediately after describing the dedication of the infant Jesus according to the law of Moses. "'Every firstborn male shall be designated as holy to the Lord,'" the law says, "and they offered a sacrifice according to what is stated in the law of the Lord, 'a pair of turtledoves or two young pigeons'" (2:23-24). Mary and Joseph were pious, obedient Jewish parents. Jesus was a true Israelite, brought up from birth in the moral and ritual life of Judaism, raised according to the traditions of his people—the same people who had been promised a Messiah. Children—especially boys after bar mitzvah at age twelve—were expected to make the pilgrimage to Jerusalem at Passover with their father, and if they did not live too far from Jerusalem, they were supposed to go up to the city for the feasts of Pentecost and Tabernacles as well, as the law required. Mary and Joseph had seen to it that Jesus did as the law prescribed. In a very tangible way, they were fulfilling their responsibilities in having dedicated their firstborn son to God. In his growing awareness of who he was, dedicated to God and to doing the things of God, Jesus' activity and response were totally natural: "Did you not know that I *must* be in my Father's house?" (2:49b) And as his ministry of authoritative teaching and compassionate healing and his sacrificial death and glorious resurrection would later reveal, Jesus was more totally at home than anyone else *could* be in the temple, for it was indeed *his Father's* house. "And Jesus increased in wisdom and in years, and in divine and human favor" (2:52). And as he did so, he claimed for himself that *special* relation to his heavenly Father which was the *real meaning* of his dedication as an infant to God. The horizon of his awareness of what it means to be faithful to God, of what it means to be obedient and dutiful, began to widen and deepen beyond the family circle in Nazareth until it embraced the entire human race, so that his life, and his death, and his resurrection, made that dedication full and complete.

None of us can claim the same intimate relationship with God that Jesus had. He was and is uniquely the Son of God, God's own self in human form, existing from before anything was created until after creation has all passed away. Yet Jesus grew and matured as *we* do, from a baby with a baby's appetite and a baby's wants and a baby's mentality through childhood to adolescence and adulthood, increasing all the while in self-awareness and in understanding of the world, becoming more and more conscious of his purpose in God's plan, and more and more trustful in yielding to it. Though Jesus' Sonship is unique in character, each of us who has been baptized in his name is *also* a child of God, dedicated to God's will. The natural place for each of us to be is in our Father's house, taking care of our Father's interests, doing our Father's business.

By the way, there is nothing here about Jesus teaching the elders. The famous painting is not scriptural. Jesus, Luke says, was "sitting among the teachers, listening to them and asking them questions" (2:46). At age twelve, Jesus was learning of God's will, not only from whatever the Holy Spirit communicated to him directly, but also from other people who had studied the scriptures—adults who were trying to live faithfully, who had experience of being the people of God in a very human world. The proper activity of anyone who is truly dedicated to God surely includes setting aside time regularly for the sole purpose of learning more *about* God and how to live faithfully as a *child* of God and within a community of faith. Jesus' understanding was so quick and profound that the teachers were amazed at what he said. But Jesus was not unique in seeking to learn, or in growing in his self-awareness of being an obedient servant of the Lord, or understanding what it means to live faithfully in the world as a citizen of heaven. Every person who has been dedicated to God *must* do the same. Every child of a Christian parent should be in church school regularly, and in church youth groups regularly, and in youth choir, learning to sing God's praises regularly, and every adult Christian should be engaged in intentional study of the Bible with other Christians, and in learning more about what it means to live faithfully as God's own people. Serious study of the Bible is not an *optional* activity for *anyone* who has been dedicated to God. So Samuel the prophet did many centuries before Jesus, serving in the temple faithfully even as a child, growing both in stature and in favor with the Lord and with the people. People of God know that there is much more to childhood than arithmetic and drug awareness and soccer and X-Box and TV, don't we? People of God know that there is much more to adulthood than the marketplace and the shop and the office and football and golf and bridge, don't we? People of God know that the answer the young Jesus gave to his parents is properly the highest imperative for *our* life, too—"Did you not know that I *must* be in my Father's house?" (2:49b).

The increasing secularism of our age and the increasing Gnosticism of our religion are such that a lot of parents and congregations are scarcely aware of what it really means to dedicate a child to God, or to have been dedicated to God when *we ourselves* were children. For one thing, some of us believe, in this age of sensitivity to individual rights, that it's not the prerogative of parents to commit children in their infancy to how they will live their lives as older teenagers and adults. But it should come as no surprise when children raised outside the church grow up caring nothing about the Christian faith. While being kept innocent from learning about the lordship of Jesus Christ over all of life from birth to death, they will daily have been immersed in the pagan belief system of a highly secular culture. Children will indeed be influenced by *some* belief system. Which shall it be?

At the other extreme, pastors' kids are at risk of saturation in the church. Night after night, the parent who is a pastor disappears from home for a church meeting or a pastoral call; in the case of my children, that was compounded by *both* parents being pastors. Family time is rare, and someone or other in the congregation always has a knack for making the pastor feel guilty about taking time for personal business or family activities, and children perceive that. The pastors' kids are always on display, in a sense. Almost everybody seems to have an opinion about their behavior, and some church members feel free to comment on it at regular intervals, and it is understandable that children could grow up resenting that. It concerns me greatly, the number of pastors' kids who become disaffected from the church and from the Christian faith. But *all* of us need to take very seriously what it means to dedicate our children to God in baptism, and what it means to take responsibility as godparents—in the Presbyterian Church, we are *all* the godparents of *all* the children here,—praying for our children, teaching our children, worshiping with our children, and, by our own faithful example, showing what it means to grow in the faith through study and Christian fellowship, and what it means to obey God by observing the commandments and serving those whom God loves.

Dedicating a child to God will lead to tensions within the family as the child grows in self-identity and understanding of God's will for him or her. There are tensions in families anyway, as children mature. That's natural, and it is healthy. But how blessed is the family that deals with the inconveniences of getting the kids to worship and church school and youth group and choir practice. How blessed are the parents whose children, through the parents' prayers and the parents' counsel and the parents' example, think not about what is easy and what is popular and what is self-promoting, but what is right and what is faithful and what is Christlike. How blessed are the parents whose children increase in wisdom as they increase in years, and in divine and human favor, but especially divine.

Second Sunday after Christmas Day
First Presbyterian Church, Dodge City, Kansas
January 5, 1992

Jeremiah 31:7–14
Ephesians 1:3–14
John 1:1–18

"Does the Light Still Shine?"

For many of us at this time of year, it is hard to understand how anyone could *not* believe that Jesus Christ is the Son of God. The story of his birth is so beautiful and so heart-warming; the message of joy and peace is so urgent and so welcome; the hopes of a new beginning for benighted humankind are so fervent and so strong. Since early childhood, the annual ritual of candlelight worship, the yearly gatherings for feasting and gift-opening, have provided a rhythm for our lives, a way of doing things and a way of thinking about things. Our calendars would now seem very empty indeed without Christmas; our Decembers would be oppressively cold and gray without the Feast of the Nativity and all of its sights and sounds and smells. Think of the hint of that we endured last Christmas, with so many opportunities denied and customs curtailed, snowed in and snowed out as we were for the holiday. The very repetition of the celebration from year to year tends to convince us that the truth of God's coming in Christ is undeniable. And if we venture *beyond* Christmas, if we listen not only to the story of the *manger*, but also the story of the *cross* and the *empty tomb*, we seem to have the complete proof of the Christian confession that Jesus Christ was God *with* us and God *for* us. "The Word became flesh and dwelt among us, full of grace and truth; we have beheld his glory, glory as of the only Son from the Father" (John 1:14 RSV). That is the Christmas story in the Gospel of John—succinct and to the point. That is the central testimony of the evangelist—God was in Jesus Christ in a unique completeness and intimacy. And the Gospel that he has left us bears out his claim of faith, in the wonders that Jesus performed and the truth that Jesus spoke.

One commentator has observed that we are inclined to dwell on the accounts of the *earthly* Jesus—the testimonies to the miracles and the teaching of our Lord—as the basis of our Christian faith, starting, of course, with the miracle of his birth.[1] So it comes as a *surprise* when we examine Paul's letters and the other New Testament epistles written by church leaders to individuals and congregations in the first decades of Christianity, and notice that they give so little attention to the birth of Jesus, or to the Sermon on the Mount, or to the parables, or to the miracles, or to the other episodes that filled the hours and days and years between the stable in Bethlehem and the cross on Calvary. No, when the apostles wanted to offer the most impressive proof of the claims of Christianity, the clearest evidence of the relationship between Christ and God, they pointed to themselves and their congregations. They started not with past history, not even the history of the comparatively *recent* past, but rather with the evidence of Christ's *present power*, and Christ's *powerful presence*. Their appeal for conversion to the new faith was first of all a witness to what Christ *had done* and was *continuing* to do in their *own* lives, and in the life of his *church*. For them, Christ was not merely an exemplary holy man from the past, a revered teacher and fondly remembered preacher famous for his impressive signs and spectacular wonders. For them, Christ was a *contemporary reality*, working miracles in their own lives and in the life of the church every bit as great as any that the Gospels record.

The stories that were shared about the earthly career of Jesus and the accounts of eyewitnesses who had personally seen his miracles no doubt were of great interest to potential converts. But what impressed them the *most*—what they commented on among themselves and what attracted them to the faith and to the faithful—was not memories of the *past* accomplishments of Jesus so much as the life-transforming experiences of Christian believers in the *present*. There was a new and powerful force at loose in the world at large and in each receptive heart—a force that was awakening people to great possibilities, that was empowering them to do courageous deeds and inspiring them to speak bold words and exciting them to plan imaginative enterprises of love and compassion and adventure.

Those early Christians saw it and felt it and their neighbors commented upon it; beyond question, miracles were happening in their midst—miracles of healing, miracles of generosity, miracles of forgiveness, miracles of hope.

---

1. Wedel, "Epistle to the Ephesians," 631.

The proof of Christ's intimate relationship with God was there in front of their own eyes, not dusty histories about the Jesus of pleasant memory, but daily occurrences of wonder and amazement when people called upon the name of the living Christ. Life among the faithful was a continuous demonstration of what it meant to be destined by God in love to be his sons and daughters through Jesus Christ, and to experience God's grace bestowed so freely in his Son.

In a very real sense, the evangelist could witness to the light that had come into the world in Christ based on the experience of his own community of faith—the transformation that had come over people who had sealed their profession of faith by being baptized, people who were discovering daily the abundant resources of grace that enabled them to relate to one another as sisters and brothers and to face persecution with quiet courage and to resist temptations that had always before seemed more powerful than the force of their will. The evils in the world, the ungodly fears and suspicions and hatreds that were arrayed against the Christian church, were a great dark force that yet could not extinguish its life. "The light shines in the darkness," John could write with confidence, "and the darkness has not overcome it" (1:5 RSV). Indeed, the more fierce the opposition to the Light, the gloomier all appeared around it, the higher it rose, the brighter it shined, the more it illumined. The miracles of Christ were still happening in the life of his church: the lame walked, the outcasts found welcome, the sin-burdened discovered forgiveness, the blind received new sight, the friendless were embraced in the fellowship of believers. The "riches of his glorious inheritance in the saints" (Eph 1:18 RSV), we read in Ephesians, were visible every time the church gathered to worship and to share fellowship and to pray and to serve. And the only explanation that those early Christians could offer was "the immeasurable greatness of [Christ's] power in us who believe" (1:19 RSV), as it says just a little later in the chapter.

Many of us Presbyterians have been suspicious of what is known as the "Church Growth Movement." Quite a few of the rapidly growing congregations in this country that advertise themselves as vibrant churches have seemed, to those of us in the Reformed tradition, to cross the line from celebrating the presence of the risen Christ to irresponsibly manipulating emotions, to cross the line from heartfelt praise to entertaining spectacle, to cross the line from inclusiveness to shallow theology. But in the New Testament church, vibrancy and growth went hand-in-hand with participative worship and loving fellowship and genuine joyfulness and rigorous discipline and sound teaching, and with the strong conviction that Christ was present in his church with power, producing miracles in abundance. So, people in the church shared freely with each other all that they had, and masters and slaves sat at the same table and partook of the same loaf and the same cup, and those who had been cast out by their family or their little social circle found warm acceptance in the family of faith and a fellowship which knew no requirements of class or race or nationality. With them, the power of Christ was no theory; it was no tale told in an ancient book. It was a current event, happening now, giving meaning to people's lives, bringing joy and hope to folk who had never *known* joy and hope, offering new birth to those whose past lives were stained and distorted, promising eternal life to men and women whose worldly cares seemed overwhelming and incapable of being relieved. This new thing, this Christianity, was more than just another religion of the mind; it demanded a new way of living, a complete change of heart, an openness to the power of Christ. And then see what *could* happen and what *did* happen!

That is how the church grows today, and how congregations grow. Christianity in our time is spreading rapidly across Central and Southern Africa and across Southeast Asia not simply because of the beautiful story of what happened two thousand years ago. Christianity in our time is spreading because of what the power of Christ is doing in the hearts of believers and in their life together *now, today.* Many of these new Christians face opposition not unlike the opposition encountered by the very first believers. Many of them live in conditions and in places where all appears gloom and hopelessness. But they are discovering the bright truth of the light of Christ—once again, the lame are being helped to walk, the outcasts are finding welcome, the sin-burdened are discovering forgiveness, the blind are receiving new sight, and the friendless are being embraced in the fellowship of believers. I once heard the stated clerk of the Church of East Africa—the Presbyterian Church in Kenya and Tanzania—speak of the miraculous growth of the Christian faith in those countries, of the tremendous and empowering changes that the church has made in people's lives, of how lay people are ministering to each other in loving and caring ways. The Light is still shining in East Africa, and the darkness has not overcome it—neither the darkness of superstition and persecution and fear, nor the darkness that results when worship becomes routine and theology becomes the exclusive province of the pastors and the church no longer expects miracles and church membership evokes neither sacrifice nor commitment, nor produces a fundamental change of attitude and behavior. Unless we believe that Christ is present even now in power, and unless we *experience* his powerful presence, we may find the coming of Christ at Christmas to be charming and heart-warming, but ultimately it will remain a once-upon-a-time sort of story.

The question that I pose for us today is one that each congregation must periodically ask itself: "Does the Light still shine?" Is the stranger genuinely welcome and accepted here? In our fellowship, are past sins forgiven and grudges set aside and encouragement offered so that people can experience firsthand the redemption of Jesus Christ? Do we expect miracles—people discovering and making use of talents they never suspected in themselves, an outpouring of generosity in giving and compassion in listening, such as is seldom witnessed in the world? Do we pray fervently for each other and for the world community beyond our walls, both when we are gathered here for corporate worship and when we are at the dinner table and at bedside? Do we tell other people at school, at work, at the club, about the joy and hope we have come to know in Jesus Christ? If not, why not? I ask the same questions of myself. Is the Light growing dim among us? Are we unconvinced that Christ is present with us in power, and that he can do a mighty work among us and through us? As I said, these are questions that every congregation must periodically ask of itself.

We Christians and church members must continually be getting to know each other better and enjoying each other's company. Together we must review the past to identify new opportunities for ministry. We must consider what it means to be an inviting church, genuinely welcoming new people into the congregation, convinced that Christ is alive and present and eager to accomplish a mighty work in our midst. I encourage us to pray for our Session and for our congregation, that Christ's light may shine in and through us in mission, in education, in worship, and in service; that we will be in this new year a family of faith that is a testimony to the present power of Christ, convinced *we* have seen—see firsthand, daily—Christ at work within us as individuals and as a church, yielding lives of joyful devotion and generous compassion and unbounded hope. "The light shines in the darkness, and the darkness has not overcome it" (John 1:5 RSV). Let it shine brightly among us to illumine a world still and much in need of the love of Jesus Christ.

Epiphany of the Lord
Isaiah 60:1–6
Ephesians 3:1–12
Matthew 2:1–12

"Two-Way Evangelism"

In worship services on certain days of the Christian year, you can pretty much count on the congregation being asked to sing particular hymns. Christmas Eve almost universally calls for "Silent Night," and a lot of people would be sorely disappointed if they didn't have a chance to sing it amidst candlelight and the beloved story of Jesus' birth as told in Luke's Gospel—no room in the inn, angels, shepherds, manger. Although my practice has been to alternate it with Charles Wesley's hymn "Christ the Lord Is Risen Today," in most churches you can dependably predict that the congregation will be singing "Jesus Christ Is Risen Today" every Easter Sunday. So, most of the many other Easter hymns in nearly every hymnal are unfamiliar to most people. On Trinity Sunday, what could be more commonly sung than "Holy, Holy, Holy! Lord God Almighty"?—though, of course, it is heard many more times a year in a lot of churches, with or without the choir singing the soaring soprano descant. And on or near the feast of the Epiphany, "We Three Kings of Orient Are" is a fixture known by churchgoers and non-churchgoers alike, despite the oft-observed fact that the Bible claims neither that the foreign visitors to the home of the newborn king were themselves kings, nor that there were as many as or only three of them. Hymnal committees and editors have tried to broaden the Epiphany repertoire and dilute the erroneous indoctrinating effects of the popular hymn by including a wider variety of choices, with only modest success. I know of only one denomination that has dropped "We Three Kings" from its principal hymnbook despite its inaccuracies—and that must certainly have been an unpopular move. I have long maintained that the hymns we sing, and that we enjoy singing, have a much greater impact on our faith, or on the details of the story we remember and repeat, than the claims of theological doctrine or even the actual words of scripture. Just ask the average person on the street, "How many wise men came to Bethlehem when Jesus was born?" And if asked to draw the scene, each of the three supposed kings would be holding in his hands one gift each of gold, frankincense, and myrrh, though the would-be artists might be a little fuzzy on exactly what "myrrh" is. Woe be it to any pastor or music director who ventures to mess with what we like to sing and what we choose to believe.

There is another hymn associated especially with the theme of Epiphany, however, that was very popular in my childhood Sunday school days and that we sang from a special brownish-pinkish Presbyterian Sunday school hymnbook, but which has not appeared in our congregational hymnal since 1955. Epiphany is the time of year when our mission emphasis turns to evangelism, the proclaiming of the good news of Jesus Christ, the manifestation of Christ's unique holiness and authority associated with travelers from distant lands who came seeking the truth of God entering the world as an infant king, unrecognized by those who *should* have known, but acknowledged and honored by *strangers* intent on studying God's ways. Not just at Epiphany, in fact, but virtually every Sunday, it seems, children from the range of elementary grades at First Presbyterian Church in El Paso gathered to sing "We've a Story to Tell to the Nations." Its words and music, both by Henry Ernest Nichol, a British civil-engineering-student-turned-children's-hymnwriter, dated to 1896, during what has been dubbed the great century of Christian missions. In his *Companion to the United Methodist Hymnal*, hymnologist Carlton Young has observed that "We've a Story to Tell to the Nations" typified the hundreds of hymns "written to express the determined, dynamic, energetic, and expansive attributes of . . . Christian missions."[1]

Hymns like "We've a Story to Tell" reflected a common interpretation of Western, and especially Anglo-American, Protestantism as being superior not only to Islam and Buddhism and Hinduism, but even to Roman Catholic and Orthodox and Coptic and other forms of Christianity prevalent and normative in foreign cultures. American evangelicalism already had a tendency to interpret evangelism in terms of carving notches in one's spiritual belt, the genesis if not confirmation of our prescribing, sometimes insistently and even gracelessly, the urgent necessity of coming to Christ to be saved.

The problem wasn't the saving truth of Jesus Christ. The problem was the dichotomy of "us" and "them" that engendered an attitude of evangelical Protestant superiority to everybody else's inferiority, manifest not only

---

1. Gealy et al., *Companion*, 686.

in religious beliefs but in everything from their language to their clothing to their table manners. Even the name that Henry Ernest Nichol gave to his hymn tune, MESSAGE, tips the evangelical origin of the hymn and suggests that evangelism a one-way conversation. Each stanza begins with w-e-apostrophe-v-e, so that no matter what the "message" is, the repetitive focus on "us" hazards diminishing the inherently winsome and inviting and universal nature of Christ's gospel, which each Christian is authorized to share only with the humility and respect that characterized Jesus himself.

> We've a story to tell to the nations
> That shall turn their hearts to the right,
> A story of truth and mercy,
> A story of peace and light.
> A story of peace and light.
> For the darkness shall turn to dawning,
> And the dawning to noonday bright,
> And Christ's great Kingdom shall come on earth,
> The Kingdom of love and light.[2]

The subsequent stanzas give voice to many great truths, challenges, and hopes of Christian discipleship, but the text is dominated by the repetitive "We've"—"We've a story to tell," "We've a song to be sung," "We've a message to give," "We've a Saviour to show"—all to "the nations," which sounds like "those other people," living even in places where Christianity had deep roots centuries before Europeans came to North America and North American Christians started sending missionaries to Africa and Asia and South America and the Pacific, and more recently to traditionally Orthodox nations formerly behind the Iron Curtain.

In the latter part of the twentieth century and now in the twenty-first, there has been a growing and penitent awareness in many Christian quarters that mission is best engaged in as a shared endeavor. We are finally recognizing that Christian mission is not a matter of imposition but a matter of mutual understanding, one of sacrifice rather than entitlement. And evangelism is a witness to the fullness of the crucified and risen Christ rather than attaining personal spiritual prestige by "winning souls" at whatever cost to human dignity and common mutual respect. The "message" that "we" are to give "to the nations," after all, is

> [t]hat the Lord who reigneth above
> Hath sent us His Son to save us,
> And show us that God is love,

---

2. Sterne, "We've a Story to Tell to the Nations."

And show us that God is love.[3]

The greatest evangelist in Christian history, the one who first accepted the challenge and took the risk of venturing to give witness to the gospel in foreign lands where most people were unfamiliar with the Jewish heritage from which Christianity arose and for whom "Lord" was a title reserved to honor very un-Christlike *rivals* to God, was Paul. Paul, or someone close enough to his thinking that he could, without challenge, it seems, write letters in Paul's name, wrote a letter to the Christians at Ephesus, who lived in the very shadow of the revered temple of the mythic goddess Diana. He declared that "the Gentiles have become fellow heirs, members of the same body, and sharers in the promise in Christ Jesus through the gospel" (Eph 3:6). Did you hear those words—"fellow," "same," "sharers"? And while the writer goes on to say, "[T]his grace was given to me to bring to the Gentiles the news of the boundless riches of Christ, and to make everyone see what is the plan of the mystery hidden for ages in God who created all things" (3:8b–9), it was "so that through the church the wisdom of God in its rich variety might now be made known to the rulers and authorities in the heavenly places" (3:10). That role of the church in which people from vastly different backgrounds, different cultures and different habits, meet to worship and learn and serve and celebrate, Ephesians immediately goes on to say, is according to the eternal purpose of God. Through faith in God, every evangelist has bold and confident access to God, but the call to evangelism is in no way a commission or excuse to deal with others arrogantly or rudely or with disrespect or even an attitude of superiority in any manner. And Paul himself, so far as we know, was never coercive. If he was sometimes blustery, it was toward those of his very own tradition, not to the Gentiles whom he understood himself graciously directed to serve, even if it meant being imprisoned for his witness to God's love made manifest in the blood of Christ, shed in exposure of human sin and offered in testimony of human salvation.

A few verses earlier in Ephesians, it says, "Now in Christ Jesus you who once were far off have been brought near by the blood of Christ. For he is our peace; in his flesh he has made both groups into one and has broken down the dividing wall, that is, the hostility between us" (2:13–14). The reconciliation that we have through Christ is not just with God, though it begins there. It is also with each other. It may be that Gentiles started out far off from the truth that is in Christ while the Jews were closer to it, but neither was already at the goal, and even those who were quite near may in fact have been stubbornly resistant to it. Both were, are, in need of reconciliation. Both were, are, in need of salvation. Both were, are, saved only through

3. Sterne, "We've a Story to Tell to the Nations."

God's grace, which the Holy Spirit is as likely and capable and desirous of bestowing upon someone else as upon you and me. Loving acceptance needs to flow both directions between us, between me and you, whoever you are, long-time Christian or someone who is new or even avowedly alien to the faith. Each of us needs God's loving forgiveness, each of us is equally a candidate for it, each of us has love and life to share. "Through him," says Ephesians,

> both of us have access in one Spirit to the Father. So then you are no longer strangers and aliens, but you are citizens with the saints and also members of the household of God, built upon the foundation of the apostles and prophets, with Christ Jesus himself as the cornerstone. In him the whole structure is joined together and grows into a holy temple in the Lord; in whom you also are built together spiritually into a dwelling place for God. (2:18–22)

The kingdom of God is not a tract of spiritual real estate to be protected behind trenches and walls. The church of Jesus Christ is not a club with membership certificates and secret handshakes. And the truth for which it exists to give witness in words and, emphatically, in deeds is not a private possession to be guarded except when dispensed to the worthy or the few, those of certain pedigree or manners. It is a truth that, imparted freely by the Holy Spirit, is an awakened understanding as likely to emerge from the experience and perception of a Muslim or Hindu or Buddhist or whatever as it is from a Catholic or a Baptist or a Presbyterian, once that person has become receptive to that truth that is the possession or entitlement of no single individual or creed. The love and mercy of Jesus Christ can be detected in the words and deeds of those even who have never heard the story of the gospel, and we who have known the gospel story for a long time need to be sensitive to hearing and accepting it through voices and actions of people who may seem to us unlikely messengers of the truth of God.

Evangelism is a two-way experience, or should be. By the wondrous working of the Holy Spirit, the truth of God may come from unexpected evangelists, messengers without the normal credentials, contributing to the building of an enlarged and even more perfect temple to God's holiness. And so, in the church, the new member of the community does not "join us." Rather, we are joined to one another, with complementary gifts and enriching perspectives, to become a new, more complete family of faith, enlarged in our capacity to minister in the name of Jesus Christ to the world in need of the forgiveness that Christ offers, the unity that Christ wills.

We've a story to tell to the nations, yes. It is a story of how each of us meets the other most truly in Jesus Christ, who welcomes and embraces and loves despite and beyond even our most cherished traditions and our most ancient creeds, and in whom we are one with each other and at peace with God.

BAPTISM OF THE LORD

Spanish Springs Presbyterian Church, Sparks, Nevada

JANUARY 10, 2010

Isaiah 43:1–7
Acts 8:14–17
Luke 3:15–17, 21–22

"What Do You Expect?"

The writers of the Gospels and Acts, as probably the Old Testament writers before them, seem often to have reduced into a single episode speeches and activities that actually took place over a period of time. What they report Jesus or one of the apostles saying or doing on *one* occasion might actually be a composite of *several* sermons or characteristic activities. And, so, it is probable that John the baptizer preached over a number of months or years in a variety of locations the things that Luke attributes to him in the third chapter of the Third Gospel. "Bear fruits worthy of repentance. Do not begin to say to yourselves, 'We have Abraham as our ancestor'; for I tell you, God is able from these stones to raise up children to Abraham. Even now the ax is lying at the root of the trees; every tree therefore that does not bear good fruit is cut down and thrown into the fire" (Luke 3:8–9). And when the crowds asked him, as they surely did whenever he spoke, what they should do, he must often have said things like, "'Whoever has two coats must share with anyone who has none; and whoever has food must do likewise'" (3:11), depending upon his audience that particular day. We have a glimpse of how he must have tailored his preaching to the sort of folk who were there; Luke reports that "[e]ven tax collectors came to be baptized, and they asked him, 'Teacher, what should *we* do?' He said to them, 'Collect no more than the amount prescribed for you'" (3:12–13). And soldiers appeared from time to time. "'And we, what should *we* do?' He said to them, 'Do not extort money from anyone by threats or false accusation, and be satisfied with your wages'" (3:14).

Notice how every one of these answers addresses a social relationship and boils down to economics and taking care of physical needs. For John, anyway, these things were all very necessary if the way of the Lord was to be prepared and his paths made straight, if every valley was going to be filled and every mountain and hill be made low and the crooked be straightened and the rough ways smoothed out. And, although any straightforward reading of the prophets would seem that it ought to lead all people to the same conclusions, apparently not too many other folks at the time understood that faithfulness to God means inconveniencing oneself in order that the needs of another might be met.

When we read or hear the Gospel accounts of John the wilderness prophet baptizing Jesus, and the Holy Spirit descending upon him, some strong images appear to our mind's eye. Sometimes they can be so vivid that we don't see or hear some of what the Gospel writer reported. For instance, although I have read this passage many times, and its counterpart in the other Gospels, I had never before really noticed the first phrase in today's reading: "As the people were filled with expectation . . ." (3:15a). I always jumped ahead to the next part: ". . . and all were questioning in their hearts concerning *John*, whether *he* might be the Messiah . . ." (3:15b). We learn later on that there was something of a rivalry between the followers of John and the followers of Jesus, despite John's acknowledgment: "'but one who is more powerful than I is coming; I am not worthy to untie the thong of his sandals'" (3:16b). But it seems that John had done such a good job of preaching that there was about to be a fundamental change in the way things were, had convinced so many people of the need to amend their ways and especially their dealings with each other (which meant that there was going to be a change in the way in which people of power and wealth dealt with *them*), that some of them started to attach their hopes to John *himself.* They grew hungry for the new age that John said was about to dawn. They yearned for a world filled with righteousness and dignity and mercy and peace rather than one doomed to greed and lust and hatred and war, in which the powerful took with impunity and the worldly cared nothing about the eternal truths of God. So "the people were filled with expectation" (3:15a), hoping that the Messiah was near and that the promises of God were about to be fulfilled.

Another thing some of us may have missed is that, in Luke's account, it was not while Jesus was being *baptized* that "the heaven was opened, and the Holy Spirit descended upon him in bodily form like a dove. And a voice came from heaven, 'You are my Son, the beloved; with you I am well pleased'"

(3:21b–22). It was *after* he had been baptized, while he was *praying*. In Luke, the coming of the Holy Spirit is often connected with prayer. And the voice may not have been thunderous, as Hollywood would have depicted. The early rabbis often spoke of the sound of a voice from heaven being like the cooing of a dove—something that, perhaps, were it not expected, might easily go unnoticed, or if one's prayers are customarily a one-way communication, filling God's ears with entreaty or complaint enough to drown out the gentle reply. In *Jesus'* case, after his prayer following his baptism, and having returned from the Jordan, he was "full of the Holy Spirit . . . and was led by the Spirit in the wilderness, where for forty days he was tempted by the devil" (4:1, 2a).

We have been raised on too many superheroes to find this a very satisfying sequence of events. It would seem that the Holy Spirit should be a little more like spinach or a cape and leotards or a radioactive spider bite, and apparently John and his followers had some such notion, too. When Jesus didn't immediately launch a campaign to rid the world of sinners and instantly right all wrongs, but rather forgave sinners and healed even the slave of a Roman centurion, John was disappointed, and he sent messengers to inquire of Jesus whether he was the one John had been predicting. "Go and tell John what you have seen and heard," Jesus replied: "the blind receive their sight, the lame walk, the lepers are cleansed, the deaf hear, the dead are raised, the poor have good news brought to them" (4:22)—all the sorts of things Isaiah had prophesied, and that Jesus did personally, one-*on*-one and one-*by*-one. We never learn what John's reaction was when he heard report of Jesus' answer. Was he *still* disappointed that Jesus didn't meet his expectations, or did he decide that it was *his* expectations that were wrong?

Too often, we tend to think of prayer as a way of securing *favors* from God. Jesus regarded prayer as an opportunity for *fellowship* with God, and of opening himself to *illumination* from God, and the channel for receiving *power* from God to do God's *will*. Now baptized, having submitted like others to the public ritual that demonstrated acknowledgment of one's need for God, Jesus prayed in confident expectation that God would aid him to be completely ready for the life of obedient servanthood he was about to undertake. As the *other* people who gathered at the Jordan were filled with expectation about what God would do *for* them, *Jesus* was filled with expectation that God was going to do something *through* him. What it would be, exactly, what all it would entail, he probably did not know. But by yielding himself obediently to serve others in the way of ministering to their needs, and opening the minds and hearts of those around him to the needs of others, and to experience God's love and to reflect God's love, Jesus showed himself to *be*, and himself came to understand that he *was*, the Son of God, the Messiah, the one *through* whom and *in* whom all of the prophecies were fulfilled and the world would know most perfectly what it meant to worship God and obey God's commands.

If we do not live expectantly, we are not going to recognize God's activity in the world, will not perceive that God's will is unfolding before us. But if we expect to be *observers* of God's activity without preparing and offering ourselves to be the instruments through which God's will is *accomplished*, we will fail God and will ourselves be disappointed.

What do *you* expect? To be pious but think that we can remain on the sidelines of life, observing and benefiting but not really participating and sacrificing, will yield paltry results and lead us to wonder, as John and his followers did, why all the marvelous promises haven't seemed to come to fruition. It's rather like when people in a church ask why there aren't more children visible in the church, more families in the congregation, but they themselves haven't offered to teach church school or lead the youth group or help with vacation church school or even just pick up the telephone and call and ask how the kids are doing in school.

The people who came to listen to John preach and be baptized by him clearly thought that things were not totally right in their lives or in the world around them, wanted the promises of God and the prophecies of the Old Testament to be fulfilled, but didn't understand that *God* had expectations, too—expectations for *them*: their sharing a coat with someone who had none, their sharing their food with someone who had none, not abusing the poor, living modestly so that others may live adequately. The *people* were expecting *God* to work a *revolution*, a turning of history, through the Messiah. But *God* was expecting *them* to *repent*—to prepare the *way* for a revolution, a turning of their hearts, through their own obedient deeds of love and mercy. That is the way through which the Holy Spirit *still* opens eyes, lifts the disabled, restores the outcast, communicates with the unhearing, summons the despairing, blesses the poor. And for each of those people, there is no doubt that through their experience of Jesus Christ in the voice, hands, feet, and commitment of his disciples, the Messiah *has* come, the one for whom the world has been waiting, the one whom all those who love God have been expecting.

Today, we are ordaining and installing church officers, elders and deacons, to lead this congregation by encouraging us to expectancy and demonstrating what it means to serve in Christlike ways. The fact that *some* church members are designated for specific tasks of ministry is no reason for the *rest* of us to sit back with arms folded, waiting for the world to be righted and the chairs to be filled. In them we will have an example, after hands are laid on them, after prayers have been offered. But the work of

Jesus Christ is something in which *all* of us who have been baptized are to be engaged, confidently expecting that God has visited the Holy Spirit upon us, and pronouncing that we, too, are God's children, beloved, and now equipped, in response to serious prayer and genuine longing and winsome humility, to bring good news to the poor, to proclaim release to the captives and recovery of sight to the blind, to let the oppressed go free, to proclaim the year of the Lord's favor, because the Spirit of the Lord is upon us. Is that what you expect from your commitment to God through Jesus Christ? I think that's what God expects of *us*.

Second Sunday in Ordinary Time
First Presbyterian Church, Ponca City, Oklahoma
January 20, 2013

Isaiah 62:1–5
1 Corinthians 12:1–11
John 2:1–11

"Not Just Another Wedding"

I don't know exactly what we expected that afternoon at Cana; perhaps we were not expecting anything out of the ordinary. We were only just getting to know each other, really. Jesus had invited us all to come with him and we, each of us, had followed without even knowing where we were going, but were looking for something different from the daily routine, looking for something more from life than what we seemed to have on the fishing docks, at the market, in the shop. We were tired of monotony, of limited horizons and narrow expectations. We were seeking adventure, I guess, even if it was just the adventure of doing something different and slightly irresponsible. Why else would we have followed along after someone from Nazareth, of all places? And yet, there is something special about him—all of us feel it, when he comes up to you and looks at you, when he walks with you, when he says, "Follow me." It is as if he could reach right down inside of you and bring you out of yourself, so that you feel like a new person—the same *you*, but *not* the same *you*—somehow more aware, somehow more eager, somehow more daring, somehow better, somehow all that you could be. You may well ask any of us how we could leave our jobs, our families, our homes, our security so easily. We just did! And, I suppose that if *you* were invited by him to follow, you could do it, too. Oh, I know, you are respectable, you are cautious, you have responsibilities. Well, we were all well-thought-of, hard-working lads who could expect to get along in life, looking out for our families, saving what we could against a bad catch or a season of drought. That's the way we had always been taught. That's how our parents lived, and how their parents lived before them—cautious, prudent, honoring the tradition by being skeptical of change, careful that others might think well of us. But when he came and invited us to follow along....

Well, that's not really what I had in mind to tell you about. We've had many adventures with Jesus now, but one of the most unusual ones was going with him to this wedding. Jesus was a friend of one of the families, I think, or maybe some relation to them. At any rate, his mother was there and seemed to know quite a number of the guests. Of course, it's not unusual to be invited to tag along to a wedding. At my cousin's wedding a couple of years ago, during the course of the week, they entertained hundreds of people; nearly everyone in town was there, as well as folk from ten, fifteen, twenty miles away, and they all brought some kind of present for the couple, and all took full advantage of the refreshments, I'll tell you. It seems that we can't get away from work to go for a friendly visit, but whenever the wine is flowing.... Well, you know how it is. And everyone wants to give their blessing to the couple and their new life together. So it didn't bother us too much that we might not know anyone at the wedding; we were getting to know each other by that time, even though it had only been a few days that we had been together, and just being with Jesus was our main interest. Every moment with him is special—he really knows how to help people enjoy life and to help make everybody feel important and accepted. We didn't have to worry about feeling out of place at the wedding as long as we were with him. And, besides, everyone at the wedding would have been pretty friendly by then, if you know what I mean, after several days of celebrating. The couple's parents would expect drop-in guests at a wedding, and usually provide amply for people like us. After all, they would be judged pretty harshly by their relatives and neighbors if they didn't do it up right. We had all been to weddings; we knew how it would be.

Well, we arrived toward the end of the week of celebration, and after the polite introductions and greeting the bride and groom and the hosts, we were invited to enjoy the hospitality. We were somewhat fatigued by our journey that day, and we were eager for refreshment, so, rather than mingle among the other guests right away, most of us were content to sit and be served wine and the various delicacies that had been prepared for our feasting and enjoy the entertainment. It seems that there's always a lot of gossip at weddings, and comparing the wedding and the food and the wine to other weddings and the food and the wine that were served at *them*. I must say that *this* wine was not particularly *good*—it was not bad, but it was certainly second-rate compared to what one might have *expected* on the *first* few days of the celebration. It probably went without notice by those who had been celebrating for *several* days, but I suspected that the hosts had spent their *best* wine and food already long before *we* had arrived, and now were counting on the likely impairment in the ability of most of their guests to judge the quality of the refreshments. By temperament, we Galileans are generally a sober and industrious lot, but when we go to a party, well . . . we like to celebrate.

While we were having our fill, Jesus, who knew several of the people there, was visiting in the crowd. And then, suddenly, there was some sort of commotion in the house between one of the servants and one of the hosts, and word soon spread that they had run out of wine! What a disaster for the party! What an embarrassment for the hosts! What a disappointment for us! Someone must have badly miscalculated the amount of wine needed, if even the second-rate stuff had been exhausted. The topic of conversation among all the guests quickly turned to the wine situation. Some threatened to leave the party immediately; some proposed to inspect the premises to see if they could turn up anything that the hosts might be holding back for themselves; some pronounced the wedding an unqualified catastrophe.

Well, after a short while, I noticed that Jesus' mother came through the disgruntled crowd and up to him, and they had a little discussion about the situation. I did not know at the time just exactly what was being said, but was later given to understand by people who overheard the conversation that she had informed him of the crisis and that his reply was not altogether courteous—whether he didn't think that someone else's social blunder was his problem, or whether he was just asserting his independence from his mother, I'm not certain. It seems to have had something to do with timing—whether it was just the right moment for him to be dealing with such an emergency. Jesus is the sort of person to whom people would naturally turn in a crisis, someone you would expect to have a solution for any dilemma. Certainly, I have always known Jesus over these past several weeks and months to be very helpful, even to people he did not know, people who were in any sort of need. Maybe he just had no idea what his mother expected him to do about the situation—offer to go out and buy more wine somewhere, when the hosts had probably already exhausted the stock of every wine merchant in the district? I have frequently hoped that it wasn't *our* presence that had caused the shortage or created an embarrassment for Jesus' mother, especially since we didn't bring any wedding gift. But as for her, I think that just having talked to Jesus was enough to set her into motion. There was a group of servants standing near me just then, bewildered at the awkwardness of the situation and talking excitedly among themselves. Jesus' mother came over to them, and I overheard her instruct them to do whatever Jesus might tell them to do. It was clear that she was confident that Jesus would do *something* to help the situation and redeem the wedding celebration.

Sure enough, a few minutes later, Jesus came over to the servants and gave them instructions of some sort. The next thing I knew, they were carrying water in jars, and pouring it into these much bigger jars—you know, those jars that you see in Jewish homes that hold water for our purification rites. There were six of these huge stone jars there in the courtyard, and they filled each one to the very brim with *water*. That took quite a while, and many of the guests were curious about what was happening, but then some of them lost interest, especially since the wine was having an effect on their ability to stand and watch for so long. When the servants finally finished their task, Jesus said something to them, and one of them drew out from one of the jars into a cup and took the cup over to the master of ceremonies. By this time, I had pushed myself through the partygoers so that I was able to follow the servant; I could not understand what purpose there might be in pouring the water into the jars and then taking some of it over to the master of ceremonies, but I knew that there must be *some* purpose, for it must have had to do with the instructions that Jesus had given to the servants.

Imagine my astonishment—you are going to find this hard to believe, I know, but I heard it with my own ears: The master of ceremonies asked, "Where did you get this wine?" It was *water* that the servants had put into the jars—I had seen them *do* it! But, "Where did you get this *wine*?" And when people heard the word "wine," everyone turned toward the master of ceremonies. But by this time, he was chiding the bridegroom—good-humoredly, but in obvious seriousness. "Everyone serves the good wine first," he said, "and then the inferior wine after the guests have become drunk. But you have kept the good wine until now" (John 2:10). And at that, all the guests flocked to the jars—the water jars—I mean the wine jars—I mean.... They all filled their cups and agreed that it was some of the best wine that they had ever tasted, certainly better than what they had *already* consumed at the wedding. I looked for Jesus and spotted him at the far side of the crowd, and saw the servants looking at him, too, in amazement. But Jesus was just smiling at the happy people crowded around the jars, each person holding out a cup to get some of the good wine.

It was certainly not just another wedding that we had attended with Jesus. None of us who were with Jesus said anything to him—we just looked at each other dumbfounded, as the story I have told you spread from one of us to another. This all happened not so very long ago, but since then we have seen so many other strange and wonderful things as we have followed Jesus around Galilee that one almost *expects* miraculous things to happen when one is with Jesus—and always things that are helpful to people who are in difficult situations.

I am sure that none of us could *ever* leave him now, no matter what might happen to us or to him. Forgive me if this sounds blasphemous, but if *God himself* were walking with us, I think it could not be more wonderful and exciting than being with Jesus. Indeed, he speaks with such authority, such power and gentleness at the same time, such truth and honesty, that some of us have begun to question among ourselves whether he might not be a prophet. But in so many ways he is much *more* than a prophet; he is so personal and so sensitive to everyone's needs—he is our friend. In fact, I have sometimes thought about what happened that day at Cana: wine in abundance, good wine—the rabbis speak of such things as a sign of the day of salvation, of the time of the Messiah. It's almost as if Jesus . . . . All I know for sure is that these weeks of being with Jesus have been more joyful than any days I had known before; so different, as if I were experiencing true life for the first time, as if the whole world must wake up and discover what life is really about, as if everyone must come to trust him and listen to him and be made over by living as he says, as if all the days that I spent before Jesus came along were as common as . . . water, and now he has changed all my days to wine.

Third Sunday in Ordinary Time
First Presbyterian Church, Dodge City, Kansas
January 18, 1998

Nehemiah 8:1–3, 5–6, 8–10
1 Corinthians 12:12–31a
Luke 4:14–21

"Job Description"

He could have had any personal satisfaction that he wanted, but he knew that "'[o]ne does not live by bread alone'" (Luke 4:4b). He could have exercised every sort of power, if he had just compromised his loyalty to God, but he knew that only *God* is worthy of *worship*, and that obedience to God must come before any personal prestige, any personal gain, any personal glory. He could have avoided all the frailties of human life, even death itself, but he realized that faithfulness means living thankfully by the blessings of God's gracious hand, not demanding them as one's right, as one's due. And after forty days in the wilderness, which is the Bible's way of saying "a long time," wrestling with sober questions of his identity and his vocation and his faith, Jesus, then about thirty years old, began his ministry by teaching in the synagogues of Galilee, filled with the power of the Spirit, and he was praised by everyone—at first, anyway.

> When he came to Nazareth, where he had been brought up, he went to the synagogue on the sabbath day, as was his custom [for Jesus knew that God should be worshiped every sabbath]. He stood up to read, and the scroll of the prophet Isaiah was given to him. He unrolled the scroll and found the place where it was written:
>
> > "The Spirit of the Lord is upon me,
> > because he has anointed me

"Job Description"

> to bring good news to the poor.
> He has sent me to proclaim release to the captives
> and recovery of sight to the blind,
> to let the oppressed go free,
> to proclaim the year of the Lord's favor."
>
> ... The eyes of all in the synagogue were fixed on him. Then he began to say to them, "Today this scripture has been fulfilled in your hearing." (4:16–21)

The promised day of salvation, of healing and deliverance, of mercy and grace, has come, Jesus said. For he himself was the promised Savior, the healer and deliverer, merciful and gracious, appointed to the task by God, equipped for the task by the Holy Spirit, fulfilling the task regardless of personal consequence. The servant who first spoke these words in Isaiah ended up despised and rejected, wounded and crushed, oppressed and afflicted. And so, of course, did Jesus. That is what one must expect in a sin-drenched world when one brings good news to the poor, for good news to the poor always seems to be a threat to the affluent; or when one proclaims release to the captives, for releasing the captives will enrage those who imprisoned them; or when one declares recovery of sight to the blind, for many would prefer that their deeds not be scrutinized by anyone; or when one lets the oppressed go free, for true justice is dangerous for the powerful; or when one proclaims the year of the Lord's favor, for a lot of people benefit from the long-engendered belief that the kingdom of God exists only in the future, far off and indefinite. But Jesus knew who he was. Jesus knew what he must do. And Jesus knew that his followers must learn to do the same.

In these few verses, which tell of an episode at the beginning of Jesus' ministry, Luke sets forth Jesus' job description. Jesus was the Messiah, the anointed one. He would reverse the fortunes of the poor and the rich. He would establish justice and equity. He would end oppression and prejudice. He would humble the proud and the self-satisfied. He would abolish boundaries of nation and race. Luke had hinted at it earlier, in the song that Mary sang in praise to God when Elizabeth greeted her, and in the song that Zechariah sang in praise to God when his son John was named—he who would be the prophet of Jesus,—and in the song that Simeon sang in praise to God when Jesus was dedicated in the temple, and in the preaching of John in all the region around the Jordan. And then, finally, Luke puts it on Jesus' own lips, this job description. "Then [Jesus] began to say to [those gathered in the synagogue], 'Today this scripture has been fulfilled in your hearing'" (4:21).

In the synagogue at Nazareth, Jesus was speaking to people steeped in the Bible. They knew the requirements of the law. They knew the warnings and promises of the prophets. They knew that God declares over and over again that it is the obligation of societies to care for the poor and ensure justice for the powerless and vindicate those who are oppressed. They knew that, having once been sojourners looking for food and shelter in a strange land because things were bad in their own country, now God required *them* to offer hospitality to foreigners. They knew that when they succumbed to the temptation to suppose that their well-being was all the result of their own ingenuity and their own toil, they were venturing over the threshold of idolatry. They knew that their ancestor Abraham had been blessed not for his *own* sake, but in order that *all* people might experience God's blessing through his offspring. They knew that God had promised a Messiah to inaugurate the realm of God over all the earth and in every heart. "Today," Jesus said, "this scripture has been fulfilled in your hearing" (4:21b). Today, Jesus was saying, I have inaugurated the kingdom of God. Today, the "*some*day" of wholeness and justice and peace and fairness and equity has arrived.

I try to avoid talk radio. Occasionally, though, I hear bits and pieces of it while waiting for the news or while searching for something entertaining as I travel in the car. I remember one day a couple of years ago I heard a talk show host praise some caller for saying, "Once upon a time, I believed that it was my job to help the poor, to sacrifice something for African-Americans and Hispanics and the rest" (actually, he used some other words there), "and to pay taxes so that guys who are on trial but can't afford a lawyer will have one, but then, eventually, I grew up." Later on in the program, another caller was complaining about the lack of prayer in school since, as she said, everyone knows that this is a "Christian" country. That, too, won the approval of the talk show host, who seemed not to have the slightest regard for the irony of agreeing with both of those statements. Does not being a Christian have something to do with fulfilling the priorities of Jesus Christ? Do "Christian" nations allow children to go hungry, or tolerate wide disparity in conviction rates and sentences between blacks and whites, between so-called white-collar crime and other forms of crime, or punish people for trying to go where they can get a job that will feed their family?

Some people will undoubtedly dismiss this sort of sermon as "political," though I don't know how a faithful minister or a faithful congregation can be oblivious to the clear implications of the gospel. It has little to do with whether a person chooses to be a Republican or a Democrat. Presidents and governors and legislators of both parties, history has shown, can embrace or ignore the teachings of Jesus and the commandments of God. Fundamentally, it is not "political"; it is *theological*, and, specifically, it is *biblical*.

It has to do with the job description that Jesus understood he was working under as the Son of God. And, since Jesus told his disciples to follow him, to put their allegiance where he did, to do even greater works of forgiving and healing and feeding and championing and confronting than he did, it has to do with *your* job description and *mine* as Christians.

There was a time in the not too distant past when the Christian church had something of a consensus about that. There was a time not too long ago when the Christian church understood that no one can say "I love Jesus" without taking responsibility for the living conditions of one's neighbor, physical needs as well as spiritual. Strategies were debated, but the basic Christian responsibility was never denied, and it was not evaded. Some things that were tried did not have the anticipated result. Human sin being a factor in everything, some programs were abused. Others worked wonderfully and changed people's lives dramatically for the better. Even if it achieved only a short-term result, it was a faithful deed. We do not know that each of *Jesus'* deeds of compassionate ministry had a lasting effect for the individual involved. Jesus fulfilled his job description wherever he saw need, whether it be hunger or despair or sickness or infirmity or cruelty, and he did so spontaneously, hopefully, leaving the long-term result to God.

Now, when I read some church-related publications, or listen to some self-styled "Christian" television and radio programs, it sounds as if being poor is a sin, as if some being hungry is God's will, as if sickness is punishment, as if economic survival of the fittest is sacred doctrine, as if forgiveness is something to be earned, as if Mary's song and Zechariah's song and Simeon's song and John's preaching and Jesus' own words about who he was and what he was doing have been struck from the Bible. And I think, where in all this "Christian" talk is the compassion of Christ that permeates the Gospels? Where is the faithful response to the special concern of God for the poor and the oppressed and the outcast that thunders through the prophets? Where is the humble gratitude for God's gifts and God's forgiveness that must make the people of God servants and not bullies, compassionate and not arrogant, repentant and not prideful?

Jesus passed on his earthly ministry to his disciples. Jesus' followers have inherited his job description. It is now *our* job to do as *Jesus* did, by the power of the Holy Spirit. But so many poor are still waiting for *good* news, not just more *bad* news, *today*. So many sin-ridden still wait for *forgiveness*, not more *condemnation, today*. So many captives still wait for release *today*. So many who are blind, both physically and spiritually, still need their vision restored *today*. Oppression continues abroad and, more subtly, in our own land, and it *is* our business to do something about it *today*. And God has never erased from the Bible his law about giving the poor a new start, an even start, even a head start, in the year of Jubilee. And it's not a matter of a "liberal" preacher here and there—a perfectly good term that has been spun into a four-letter word lately. It's a matter of God's Word.

Feeding the hungry may not be for us today just a matter of multiplying five loaves and two fish, though it *might* be. Restoring sight to the blind may not be for us today just a matter of laying hands on the person who is afflicted, though it *might* be. The job description has remained unchanged for nearly two thousand years. It will not be rationalized away by economic predictions or political theories or sociological statistics. It is the daily assignment of the Messiah and anyone who believes that the Messiah has come. And everyone who loves Jesus has been gifted by the Holy Spirit to do an important ministry that Jesus did, graciously, confidently, hopefully, faithfully. It is the job description of *each Christian*. It is the job description of the *whole church*. It is the job description of *every* church. It is the job description of each of *us*. It is the job description of the Presbyterian Church (U.S.A.). It is the job description of First Presbyterian Church of Dodge City, Kansas. It is the job description of a Christian people.

Fourth Sunday in Ordinary Time

Spanish Springs Presbyterian Church, Sparks, Nevada

January 31, 2010

Jeremiah 1:4–10
1 Corinthians 13:1–13
Luke 4:21–30

"Pride *Is* a Deadly Sin"

It is a profound irony that perhaps the greatest passage in all of literature on the subject of *love* was occasioned by a habit of behavior that was love's exact *opposite*. "[L]ove is *not* envious or boastful or arrogant or rude," Paul wrote. "It does *not* insist on its own way; it is *not* irritable or resentful; it does *not* rejoice in wrongdoing" (1 Cor 13:4b–6a). Instead, Paul reminded his audience, "Love is *patient*; love is *kind* . . . . It *bears* all things, *believes* all things, *hopes* all things, *endures* all things" (13:4a, 7).

Those words, of course, are from the thirteenth chapter of First Corinthians, a letter that must have been very difficult for the apostle Paul to write, and painful. The church at Corinth, which *should* have been behaving as a beacon drawing people to the gospel, the good news of Jesus Christ, was *instead* acting in such an un-Christlike manner that it very probably was driving away good pagans who had begun to inquire about Christ. Specifically, some members of the church seem to have been claiming spiritual superiority to one another, and more generally were giving and taking offense over claims of entitlement and privilege. Judging from Paul's comments about thinking and reasoning "like a *child*" (13:10), the *adults* in that congregation were behaving as *juveniles*, in a way that even *non*-Christians would regard as immature, talking each other down, triangulating and manipulating in the way that we associate with prideful and jealous and insecure adolescents. Even the sacrament of the Lord's Supper, the table of reconciliation, had become a zone of contention—an extreme scandal to the body of Christ and an appalling disregard of his great sacrifice on the cross.

That was not what the church was supposed to be like—dissension, jealousy, backstabbing, and backbiting. Christians were to exhibit a more excellent way. And as long as the motives of the Corinthians were pride and the jealousy that erupts from it, nothing that they did, no matter how great an achievement, would be of any worth, would be any credit.

The state of the Corinthian church is one that many of us have experienced in our own histories of churchgoing. It is surprising, perhaps, that such a condition could exist in such a *young* congregation, which *should* still have been fired with enthusiasm to be spending its energies on evangelism and reveling in the new thing God was doing with them and among them. There was plenty of work to be done in a city not much in tune with the ways of God. Scholars think that the letter was written in the year 54 or 55 to this congregation that had only just been established in the year 49; the church, in other words, was only five or six years old, roughly the same age as our own Spanish Springs congregation. What things *weren't* getting done for Jesus Christ, because the sins of the ego were asserting themselves so destructively, because turf was being protected so assiduously, because love, the most important ingredient for Christian living, was in such short supply? It seems that the motives and manners of Greek culture were infecting the *congregation* more than the congregation was modeling the ways of Christ in order to transform Greek *culture*. Even the gifts of the Holy Spirit, bestowed for the purpose of building up the church in love and devotion and effectiveness, had been turned into ammunition in the contentious congregation!

The love that Christians are supposed to display and that is supposed to be their motive is, of course, the very *antithesis* of self-importance or self-display or self-assertion. The Christians in Corinth *were* to be living in humble submission to *God* and to *one another*, patterning their behavior on the obedient servanthood of Christ, rejoicing in the power and accomplishments of the Holy Spirit, *whatever* channels it chose to use. But the jealous factions that had developed in the Corinthian congregation were bringing *disrepute* to the gospel, not *advancing* it, and so Paul, when he heard that the church was exhibiting the fruits of *pride* rather than the fruits of the *Spirit*, wrote a long letter, probably from Ephesus, trying to *correct* the misdirection of the young congregation by drawing its attention to the marks of Christian love.

John Cassianus, a monk who lived in the late fourth and early fifth centuries, once identified eight sins, categories into which, he taught, all transgressions essentially fall. Pope Gregory the Great, two centuries later, refined the number into seven, putting pride at the head of the list. Many theologians since that time have recognized pride as, in fact, the motive from which all *other* sins really *flow*. There is no list of "seven deadly sins" in the Bible, and the Bible nowhere specifies *some* sins as being any more heinous than *others*, except to say that blaspheming the Holy Spirit is unforgivable. Biblical writers were more concerned to attack sin as the basic condition of human rebellion against God rather than listing all the specific activities through which it is manifested. And as the basic condition of rebellion against God, sin is virtually synonymous with pride. It is placing ourselves at the center of the universe, trumpeting our desires over God's purpose, counting our wisdom as superior to Christ's, to the point of thinking that our goals—even those that, on their face, match God's hopes—justify un-Christlike means, anything from gossip and fraud to war and extermination. *All* sins are equally deadly, as far as the cause of the gospel is concerned. *All* of them are destructive to the relationship we ought to have with God and with each other. *All* of them violate the law of love.

When Jesus rolled up the scroll of Isaiah and handed it back to the attendant and sat down and announced that the prophecy had been fulfilled that day in the hearing of those gathered in the synagogue at Nazareth—the prophecy about the Spirit of the Lord being upon the servant who had been anointed to bring good news to the poor and to proclaim release to the captives and recovery of sight to the blind and to let the oppressed go free and to proclaim the year of the Lord's favor,—the response was quite *different* from what it *should* have been. Scholars disagree whether the murmuring among the worshipers was approval or criticism—"Is not this Joseph's son?" (Luke 4:22) could be taken either way, and perhaps Luke intended for it to be ambiguous. But *Jesus*, at least, understood that there was a potential for the hometown folks to respond to him out of wounded *pride* rather than joyous *approval*. People who had been praying for the coming of the Messiah *should* have answered his announcement with shouts of "Thanks be to God!" or "Isn't it wonderful!" or "Finally!" But these good religious people tried to throw Jesus off a cliff! They were in a jealous rage because he had reminded them that the prophets Elijah and Elisha had performed wonders for *Gentiles* rather than *Jews*, though *Jews* were *also* in need at the time of Elijah and Elisha. God's promise of blessing upon Abraham had been warped into a sense of privilege and entitlement, so that good synagoguegoers could not bring themselves to rejoice at the news of the *boundlessness* of God's *love* and the *limitlessness* of God's *salvation*. And yet, God's promise to Abraham had been that he and his descendants would be blessed in order that they might in turn be a blessing to *others*. There was to be nothing exclusive about God's blessings—they did not constitute a privilege, but were instead a commission to go out and *spread* the blessing; as Luke later says, the good news of Jesus Christ was to *start* from Jerusalem but then to *spread* to all Judea and the despised country of Samaria and finally to the ends of the earth, even to Rome itself. There was nothing *new* in that scope of God's concern. Even the great prophet Jeremiah, God appointed to be a spokesperson "to the *nations*" (Jer 1:5).

The Corinthians had themselves been beneficiaries of God's indiscriminate care and Paul's conviction that the grace of God is in no sense a private possession, that no one is more deserving of God's salvation than another, that no church member is entitled to greater deference than any other, that no skill or talent is more indispensable to Christian community than any other. Of all people, those who had once been on the *outside* of God's covenant should know how *deadly* pride can be, cutting others off from full access to God's grace, should know what it means to suffer from denial of the inclusive sweep of God's love. And yet, here they were, turning faith into a competition and turning good news into heartache, or at least heart*burn*. "Now I appeal to you, brothers and sisters, by the name of our Lord Jesus Christ, that all of you be in agreement and that there be no divisions among you, but that you be united in the same mind and the same purpose" (1 Cor 1:10), Paul wrote. To divide the body of Christ is to tear Jesus apart. It is to crucify Jesus again. And wasn't it *pride* that put Jesus on the cross the *first* time?—the pride that condemned him for befriending the poor and forgiving sinners and healing on the sabbath and announcing the nearness of the kingdom of God?—the pride of those who claimed the authority to ration God's bounty and regulate God's grace and restrict God's salvation and decide when and where God would meet his people? Pride!—the inordinate love of one's own excellence, and all the things that flow from it, which deadens us to God and deadens us to one another, and can deaden even the witness of the church. Why, it can even motivate good religious people to throw God's own Son over the cliff, or execute him as a criminal.

"If I speak in the tongues of mortals and of angels, but do not have love, I am a noisy gong or a clanging cymbal. And if I have prophetic powers, and understand all mysteries and all knowledge, and if I have all faith, so as to remove mountains, but do not have love, I am nothing. If I give away all my possessions, and if I hand over my body so that I may boast, but do not have love, I gain nothing" (13:1–3). If I am the most religious, talented, wise, dedicated person imaginable, but am not *acting* out of love, *demonstrating* love, *speaking* love, I am very likely acting out of, demonstrating, and speaking from *pride*. I put myself at the center of the universe. Whatever *I* do is *God's* will, whatever *I* say is *God's* truth, whatever *I* decide is *God's* judgment. In fact, I *usurp* God, put *myself* in God's place. Even if the poor and the captive and the blind and the oppressed *are* ministered to, I become resentful of them, I keep them at arm's length, I secretly believe that I am more deserving of God's favor than they.

To a church that, in a few short years, had become contentious and divided and territorial, careless to injure and quick to perceive insult, Paul the apostle, himself so often provoked, accused, slandered, wrote, "Love is patient; love is kind; love is not envious or boastful or arrogant or rude. It does not insist on its own way; it is not irritable or resentful; it does not rejoice in wrongdoing, but rejoices in the truth. It bears all things, believes all things, hopes all things, endures all things" (13:4–7). Surely, love wants only the *best* for others—*all* others—and *rejoices* at news of healing, of forgiveness, or restoration, of wholeness, of salvation. It is the opposite of pride, and so, where love is present and active, jealousy and dissension and all the rest have no opportunity to sprout and grow and destroy. Pride *is* a deadly sin. Love is the more excellent way.

Fifth Sunday in Ordinary Time

Spanish Springs Presbyterian Church, Sparks, Nevada

February 8, 2004

Isaiah 6:1–8
1 Corinthians 15:1–11
Luke 5:1–11

"Truth in Advertising"

Shortly after I arrived in Nevada and assumed my position as organizing pastor of the Spanish Springs new church development, I was sent to a conference about starting new churches. There were hundreds of people there—pastors, seminarians, consultants, staff personnel from various denominations and *un*-denominations, and quite a crowd of vendors selling everything from canned sermons to promotional packages to recorded music to audio-visual equipment—all very slick, all very programmed, all very loud. After the three days of the conference, my head was reeling. I felt like I had landed on an alien planet. I felt sick in my soul. I just wanted to leave. I had been thrust into the bold new world of marketing Jesus, of church as big business, of selling the Christian faith, and, frankly, I was appalled. The church must always be able to speak *to* the culture, to make connections *with* the culture, but the gospel of Jesus Christ is always a judgment *upon* the culture, and must never succumb *to* the culture. But it seemed to me that everywhere I turned, everything I heard, everything I saw was an uncritical embrace *of* the culture—shallow glitz, loud hype, domineering showmanship, "If you don't buy this then you ain't serious about Jesus." There was nothing at the conference that taught anything about holding the hands of parishioners who are journeying through dark nights of the soul; there was nothing at the conference that suggested at all that being a disciple of Jesus Christ *might* and inevitably *does* come at some *cost*. There was certainly nothing at the conference that even *hinted* at the *prophetic* side of Christian responsibility—of God's truth standing over *against* the materialism, the wastefulness, the greed, the brashness, the artificiality of our age. In fact, the conference struck me as a *celebration* of *those very things*, only thinly disguised by stamping the name "Jesus" all over it.

In a culture that seems to gauge just about everything in purely *economic* terms, perhaps we should not be surprised at the pressures to commercialize the Christian faith, but we should at least be alert to the *truth* of what is happening, and name it for what it *is*. And commercialization brings with it all of the techniques of advertising—the art of creating a market for a product or a service and making people feel inferior or out of step or unpopular or ignorant if they don't buy it. In such an atmosphere, the gospel itself is in danger of being warped and twisted to meet the modern consumer's desires—desires that certainly have little to do with confessing our sin or enduring suffering or sacrificing for others or occupying the position of a servant. So, commercial Christian music doesn't talk about such things. In conferences such as the one to which I was sent, pastors are advised not to preach about such things. And I have yet to see a full-color glossy church mailing that includes the advisory, "Warning: Following Jesus Christ may be hazardous to your comfort level and accustomed standard of living," certainly not, "Beware: Christians have been persecuted, tortured, and killed."

Faithfulness to God, to whom Jesus Christ always pointed those whom he taught, those whom he forgave, those whom he healed, those whom he fed, begins with a sense of unworthiness and gratitude. That is far *different* from our modern Western assumptions of superiority and entitlement. Simon the fisherman surely took no guff from anybody, would never have allowed anyone to think for a minute that he was any less a man than anyone else on the boat, or perhaps in the tavern, would never have doubted his ability to match any other fisherman's skills or bravery. But one day, after Simon and his crew had had a discouraging night on the lake, Jesus came walking along the shoreline and climbed into one of their boats that was beached there and began teaching the people who gathered to hear him, and then he said to Simon, "'Put out into the deep water and let down your nets for a catch'" (Luke 5:4b). It may be that Luke has toned down Simon's reply, has made it a little more respectful and cooperative. "'Master, we have worked all night long but have caught nothing. Yet, if you say so, I will let down the nets'" (5:5–6). At the very least, Simon must have rolled his eyes when he called his crew back to the boat, reloaded their nets, pushed it back out into the water, jumped aboard, began rowing and perhaps hoisting the sail, Jesus sitting quietly in the boat all the while. We can just imagine that, fifty yards out or so, Simon probably looked at Jesus with an expression that said, "Is this far enough?," and Jesus didn't change *his* expression, and so they went out another fifty yards or so, and then he looked at Jesus with an expression that said, "Well, is *this* far enough?," and Jesus *still* didn't change *his* expression, and so on until they were much farther out, beyond earshot of Simon's friends and comrades standing on the shore looking out toward the boat, now just a small object and its crew barely visible, casting their nets over the side. "When they had done this, they caught so many fish that their nets were beginning to break. So they signaled their partners in the other boat to come and help them. And they came and filled both boats, so that they began to sink. But when Simon Peter saw it, he fell down at Jesus' knees, saying, 'Go away from me, Lord, for I am a sinful man!'" (5:6–8)

Suddenly, Simon recognized the holiness of Jesus; that this man sitting quietly in his boat was like no other, that despite his appearance of being just another Galilean peasant, he was in fact God-like in his power and his wisdom and his authority, that Simon, rough in speech and quick in temper and casual in his observance of the sabbath, had no business being in the same place with such a man. No one in Capernaum had ever witnessed a catch like this before. It was a miracle, undeserved and, after a long night of disappointment, very much appreciated. "For [Simon] and all who were with him were amazed at the catch of fish that they had taken; and so also were James and John, sons of Zebedee, who were partners with Simon. Then Jesus said to Simon, 'Do not be afraid; from now on you will be catching people.' When they had brought their boats to shore, they left everything and followed him" (5:9–11).

I can think of only one case in the Bible where someone thought that he or she was worthy to follow Christ, was deserving of being called by God to a ministry of any kind, and Jesus turned *that* person *away*. Among all the patriarchs, among all the prophets, among all the disciples, among all the apostles, there was not *one* who assumed that he or she was worthy or even able to carry out the task that was being assigned. "Woe is me!" the prophet Isaiah confessed when he realized that he was in the presence of God that day in the temple. "I am lost, for I am a man of unclean lips, and I live among a people of unclean lips; yet my eyes have seen the King, the Lord of hosts!" (Isa 6:5) He knew that he had no right to be looking even upon the *robe* of God—the vision he saw as the smoke from the altar and the burning incense drifted up and down in the sunlight that penetrated the holy place,—holy as God is, and sinful as he was. Already, the very hinges of the doors had shaken with the testimony to the holiness of God.

> Then one of the seraphs flew to me, holding a live coal that had been taken from the altar with a pair of tongs. The seraph

touched my mouth with it and said: "Now that this has touched your lips, your guilt has departed and your sin is blotted out." Then I heard the voice of the Lord saying, "Whom shall I send, and who will go for us?" And I said, "Here am I; send me!" And he said, "Go and say to this people:
>'Keep listening, but do not comprehend;
>keep looking, but do not understand.'
>Make the mind of this people dull,
>>and stop their ears,
>>and shut their eyes,
>so that they may not look with their eyes,
>>and listen with their ears,
>and comprehend with their minds,
>>and turn and be healed."

Then I said, "How long, O Lord?" And he said:
>"Until cities lie waste
>>without inhabitant,
>and houses without people,
>>and the land is utterly desolate;
>until the LORD sends everyone far away,
>>and vast is the emptiness in the midst of the land." (6:6–12)

Not only was the presence of God a frightening notion to Isaiah, but his commission from God, when it came, was a terrifying one, too: preach to the nation so that their hearts are hardened toward God and their ears are deafened toward God and their eyes are shut toward God, so that they will refuse to repent, and keep doing it until their cities are destroyed and their land is devastated and they have been carried off into exile! In other words, preach the radical countercultural reality of God, and *keep* preaching it until the people are judged and punished for their very refusal to listen to and obey his commands about right worship and turning from idols and caring for the poor and removing the yoke of the oppressed!

Not a very happy job description for Isaiah—not one calculated to make him popular, but one that would quite likely cause him to be despised and rejected (and, we see from the rest of the book of Isaiah, he *was*). And six hundred years later, Simon Peter, as we are told, was crucified upside down for his faithfulness to Jesus and to Christ's gospel. It seems that not many of the ancient prophets or the early apostles died of old age. And in our own time, there are *still* followers of Christ who are being killed for their faith—Dietrich Bonhoeffer in Nazi Germany, Martin Luther King Jr. in segregationist America, Bishop Oscar Romero in dictatorial Guatemala, and those whose names are lesser known—a young seminary graduate who was killed while working in the South during the civil rights movement, a teenaged believer at Columbine High School gunned down when she acknowledged her loyalty to Christ.

I have shared with some of you my amazement over a commercial currently running on television about a new church that meets on Tuesday evenings—nothing wrong with that—which explains that it is so people can enjoy their weekends—have their Sundays free for recreation instead of worshiping God. Surely, God can be worshiped anywhere and anytime. But what is the message being conveyed to people about the potential *cost* of being a disciple of Jesus Christ, about the mystery and awe of God, which surely requires more of us than "Let's do lunch sometime"? The study book that we are using for our midweek class on Isaiah quotes writer Annie Dillard's warning about not taking worship lightly—about not being casual with God. "Does anyone have the foggiest idea what sort of power we so blithely invoke?" she asks. "We should all be wearing crash helmets. Ushers should issue life preservers and signal flares; they should lash us to the pews."[1] *That* would be truth in advertising—at least, if we are talking about genuinely encountering the God who created everything that is, whose holiness is absolute, whose decree is uncompromising, whose urgent love compelled him to sacrifice even his own Son for our salvation, and to whom we should be so *grateful* that *no* inconvenience should prevent us from giving all of the praise and honor and loyalty and obedience we can muster, both *inside* God's house on the *sabbath* and *outside* God's house all through the *week*.

An acknowledgment of our unworthiness and a profound sense of gratitude—these are the motives that fashioned all of the faithful servants of God, all of the disciples of Jesus Christ, in the scriptures, and that still fashion faithful servants and faithful disciples today. "Woe is me! I am lost, for I am a man of unclean lips, and I live among a people of unclean lips; yet my eyes have seen the King, the LORD of hosts!" (6:5), cried Isaiah when he recognized himself to be in the presence of God. "Go away from me, Lord, for I am a sinful man!" (Luke 5:8b), cried Simon Peter when he recognized himself to be in the presence of God. "Go and say to this people . . ." (Isa 6:9), God commissioned the prophet. "Do not be afraid; from now on you will be catching people" (Luke 5:10b), the Son of God commissioned the disciple. The truth is, it's not about marketing hype. It's about reverence for the holiness of God. It's not about working Jesus into our schedule. It's about giving up everything and following him. It's not about living the good life in a consumer's paradise. It's about dying to ourselves and rising with Christ to eternal life.

---

1. Dillard, *Teaching a Stone*, 52.

Sixth Sunday in Ordinary Time

First Presbyterian Church, Dodge City, Kansas

February 15, 1998

Jeremiah 17:5–10
1 Corinthians 15:12–20
Luke 6:17–26

"The Guarantee"

"For I handed on to you as of first importance what I in turn received: that Christ died for our sins in accordance with the scriptures, and that he was buried, and that he was raised on the third day in accordance with the scriptures, and that he appeared to Cephas, then to the twelve. Then he appeared to more than five hundred brothers and sisters at one time.... Then he appeared to James, then to all the apostles. Last of all, as to one untimely born, he appeared also to me" (1 Cor 15:3–8). So the apostle Paul, in what we know as his first letter to the young Christian church at Corinth, described the substance of his preaching as he spread the gospel in the cities and towns of Greece. He and the other apostles proclaimed a message that has come to be known as the "*kerygma*"—they proclaimed the death and resurrection of Christ, and they proclaimed it with passion and zeal. And none of them preached more passionately or more zealously the death and resurrection of Christ than Paul, and nowhere did he preach it more passionately or more zealously than at Corinth, among both Jews and Greeks.

For Paul and the other apostles, the death and resurrection of Christ was the foundation of their faith in the character and purpose of God and the foundation of their faith that Jesus was the *Son* of God. So, when Paul heard from some source that the Corinthians were disputing among themselves in a way that impinged upon the belief in Christ's *resurrection*, the apostle wrote to them not only in order to defend the doctrine that he preached among them, but in order to preserve the very underpinning of the Christian faith.

Jesus was clearly a gifted teacher and healer. Even his enemies admitted that. His teaching and healing attracted large crowds of people who had been impressed and sometimes disappointed by *other* teachers and healers, itinerants offering wisdom and cures, perhaps even following them from town to town as they traveled around Galilee and Judea. As some of the Jews of Galilee and Judea did, as some of Paul's ancient Greek audience did, we moderns easily become impressed by the accounts of the words and deeds of Jesus. Some of us find that we admire his teachings and his generosity and his kindness, yet without committing ourselves to believe that this man from Nazareth was God in human flesh. Some of us find ourselves deeply moved by Jesus' unjust and submissive death on Good Friday, yet cannot quite believe that he was raised from the dead on Easter Sunday. The gospel story has great power to affect us at a sentimental level. It may lighten our daily load with its quotable moralisms. But Paul discerned how the real *significance* of Jesus' words and deeds ultimately depends upon the *fact* of Jesus' resurrection, and how *confidence* in the eternal truthfulness of Jesus' words and deeds ultimately depends upon *faith* in Jesus' resurrection.

It is not clear how the issue had arisen at Corinth, but it seems that several of the Corinthian church members were saying that they did not believe that their friends and relatives who had died or would die before Christ's return would be raised from the dead. Ancient Greeks would have had difficulty understanding and accepting the concept of the resurrection; in fact, they would have been rather offended by it. Many of their greatest philosophers over the centuries had taught that the soul is immortal and good, but the body is crude and repulsive—an earth-bound hindrance to the soul, preventing the soul from achieving its destiny. Anything that emancipated the soul was beneficial. Anything that restricted the soul was repugnant. Since death dissolved the fleshly bonds that imprisoned the soul, the demise of the body was a welcome event. For the Greeks, any talk of resurrection—of being raised to life again in a new body—scandalized their entire concept of life after death. The Corinthians were not directly contradicting Paul's teaching that *Christ* had been raised again from the dead, but only indirectly, by denying the resurrection of anyone else.

But the logic of Paul was finer even than the logic of the Greek philosophers. Paul knew that to deny the resurrection of the dead in *any* instance was to deny *Christ's* resurrection—an event that Paul preached not as an optimistic *possibility*, but as a fundamental *fact*. "Now if Christ is proclaimed as raised from the dead, how can some of you say there is no resurrection of the dead? If there is no resurrection of the dead, then Christ has not been raised; and if Christ has not been raised, then our proclamation has been in vain and your faith has been in vain" (15:12–14). Paul was utterly convinced of Christ's resurrection. Paul had encountered the risen Christ as he was traveling to Damascus, when he was still zealous in the cause of persecuting the Christians. Paul had the proof of the way his own life had been changed by that encounter with the risen Christ. And he had the proof of the way that other people, too, were coming alive and being sustained and nurtured by the risen Christ wherever Jesus' death and resurrection were proclaimed. Paul had not been there to see with his own eyes the cross and the empty tomb. But he was daily experiencing an empowerment and forgiveness and freedom that simply could not be explained except by concluding that Christ had been raised from the dead and Christ was alive again.

How, then, could these Corinthians suggest that the dead are not raised? For if the dead are not raised, that would mean that Christ himself could not have been raised, and everything that Paul had taught them, everything that Paul himself had experienced beginning with that moment on the road to Damascus, was an empty lie—forgiveness of sin and freedom from its influence, the promise of the victory of God's love over the evil powers of pride and fear and jealousy, hope for life's fulfillment beyond the grave and reunion with loved ones and fellowship with Christ himself, staking our surrender of this life's passing pleasures upon trust in the eternal blessings of God—all of it would be an empty lie. If God permitted the goodness and love of Jesus' words and Jesus' deeds to bring him only to Calvary and no farther, if God did not vindicate Jesus by raising him from the dead, but instead allowed the evils that hoisted him onto the scaffold to have the *final* say, then in fact *God* does not rule the universe he created, but *Satan*; then God's *love* is not the ultimate value in the universe, but *hatred*; then *forgiveness* is not our destiny, but *revenge*. If Christ was not raised from the dead, then evil has finally and utterly triumphed at the cross.

But if Christ *was* raised from the dead, then *forever*, despite every appearance to the contrary in the affairs of humankind and the casualties of nature, people can put their trust in God's love and goodness and power. Christ's resurrection is God's guarantee that what Jesus said and did is true. Christ's resurrection is God's guarantee that what Jesus said and did is the model by which we can and should live, that what Jesus said and did is the unshakable source of our confident hope in this life and the life to come, that what Jesus said and did is the sign of how precious we are to God and how precious we must regard each other. Christ's resurrection is the clear and powerful seal of God's steadfast love and truth and purpose upon his creation and upon each person in it.

When the Corinthian Christians looked around them, they saw suffering, persecution, anxiety, despair. Surely, their world was at best an *equivocal* indication of God's character and power. So, to many people, our world today shows few enough signs of God's loving presence and caring involvement in events. Except for what happened at *Easter*, the basic fact of human existence is the *cemetery*—a destiny that must rob childbirth of its joy and leave every human pleasure bittersweet and render every human love pathetic. Except for what happened at *Easter*, the bloodied cross and the sealed tomb signal that the God to whom Jesus prayed is a God of cynicism and powerlessness—that this God is either unfeeling and uncaring, or simply unable to do anything about his own values and convictions. On Good Friday, it very much seemed that Jesus had been deluded, that God had failed him utterly in his hour of need. But then came Easter, and for the followers of Jesus, the doubt and the anger and the pain dissolved and gave way to faith and thanksgiving and joy. The empty cross and the empty tomb manifest a God of unlimited power and unbounded love, a God who will not let any force of evil frustrate his purpose of redemption, will not let any force of sin dissuade him from communion with his people, will not let any force of hatred destroy his feelings of fatherly love toward all creation. God will not permit suffering and death to triumph over his love for *us*.

The Gospels all insist upon the fact of the empty tomb, and each of the apostles taught the resurrection as the guarantee that their testimony on the Sonship and Saviorhood of Christ was true. For them, the resurrection of Christ was not mere words in a book, but a present experience of the church itself. God ratified the Sonship of Christ, the Saviorhood of Christ, by raising him from the dead. And those early believers experienced it firsthand; they sensed *themselves* being raised to new life by Christ's Spirit active in the church; they were no longer *bound* to hopelessness by affliction and poverty and persecution; they were no longer *doomed* to hopelessness by sin and fear and doubt. God had raised Jesus from the dead! Nothing else but Christ's resurrection could explain the forgiveness, the freedom, and the empowerment that the early Christians felt, and that Christians *still* feel when the church is *faithful to its calling*, when it prays for the Spirit of Christ to be present in power and in truth and in hope and in love. What motivated the first Christians? What caused them to hope in spite of every discouragement and every heartache? It was no mere sentimental memory of a *dead* Savior's words and deeds. It was the living Christ present in their midst and active in their lives. And what confidence it gave them! What confidence it can give *us*!—knowing that Jesus' words and deeds of mercy, of acceptance, of hope, of commission, are God's urgent agenda for the church, and God's guaranteed promise for you and me.

"The Guarantee"

One day, according to Luke, Jesus was surrounded by a great crowd of people trying to cope with the ambiguities of life. They heard their rabbis speak of the promises of God on the sabbath, and must sometimes have questioned whether any of that had to do with the daily exasperation of broken plows and the daily news of Roman atrocities and the daily heartaches of disease and disability and death. Promises, always promises. Still, they sought out the teachers, sought out the healers; still, they hoped. On this particular day, all the crowd sought to touch Jesus, "for power came out from him and healed all of them" (Luke 6:19b). And Jesus spoke to those few who had *pledged* themselves to follow him throughout Galilee, yet he spoke in such a way that people in the larger crowd could hear what he was saying, too:

> "Blessed are you who are poor,
> for yours is the kingdom of God.
> Blessed are you who are hungry now,
> for you will be filled.
> Blessed are you who weep now,
> for you will laugh.
> Blessed are you when people hate you, and when they exclude
> you, revile you, and defame you on account of the Son of Man.
> Rejoice in that day and leap for joy, for surely your reward is
> great in heaven." (6:20b–23a)

What beautiful words for people who are indigent, who are underfed, who are sorrowful, who are despised. Heavy human hearts are lightened by such promises. But in a world where poverty is spreading, where hunger is increasing, where hatred breeds more hatred, where sorrow never seems to take a holiday, are these anything but beautiful words, just another promise? In Christ's resurrection, God says to all humankind, "Everything that you have heard from Jesus, everything that you have seen Jesus do, is true. Here is the guarantee: I have raised him from the dead, and even now he is living in glory and power." Can you sense the presence of the risen and living Christ in your life, and in the life of your church?

Seventh Sunday in Ordinary Time

First Presbyterian Church, Dodge City, Kansas

February 23, 1992

Genesis 45:3–11, 15
1 Corinthians 15:35–38, 42–50
Luke 6:27–38

"Picture the Spirit"

Last Sunday, our epistle reading featured the apostle Paul's insistence upon the resurrection of Christ. Exactly what had prompted him to address the subject, we do not know. Apparently, someone or some group of people in the predominantly Greek congregation at Corinth had denied that the dead would be raised. Paul saw that such teaching jeopardized belief in the resurrection of *Christ*. Along with Christ's death, that was the *central message* of the apostles' preaching and the *central reality* of Paul's own life. From his strong defense of the doctrine of the resurrection, Paul went on in his letter to the Corinthians to address a related question, one that had not necessarily been voiced by the Corinthians but might well have been lurking in the back of their minds: What will the resurrected body be like? And although Paul had no special revelation concerning the subject, he drew on the accounts of the appearances of the resurrected Christ to his disciples, and also on the analogy of the seed, which, when planted as something rather small and insignificant, is transformed into something much greater and much more beautiful.

The seed has within it the potential to be something more wonderful than it is, but it cannot be transformed into that new thing unless and until it "dies"—unless and until it is placed in the ground and germinates and comes to life. By itself, the seed is not a living thing, yet there is within it the potential for life, which springs marvelously into being as the outer form of the seed passes away. "So it is with the resurrection of the dead," wrote Paul. "What is sown is perishable, what is raised is imperishable. It is sown in dishonor, it is raised in glory. It is sown in weakness, it is raised in power. It is sown a physical body, it is raised a spiritual body" (1 Cor 15:42-44a).

In this passage, we can easily confuse what Paul was saying about our appearance in the resurrection with his attempt to distinguish what he calls the "physical body" and what he calls the "spiritual body." The confusion is compounded by his use of the word "sown"—"what is sown is perishable, what is raised is imperishable" (15:42b). His image of the seed almost makes it sound as if, by saying that what is sown is perishable, he is talking about burial of the dead. But a careful reading of this passage discloses that what is "sown," to use Paul's word, is the soul—our personhood, our personality, that which makes us distinct individuals, and which is made a part of each person, is "sown" in our bodies, from birth.

Everybody has a soul. But what is raised at the resurrection is the spiritual, the "new creation" in Christ. And those who truly and sincerely put their faith in Christ are transformed from their dull "soulishness" into the state of spirituality. Their lives are fundamentally changed by the redeeming power of Jesus Christ. This power works a regeneration of people who are born or "sown" as souls, but who, during their earthly existence, give themselves to Christ as their Lord and Master. When life takes on the new quality of Christlikeness—when our habits, our thoughts, our desires, our actions are all transformed by being patterned on Christ himself—then we become spiritual beings, and thus, in the resurrection, we will be endowed with a *spiritual* body of God's making that corresponds to our spiritual nature.

What will this new body be like? Aside from the fact that we will still be able to recognize one another, even as Christ's disciples were able to recognize *him* after the resurrection, not even Paul wants to speculate on our resurrected appearance. What is clear is that the resurrection body will bear the marks of the spiritual nature that characterizes the habits, thoughts, desires, and actions of the person who truly and sincerely and completely puts faith in Christ. And, having looked ahead to the great change that will take place at the resurrection, all those who have put their faith in Christ will indeed be raised in spiritual bodies. But those who have truly put their faith in Christ are this very moment characterized by the qualities of the Spirit. Even now, the thoughts and actions of people who are spiritually endowed are distinguished from the motives and customs which rule the unfaithful. We may not be able to picture the appearance of the new spiritual body at the resurrection, but we have many glimpses from scripture and from Jesus himself that allow us to picture the Spirit.

Ask the average individual what a "spiritual" person looks like, and you will likely get an answer that refers to overtly *religious* activity—activity such as worshiping regularly, reading the Bible and devotional literature, spending time in prayer and contemplation. But "religious" is not the same as "spiritual," and spirituality cannot be measured by the amount of religious activity in which a person is engaged. Invariably, and perhaps inevitably, spirituality prompts us to worship, to study the scriptures and issues of faith, to pray and even to set aside time for undisturbed meditation. But spirituality goes beyond the activities that define religion, to an attitude of heart. Spirituality has to do with incorporating into one's own being the gentleness and generosity, the mercy and magnanimity, of Christ.

It would be interesting to know whether there were any scribes or Pharisees among the crowd that day when, as Matthew says, "Jesus . . . went up on the mountain" (Matt 5:1), or, as Luke says, "[Jesus] came down . . . and stood on a level place" (Luke 6:17), and preached blessings and woes and taught how people should respond to each other's needs. If so—if the conspicuously religious people had been present that day,—they must not have recognized much of what Jesus said as having anything to do with religion as they knew it. He said nothing about regular attendance at the synagogue. He did not encourage sacrifices at the temple. He did not recite the Ten Commandments. He did not call for meditation on the law and the prophets. He did not condemn sinners and Gentiles. He said none of the things that would have won him the approval and support of the people who knew how to be religious, people who prided themselves on their religious accomplishments. But Jesus said to those who would hear, "Love your enemies, do good to those who hate you, bless those who curse you, pray for those who abuse you. If anyone strikes you on the cheek, offer the other also; and from anyone who takes away your coat do not withhold even your shirt. Give to everyone who begs from you, and if anyone takes away your goods, do not ask for them again. Do to others as you would have them do to you" (6:27–31). Here was a radically different standard of pleasing God than worshiping in the synagogue or making sacrifices in the temple; here was a completely different way of living from that of the people who regarded themselves as righteous beyond question.

Like most people of our own time, both inside and outside the church, folks in Jesus' day, whether they thought of themselves as religious or not, tended to respond to other people by the axiom of reciprocity. They loved those who showed them love; they did good toward those who did good toward them; they lent money on the expectation of repayment rather than giving money away even to bad credit risks. Like most people of our own time, both inside and outside the church, folks in Jesus' day, whether they thought of themselves as religious or not, assumed some just and moral force in the universe—whether they called the force "God" or some other name—that should reward good deeds and punish evil ones, that should honor instances of gratitude and kindness and withhold favors from the selfish and the contemptible. And naturally, justice and morality required that such matters should be judged on the basis of their own standards. It is not unusual for someone to say to a minister following a sermon, "You mean that if someone lives a life of sin and then asks God's forgiveness and changes his or her ways shortly before dying, that person will be just as welcome in the kingdom as a person who has been good their whole life?" A member of one of my former congregations, without realizing it, once challenged the notion that God's love and mercy are broader than human measure. "If it is possible that even an Adolph Hitler can be in heaven," said she, "then God is not a God of justice." By prevailing standards, she was a very religious person.

But Christlikeness compels us to go *beyond* the *world's* definition of justice. The spiritual nature that fills us when we have total faith in Christ produces within us the willingness to go beyond the world's expectations of love and kindness and generosity. "If you love those who love you," observed Jesus, "what credit is that to you? For even sinners love those who love them. If you do good to those who do good to you, what credit is that to you? For even sinners do the same. If you lend to those from whom you hope to receive, what credit is that to you? Even sinners lend to sinners, to receive as much again. But love your enemies, and do good, and lend, expecting nothing in return. Your reward will be great, and you will be children of the Most High; for [God] is kind to the ungrateful and the wicked. Be merciful, just as your Father is merciful" (6:32–37). Jesus calls us to be forgetful of ourselves, our interests, our desires. Jesus bids us to love our neighbor—every neighbor—by looking upon him or her as someone who is worthy of all the best in life. Jesus commands us to submerge our anger and our pride, to resist the quick impulse to resent injury, to put aside self-assertion, to be eager to show mercy and loath to gossip, to be quick to sympathize and *never* to *condemn*.

Our soul's first impulse is to take all that can be taken in life and to give as little as is necessary, to show interest in other people in the exact same proportion that they build up our own self-esteem, to belittle our own failings while mercilessly judging the faults of others, both petty and gross. That is what is sown in each of us at birth—a weak and rapacious and carping personality, one that, if left untutored by the redemptive ways of faith in Jesus Christ, remains selfish and churlish and small. But picture the Spirit of the risen Christ alive and at work in the truly spiritual person, the person who has heard Christ and who has assumed the character of Christ himself. Will that person not be the most carefree of individuals, and yet the most caring? Will that person not be empty of self-concern, and yet the most secure? Will that person not be eager to find the good in every individual and to praise it, and never gossip complaints to friends about someone else's failings? Will that person not greet each new day with enthusiasm and expectancy, setting aside the disappointments of the past and always hopeful for the future? Will that person not be generous beyond all conventional wisdom, even toward those who seem ungrateful, and yet always be satisfied with what he has left? Will that person not immediately forget wrongs and slights committed against her, and instead radiate with a joy and a peace that no insult or misfortune can seem to take away? *That* is a picture of the *spiritual* person—the one whose behavior and attitude are prompted by the example of the God who does not hate in response to hatred, and who loves even before he is loved—a habit of being that God demonstrated for all people in the life, death, and resurrection of his Son Jesus.

And when Jesus stood among those people gathered to hear him—people who were likely victims of others' contempt and miserliness and ingratitude,—he gave them the blueprint for faithful living, a picture of the life of the Spirit: the decay of all that is crusty and hard and cold, the blossoming of all that is generous and kind and loving. "So it is with the resurrection of the dead," explained Paul. "What is sown is perishable, what is raised is imperishable. It is sown in dishonor, it is raised in glory. It is sown in weakness, it is raised in power. It is sown a physical body, it is raised a spiritual body" (1 Cor 15:42–44a). "What I am saying, brothers and sisters, is this: flesh and blood cannot inherit the kingdom of God" (15:50a–b).

Eighth Sunday in Ordinary Time
Isaiah 55:10–13
1 Corinthians 15:51–58
Luke 6:39–49

"The Resurrection Hope"

"We will not all die," wrote Paul, "but we will be changed, in a moment, in the twinkling of an eye, at the last trumpet" (1 Cor 15:51b–52a). Just like the trumpet would summon the exiles from Egypt and Assyria to worship on the holy mountain at Jerusalem back in the time of the prophet Isaiah, Paul foresaw a great blast from a trumpet signaling God's triumphant call for all to return to where they belonged—the kingdom that God purposed from before time began. "[A]nd the dead will be raised imperishable, and we will be changed" (15:52).

It is perhaps not a coincidence that this testimony of Paul occurs in the lectionary for the last Sunday before the Transfiguration, when Jesus' own appearance was changed in the presence of Peter, John, and James, and they saw him to be radiant, dazzling white, as Moses and Elijah spoke with him. They still knew that it was Jesus, and they knew that it was still Jesus. They had no difficulty recognizing him. Jesus, of course, had not yet been crucified and had not yet been resurrected, but changed he was as the disciples saw him in his glory. It was just a suggestive foreshadowing, a hint, of what Paul might have been talking about in First Corinthians, although he himself seems not to have comprehended fully. It is, after all, "a mystery" (15:51). Nevertheless, Paul understood, "this perishable body must put on imperishability, and this mortal body must put on immortality" (15:53), as had happened when Jesus was raised from the tomb and appeared to his disciples in a resurrection body, different from how they had known him before the crucifixion, but clearly recognizable, clearly identifiable, clearly still Jesus.

The Corinthians, like all their Greek cousins, generally regarded the body as an inconvenience, a distraction, an impediment, even, to the proper destiny of the soul: to be liberated from everything physical and free to float to the uncorrupted existence of the spirit. This, it was thought, happened more or less at the moment of death. It was a shared belief but an individual goal. In life, one had little responsibility for the well-being of others, and one had little involvement with the divine. The gods had to be propitiated—they had to be sacrificed to in order for human beings to receive their favors of seasonable weather and good health, of fruitful crops and the like. But there was no conception of or yearning for a personal relationship with the divine, and certainly not a relationship that would transcend the boundary between death and life. And there was no sense that life was a gift, or the human body a blessing, intimately connected to communal blessings and responsibilities and hopes. And as for the expectation that one's labor in this physical world had eternal purpose and import, what was the point if this world had no real value? It, too, was something to be escaped from, to be used and then left behind. Stewardship of the environment, caring for creation as God's great gift and the arena of God's saving history, would have had no meaning to the pagan Greek mind, whereas for the believer, acknowledging it to be something crafted and loved by the Creator endows it with great importance indeed, not something to be worshiped—nothing like that—but something to be respected, to be husbanded, to be preserved because it discloses God's character and God has declared it to be good. The Bible looks toward not the destruction of all nature, but the renewal and redemption of all creation.

It was true for Paul, and it must be true for every believer, that the resurrection is the great seal of God's approval of creation and guarantee of redemption. The Jews, the people of God, found the notion of body and soul as separate realities just as impossible as the pagan Greeks found the notion of body and soul as one inseparable creation to be objectionable. And when Paul articulated to the Corinthian Christians the heart of the Christian hope, he knew that he was preaching in defiance of an ancient philosophical assumption. No, the soul does not just sort of float upward when the body stops working. The New Testament testimony is that the bodies of the faithful will be raised when Christ returns and pronounces final judgment—soul and body together, although changed. In this life, our identity is bound up inextricably with our bodily existence, as commentator Richard Hays, professor of New Testament at Duke Divinity School, has observed, and if we are to be saved, we must be saved as embodied persons; the God who made us will finally make us renewed and whole, that is, spirit, soul, and body together.[1] But, beyond that, even, God's intention for you

---

1. Hays, *First Corinthians*, 278.

and for me and for every single creature will not be realized until all of creation is restored. The promise is of a new heaven and a new earth, not an ethereal existence without substance.

A lot of what ministers are expected to say and do at the time of someone's death has been woefully colored by the corrupting individualism of frontier revivals and the wrongheaded assumption that creation is something to be exploited, even destroyed, as, while awaiting heaven, we pursue our individual earthly comfort, amass personal wealth, notch private achievement. It's all a matter of personal salvation *from* rather than communal salvation *to*. And so we too often hear of our departed loved one being in "a better place," or that heaven needed another auto mechanic or doctor, or that dear Aunt Matilda is looking down on us now and smiling—none of which has the slightest support in scripture. And the notion that we have earned a place in paradise is flatly contrary to any promise of Jesus, and extends the notion that we need to compete with each other in this earthly life into a foreverness of winners and losers.

Paul is insistent that nothing we achieve in life, no work that we do, has any value unless it contributes to the purpose and intention of *God*. After all of his discussion about resurrection, about how the perishable body must put on imperishability and the mortal body must put on immortality, about death being defeated and finally made impotent by the resurrection of Christ, which is the pattern for *our* resurrection, Paul declares a big "therefore": "Therefore, my beloved, be steadfast, immovable, always excelling in the work of the Lord, because you know that in the Lord your labor is not in vain" (15:58). Somehow, as far as the apostle Paul is concerned, the resurrection to eternal life relates back to, has meaning because of, what happens in *this* life, not in spite of it, not instead of it, not in disregard of it. And the importance of what happens in *this* life is *measured* by the degree to which it agrees with, supports, and contributes to the work that God is up to—restoring to wholeness, to health, to goodness, the world that God created and that God loves, including everyone and every creature in it. It is not a matter of just being busy, as if our worth to God and in God's scheme of things is dependent upon how many hours we spend at the office or in the shop or in the field or in the kitchen or wherever, certainly not by how many clubs we belong to or awards we have received or cruises we have taken, definitely not by how many titles we have or how big our houses are and how many we have or how much we get paid. Working steadfastly toward the redemption of creation from all that degrades it, from all that monetizes what God made for his delight and as an expression of his love, from all that objectifies people and values them as but producers and consumers and something to accumulate more than—that is the work of the Lord, the labor that, when all else passes away, is not in vain. The resurrection puts the stamp of ultimate value on love—God's love for us, our love for one another, precious to the point that nothing about any of us is expendable, discardable, forgettable, or beyond salvation.

Sadly, the Christian hope of resurrection has been confused and even obfuscated by a good deal of fuzzy sentiment, as the Christian work ethic has been coopted by the powers and principalities to satisfy economic greed. More than sad, it is perilous to the soul and obstructive to God's purpose and the health of all creation. Our allegiance is supposed to be to God, who seeks to bring all things into eternal community with himself, not to political agendas or economic theories that claim to promise some personal benefit for an individual or a class or a tribe. The cross is the sign of the seriousness of God's intention, passionate to the degree of surrendering his own Son to the purpose of salvation, and not just for some, but for all. And the crucifixion is pointless if the flesh and the blood of the very human Christ had no ultimate value, were not important, could easily be expended and disregarded. Our very gathering at the Lord's table to feast on the symbols of Christ's humanity speaks to the dearness in which God holds us—our whole selves—and how loathe God is to lose us to the oblivion of sin and death. If the body is of no real account, then Jesus' death was no big deal and our own resurrection is not something to be hoped for.

Christian hope is not something that springs from our imagination or our dreams or greeting card cheeriness. Nor is Christian hope self-fulfilling, as if we can think our way into a custom-designed heaven. Christian hope is based solely on God's promise, articulated by Jesus Christ and attested by his resurrection. Was he just the best teacher, the kindest healer, the friendliest companion? No, although he was and is all those things. If we end his story at the crucifixion, be it ever so tragic and unjust, and therefore Jesus is a great martyr but a dead one, then ultimately all that he accomplished for the individuals that he taught and healed and befriended passed away with them, a goodness reduced to dusty memory. We would then follow his teaching, we would imitate his behavior, because it is what inclines toward our social or political or economic preferences, or simply because it is pleasant. Jesus is the Christ, the Messiah, the Son of God, and the resurrection is the seal that his words and ways, one and the same, are the words and ways of God, and the lens through which our lives—our wills and our works, which are also to be congruently the same—are to be seen. When Paul writes that we shall all be changed, he is confidently affirming that God has begun a work in believers and will bring it to completion—a work that is no individual effort and no personal achievement, but the very work of God, redeeming and bringing to fulfillment God's eternal purpose for all creation, as we minister to others in Christlike mercy, Christlike sacrifice, Christlike love.² It is not that we each have an immortal soul just waiting to be released at death to its inevitable destiny. It is that each of us has the same Creator, whose love is never-ending and whose word of salvation is eternal truth. Does our every word, does our every thought, does our every deed comport with that truth? "Therefore, my beloved," testified Paul, "be steadfast, immovable, always excelling in the work of the Lord, because you know that in the Lord your labor is not in vain" (15:58). It is the very building of the kingdom of God, blessed and eternal.

"For as often as you eat this bread and drink the cup," Paul announced in his instructions about the Lord's Supper, "you proclaim the Lord's death until he comes" (11:26). We eat and drink in remembrance of Jesus—not of his death only as a sad event in human history, but of God's working of salvation through his obedient sacrifice, the culmination of his life for others, his body now broken and his blood shed for all, fulfilling God's passionate purpose of eternal fellowship with all creation. So we proclaim, "Christ has died. Christ is risen. Christ will come again," as we receive as a gift from him and share as a gift with each other the tokens of the dear flesh-and-bloodness of the one who now reigns in his resurrected body, whose presence his disciples of old recognized by the marks of nails in his hands and his feet and his wounded side, who is known to us in the breaking of the bread. Not one of these things alone do we proclaim—that Christ has died, that Christ is risen, that Christ will come again—but all three events dependent upon each other for their significance, and all of them together the root of the Christian hope. The labor of the Christian does not die; it is not in vain. Our bodies, though changed, will be raised, together, at the return of Christ, which is certain whether it be near or far off. And what God first brought into being will be perfected, restored, renewed, complete, and at peace, as God intends and only God can achieve, and will. Sin will be no more. Death will be no more. Everyone and all together will acknowledge with their lips and demonstrate with their actions that Jesus Christ, crucified, raised, living now, is Lord. What God has brought into being, God loves and God will preserve and God will never let go. That is the resurrection hope.

---

2. See Sampley, "First Letter to the Corinthians," 991.

Transfiguration of the Lord
Spanish Springs Presbyterian Church, Sparks, Nevada
February 14, 2010

Exodus 34:29–35
2 Corinthians 3:12—4:2
Luke 9:28–43

"The Greatness of God"

I am going to begin today's sermon by asking you to recall the first scripture reading from last Sunday. That was the passage in which Isaiah the prophet had a vision of God in the temple in Jerusalem and then, having offered himself to be God's servant, he was commissioned to prophesy to the people of Judah. That episode—which, by the way, provides the pattern for our order of worship—is an example of the Jewish understanding of the vast gulf that exists between *God*, as absolute holiness, and *humankind*, characterized by sin.

The difference is more than simply "Creator" and "creation." For the *creation*—in this case, specifically, humankind—is different from the *Creator* not only in *power* and *ability*. (God is eternal, while we are mortal; no one created God, but God created us.) The *Creator* is also radically different from us in *character* and *virtue*. (God's is absolute, steadfast, and unblemished.) God the *Creator* is completely *other* from everything that God has *created*, including you and me. The colloquial way to express it is that we aren't even in the same ballpark with God. God is infinitely *greater* than we are in every way. So, when Isaiah detected that God was present with him in the sanctuary that day, he feared that he was going to die. He had seen with his own eyes the holiness of God, seated on the throne and the hem of his robe filling the temple. From ancient times, it had been said that for any mortal to look upon the holiness of God meant *death*—not as a *punishment*, but just because our *unholiness* cannot coexist in the same place with God's *holiness*. It is for our own protection, the Old Testament writers understood, that we must not look directly on the face of God. Metaphorically, they were expressing the truth of the distance between who *God* is and who *we* are.

After the first encounter that Moses had with God on Mount Sinai, wrapped in smoke, Moses, who had thrown down the original tablets of the law in disgust at the people's faithless fashioning of a golden calf, went back up the mountain to receive a *second* set of the Ten Commandments. Between the accounts of those two trips up Mount Sinai, Exodus tells us that Moses would go out to a tent he set up beyond the people's camp, and a pillar of cloud would descend and stand at the entrance of the tent, and "the Lord would speak to Moses face to face, as one speaks to a friend" (Exod 33:11a). By a gracious accommodation to Moses' creatureliness, the greatness of God, the holiness of God, the otherness of God was no longer an insurmountable barrier between God and Moses. Was it perhaps because they were united in exasperation with the people's fickleness that God permitted Moses to look upon the divine countenance unharmed? That seems to contradict the care that God had taken to shroud the mountain in smoke to protect Moses during his *first* trip up the mountain, and God's telling Moses, on his *second* ascent, when Moses had asked to see God's glory, that neither *he* nor *anyone* could see God's face, and thus God hid him in the cleft of the rock before passing by and covered him with his hand, so that Moses would not look directly upon God's glory but only be able to detect, after the fact, that God had passed by. At any rate, when Moses came back down the mountain with the two new tablets of the covenant, Moses' face was *shining* because he had been talking with God. And it *continued* to shine, reflecting the divine glory with which Moses had been in contact on the mountain. Whenever he was *not* speaking with God or telling the people what God had said to him, Moses would put a veil on his face.

It strikes us as strange and perhaps not quite consistent that God's glory should be present now in a dark cloud and now in bright, shining light, and that people had to be protected from it and yet Moses would remove the veil from his face, which shone with the reflection of God's glory, whenever he spoke to the people on God's behalf. Whatever the details of protocol for wearing the veil, the shining brightness of Moses' face signified that Moses had been in conversation with God, holy and mighty. Moses was now a mediator between God and God's people, a bridge over the gulf between divine and human, not *himself* divine, but no *ordinary* person, either, because he had been welcomed into the *presence* of God, had even entered deeply into the *mind* of God, was fully trusted to communicate the *will* of God. The glow of Moses' face was God's validation of what he said and did, evidence that he had indeed been speaking with God, confirmation that he had a special relationship with God and would now speak *for* God, and the people understood that. He truthfully represented in his words to them, when his face was unveiled, the will and purpose of God. The *greatness of God* no longer stood as an absolute barrier between God and humankind.

That is the important background for another strange case of a bright shining, when Jesus, taking with him Peter and John and James, went up a mountain to pray. Always eager to show the similarity between Jesus and Moses, Matthew says that the face of Jesus "shone like the sun" (Matt 17:2). Luke doesn't go that far. But both Luke and Matthew, and Mark, report that Jesus' *clothes* became dazzling white. Clearly, we are to recall the brightness of God's glory and the appearance of Moses after he had been talking with God.

The incident of Jesus on the mountain took place, Luke says, "about eight days" (Luke 9:28) after Jesus said how costly being his disciple would be—that it was a matter of taking up one's cross daily and following him, that it meant being willing to give up one's life. "'Those who are ashamed of me and of my words, of them the Son of Man will be ashamed when he comes in his glory and the glory of the Father and of the holy angels'" (9:26)—glory that, the Bible indicates, is often manifested in bright light. "'[T]ruly I tell you,'" Jesus had said, "'there are some standing here who will not taste death before they see the kingdom of God'" (9:27). It was to the Twelve that he said that, which would have included Peter and John and James. In the very next paragraph, Jesus took Peter and John and James up the mountain with him when he went up to pray, and "while he was praying, the appearance of his face changed, and his clothes became dazzling white. Suddenly they saw two men, Moses and Elijah, talking to him. They appeared *in glory* and were speaking of his departure, which he was about to accomplish at Jerusalem. Now Peter and his companions were weighed down with sleep; but since they had stayed awake, they *saw* his glory and the two men who stood with him" (9:29-32).

Presumably, all three disciples understood that they were looking upon Jesus' *glory* because of the brightness of his appearance. Presumably, the glory in which Moses and Elijah were seen *also* involved brightness of appearance, as if God had just momentarily opened the gates of the kingdom of heaven and they had stepped forth. Peter was so impressed with what he had witnessed that he wanted to commemorate it with three little monuments testifying to God's greatness. But even as Peter was saying that, "a cloud came and overshadowed them . . . . Then from the cloud came a voice that said, 'This is my Son, my Chosen; listen to him!' . . . On the next day, when they had come down from the mountain, a great crowd met him.

Just then a man from the crowd shouted, 'Teacher, I beg you to look at my son; he is my only child. Suddenly a spirit seizes him, and all at once he shrieks.' . . . Jesus rebuked the unclean spirit, healed the boy, and gave him back to his father. And"—listen to what Luke says—"all were astounded at the *greatness* of God" (9:34b-35, 37-39a, 42b-43a). Then, just a few verses later, the disciples jumped into an argument among themselves about which one of *them* was the greatest.

The story of the Transfiguration is almost incomprehensible when we look at it in isolation, and even when we consider it in the light of the story about Moses, which itself leaves us with questions in our mind. Surely, it has to do with God communicating that Jesus, too, shares the divine glory, opens the gates of heaven to us, is entitled to our honor and our praise and our obedience—that he speaks God's will. But *here* is a display of divine glory that results not in *death*, but *life*, doesn't threaten our *destruction* but works our *salvation*—our health and our wholeness. Jesus' identity, his true glory, is revealed in dazzling light, but it is susceptible of being misunderstood apart from his healing touch upon the daily needs of suffering humankind. Jesus' greatness, like that of God the Father, entitles him to all the display of heavenly glory we can imagine, and more, but Jesus' greatness does *not* lie in his being seen with a bright shining face or wearing dazzling white clothes, no matter how appropriate we might think it would be to enshrine him that way on the mountaintop. It was when Jesus and his disciples had come back *down* from the mountain, no longer had clothes that were dazzling white but were normal in appearance, perhaps even soiled, that "Jesus rebuked the unclean spirit, healed the boy, and gave him back to his father. And all were astounded at the greatness of God" (9:42b-43).

The *crowd* hadn't been on the mountain. *They* didn't see the sound-and-light show—they didn't know anything *about* it; Peter and John and James "kept silent and in those days told no one any of the things they had seen" (9:36b). The people weren't astounded that the appearance of Jesus' face changed, and his clothes became intensely bright, and suddenly Moses and Elijah appeared talking with him and they, too, appeared in glory. They were astounded at the greatness of God, which they recognized *not* because Jesus was bathed in a shining light but because he rebuked the spirit that was afflicting a boy with pain and making him a spectacle, and healed the boy of his convulsions and restored the boy to his father. They recognized the astounding greatness of God in Jesus' mighty deed of compassionate healing, answering the plea of a desperate parent, giving back to a miserably sick boy his childhood and his dignity. And if any of Jesus' disciples ever claimed the distinction of being the greatest, it would have to be on the basis of being humble enough to minister to very needy people caught in the cruel mess of unclean spirits, far away from scenes of pedestaled glory. No longer was God's holiness a barrier to feeling God's heavenly touch or seeing the love in God's eyes. Now God could be felt in Jesus' embrace, could be seen in Jesus' gaze. And his disciples must reach out to people in need with the *same* acceptance, must look upon people in need with the *same* love. Indeed, far from scaling the heights of prestige and privilege to bask in conspicuous approval, they must be willing to descend into the depths of pain and affliction, and perform there the obedient ministry that made Jesus *worthy* of glory.

On his way to persecute those who sought to follow the way of the cross, Saul, before he became the apostle Paul, was blinded by a light from heaven that flashed around him, and the Lord spoke to him. For three days, he was without sight, so bright had been the presence of the risen Christ that day on the road to Damascus. When the apostle Ananias put his hands upon him, something like scales fell from his eyes—or, perhaps, something like a veil—and, enlisted into being a follower of Christ and obediently taking up the cross of humble servanthood, Paul began *his* transformation into the image of Christ, from one degree of glory to another, seeing the glory of the Lord as though reflected in a mirror. And he and his fellow apostles did many acts of healing and liberation, so that many people were astounded at the greatness of God.

When you and I leave this mountaintop today, where we have worshiped Christ with organ and candles and feasting and song, we will step into the crowded world of hurt and need. And there we will have the opportunity and the obligation to demonstrate the greatness of God.

Ash Wednesday

Spanish Springs Presbyterian Church, Sparks, Nevada

February 21, 2007

Joel 2:1–2, 12–17
2 Corinthians 5:20b—6:10
Matthew 6:1–6, 16–21

"Perhaps God Will Relent"

Once upon a time, according to the Bible, when disasters befell nations or threatened to do so, leaders would call on the people to repent. The whole population was to change the direction they were headed, to alter their attitudes and their behavior, and to show their purposefulness by fasting, by wearing coarse clothing, by covering themselves with ashes. Sometimes the disaster experienced or pending was in the form of military aggression from another nation. Sometimes the disaster experienced or pending was in the form of a natural event, such as a terrible storm or a plague or a drought or an earthquake.

The Bible tells of such cases. Perhaps the most startling story is in the book of Jonah, where God directs the prophet to go preach to Nineveh, the capital of Israel's enemy Assyria, that it's going to be overthrown because of its wickedness. And eventually, after first *refusing* to do as God commanded him, Jonah *does* go to Nineveh and preaches its impending doom,

> [a]nd the people of Nineveh believed God; they proclaimed a fast, and everyone, great and small, put on sackcloth.
>
> When the news reached the king of Nineveh, he rose from his throne, removed his robe, covered himself with sackcloth, and sat in ashes. Then he published a proclamation made in Nineveh: "By the decree of the king and his nobles: No human being or animal, no herd or flock, shall taste anything. They shall

> not feed, nor shall they drink water. Human beings and animals shall be covered with sackcloth, and they shall cry mightily to God. All shall turn from their evil ways and from the violence that is in their hands. Who knows? God may relent and change his mind; he may turn from his fierce anger, so that we do not perish."
>
> When God saw what they did, how they turned from their evil ways, God changed his mind about the calamity that he had said he would bring upon them; and he did not do it. (Jonah 3:5–9)

Jonah found out that it was never God's desire that even the wicked people of Nineveh should perish—that "great city" (1:2), as God kept referring to it.

And then there is the case of which we read this evening: Joel's prophecy to Judah many years after the people had returned from their exile in Babylon but still had not established the just society that God intended for his people.

> Let all the inhabitants of the land tremble,
>   for the day of the Lord is coming, it is near—
> a day of darkness and gloom,
>   a day of clouds and thick darkness!
> Like blackness spread upon the mountains
>   a great and powerful army comes . . . .
> Yet even now, says the Lord,
>   return to me with all your heart,
> with fasting, with weeping, and with mourning;
>   rend your hearts and not your clothing.
> Return to the Lord, your God,
>   for he is gracious and merciful,
> slow to anger, and abounding in steadfast love,
>   and relents from punishing.
> Who knows whether he will not turn and relent,
>   and leave a blessing behind him,
> a grain offering and a drink offering
>   for the Lord, your God? (Joel 2:1b–2b, 12–14)

This time, the threat was a great advancing army of locusts, and Joel appealed to every single individual in Judah to assemble and call upon God for mercy.

The Bible does not assume that *every* natural catastrophe is God's punishment upon the nation, nor even every act of military aggression, and so *we* shouldn't. Unless endowed specially by God to be a prophet, none of us is in a position to judge or declare whether an event *is* or *isn't* God's intentional punishment. During a story on the evening news about the recent devastating tornado in Florida, one person from the congregation of the church that lost its building described the destructive storm as *God's* act, while another person from the *same* congregation said that the congregation wouldn't let the devil win, but would build bigger and better. Pat Robertson famously predicted the destruction of San Francisco a few years ago because of its tolerance of homosexuality, and within weeks a hurricane slammed into not *San Francisco*, but *Virginia Beach*, Pat Robertson's own headquarters. Nor does the Bible assume that every catastrophe, natural or of human making, is God's punishment upon an *individual*. Job steadfastly protested his innocence to his friends in spite of his great personal losses and physical suffering, and the book of Job says that it wasn't Job's *sin* that led to his troubles, but in fact his *righteousness*—Satan was trying to get him to curse God, which Job refused to do even after losing his flocks, his herds, his servants, his children.

There are times when whole societies, whole nations, should repent, should fast and don sackcloth and sit in ashes, even today. But it's not very likely that they're going to do so. It must have taken a lot of courage, and a great defiance of the political polls, for the king of Nineveh to say to his subjects that he and they had been going in the wrong direction and now needed to change their ways. Those who call for repentance in *our* nation generally seem to do so in order to appeal to a particular part of the electorate for their own partisan purposes, and always with their finger pointed at others, never admitting their *own* need to repent. Opinion polls repeatedly disclose that Americans want their leaders to be "strong" more than they want their leaders to be "righteous" or even "right"; not many, though, are as strong as the king of Nineveh, strong enough to be humbly repentant, even when things are very obviously going all wrong. What would have happened to any politician or, for that matter, religious leader who had dared to pose the question of whether September 11 might be a sign of God's displeasure? Or Hurricane Katrina?

In fact, acts of repentance in the Bible are not always tied to specific instances of wrongdoing. In Joel, there is no accusation of any particular sin, any one event or one behavior that has caused God to be angry with the people and punish them. There is no suggestion that they have turned to other gods, for instance. It seems to be more the case that they have just rather drifted away from God, and from their trust in God, their conscious dependence upon God, their gratefulness to God that would naturally spill over into dealing justly with each other. The day of the Lord is said to be near—presumably a day of judgment—but the day of the Lord is also presumably coming eventually anyway. "Yet even now, says the LORD"—even in the face of the advancing army of locusts, which threatens to strip the land of its crops and leave the people in famine—

> return to me with all your heart,
> with fasting, with weeping, and with mourning;
> rend your *hearts* and *not* your *clothing*.
> Return to the Lord your God,
> for he is gracious and merciful,
> slow to anger and abounding in steadfast love,
> and relents from punishing. (2:12–13)

Here in Joel, at least, the pending disaster is indeed a punishment. Acknowledging some *specific* sin, though, is apparently *not* as important as the people's need to reorient their entire *life* toward God, remembering what God has done and showing thanksgiving for it in the way they live.

But if *disasters* are not automatically a *punishment* from God, neither is God's *forgiveness* an automatic result of *repentance*. "Who knows?," asked the king of Nineveh, and not just rhetorically. "God may relent and change his mind; he may turn from his fierce anger, so that we do not perish" (Jonah 3:9). Or God might *not*. We mustn't suppose that our repentance in any way *compels* God to forgive us, or to divert the storm that is headed our way, or to cancel the volcanic eruption, or to turn aside the locusts. "Who knows whether he will not turn and relent?" (Joel 2:14), asked the prophet Joel. It was up to *God*, who, in order to *be* God, must be absolute in his sovereignty and unassailable in his justice. But Joel also testified to the *nature* of the one true God:

> Return to the Lord, your God,
> for he is gracious and merciful,
> slow to anger, and abounding in steadfast love,
> and relents from punishing. (2:13b–c)

We can't claim God's grace or mercy by right or by exchange, but the fact *is* that God *is* gracious and merciful, and that fact *alone* is reason enough for us to *turn* to God, *return* to God, no matter our particular circumstances, no matter the specific outcome.

Lent is not just about being sorry for sins that we can enumerate on our fingers and toes, committed at specific times and in specific places. Lent is about our need always to be mindful of our human tendency to drift from God, both as individuals and as societies, and about pondering our dependence upon God's grace and mercy, and about being so thankful for God's grace and mercy that we reverse the path we have been taking that leads away from him. *Specific* sins, serious as they might be, are a manifestation of a more *general* condition that plagues *all* of humankind. Fasting and wearing sackcloth and covering ourselves with ashes doesn't in any way set the balance right. But such things *can* be a way of focusing our attention on the situation, and demonstrating by external act something of our inner awareness. Adopting any or all of these disciplines was, *is,* a way of acknowledging our tendency to drift from God, our dependence upon God's grace and mercy, our gratitude for God's grace and mercy, our desire to turn around and come back to him. And, importantly, when done with *others,* it *was* and *is* an acknowledgment of the common need that should bind us one with another in seeking to be obedient to the God who has called us to be not just his *sinless individuals,* but his *faithful people.*

Jesus often called people to repentance, and he had no objection to external deeds of piety. Indeed, he *assumed* that people would *do* them—"So *whenever* you give alms . . ." (Matt 6:2a), he said. "And *whenever* you pray . . ." (6:5a). "And *whenever* you fast . . ." (6:16a). He *did* attack the doing of traditional *external displays* that have no connection to sober *inner intent.* He *did* criticize making a show of repentance that is not genuine. And he certainly *never* indicated that any of these things is a *payment* for sin; the sin, once committed, is a fact that cannot be changed. It *can* be *forgiven,* if God chooses to *do* so, and it *is* God's nature to be *merciful* as well as *just,* and Jesus promises that God *will* be forgiving toward those who *themselves* are forgiving of *others*—but nothing that the *sinner* does can *compel* God to be merciful. But for those who truly *are* repentant, who *do* change their direction, and for the *society* or *nation* that does the same thing, and is forgiving of *others,* God *does* provide us a definite answer to Joel's question, "Who knows whether he will not turn and relent?" (Joel 2:14a). And that answer lies in the cross.

First Sunday in Lent
Spanish Springs Presbyterian Church, Sparks, Nevada
February 21, 2010

Deuteronomy 26:1–11
Romans 10:8b–13
Luke 4:1–13

"Jesus Is Lord"

During my career as a professional minister, I have conducted somewhere in the neighborhood of 150 funerals and memorial services. Many of them have been very profound spiritual experiences for me. And, though it may sound strange to the ears of a lay person, many have been very *satisfying* experiences, from a professional point of view; pastors naturally want to be of service to a family in times of need, and we appreciate the opportunity to grow closer to parishioners on the occasion of a loved one's death. While we would never wish those circumstances on anyone, ministry at the time of a death can be important in forming and strengthening personal relationships. It is always a blessing to learn more about a person's life and how that life touched and intertwined with the lives of others, and to think about how, in a sermon, to weave *that* individual's story into our *shared* Christian story of being God's people in the world—how *each* person of faith stands amidst *others* in the great parade of witnesses to Jesus Christ, the spiritual genealogy that leads from Abraham and Sarah on to God's final consummation.

But I must say that ministering at a time of death *can* be an occasion for sadness *beyond* the *normal* reasons for grieving. Sometimes, when I am visiting with a family in preparation for the service and I ask them to tell me what they knew of their loved one's faith and how it influenced his or her life with other people, my question is answered with a blank stare, or I get a sort of generic, "Well, so-and-so believed in God, and was a good person." And sometimes that's all the family can *tell* me about their loved one's faith. At least when, in premarital counseling, I ask a couple how their getting married is an expression of their Christian faith, if they *haven't* thought about it or spoken to each other about it—which is often the case,—they still have an opportunity to *do* so. But after someone has *died*, the opportunity to talk with him or her about matters of faith has *passed*. It may be, of course, that he or she *thought* about God, *prayed*, maybe even went to *church* occasionally or regularly. But if even the closest family members have nothing to say about how the person's faith influenced the way he or she lived, how he or she spent time, what the person thought and spoke about, what fruits of the Spirit he or she demonstrated in word and in deed and in relationships, then the person's death, no matter its cause or at what age, is tragic indeed.

Presbyterianism, and the entire Reformed church movement, stands within the "confessing church" tradition. Some worshipers may wonder why, in every worship service, we have an affirmation of faith, either one of the ancient creeds or a statement of belief from the Reformation era or one of the more recent confessional documents that the Presbyterian Church here or in some other country has adopted as authoritative. From time to time, I hear of somebody objecting to that part of our order of worship, that he or she doesn't like being asked to state something out loud that they consider to be essentially private. Historically, our spiritual ancestors have considered it important to declare before *others*, and before *God*, what we *believe* about God whom we have come to know in Jesus Christ. The book of Deuteronomy, in our reading this morning, commands that God's people declare at least annually the faithfulness of God in leading them into Egypt and blessing them there, and then saving them from slavery when the Egyptians treated them harshly, and bringing them into a land where they prospered, all being reason to make a yearly offering to God of the first fruits of the land.

It has long been considered appropriate in worship to declare our shared convictions together and in public, and never more so than at a Christian funeral, the completion of our Christian baptism, when we typically say together, in witness to our resurrection faith, the Apostles' Creed, which was originally a statement of belief proclaimed publicly at baptism. *Do* we or do we *not* believe that the most important thing that can be said about us or that we can say about ourselves is that we belong to God?—a relationship sealed by the death and resurrection of his Son Jesus Christ and celebrated in our baptism and nurtured regularly at the Lord's table and apparent to all by our words and our actions, our loyalties and our sacrifices, the *faithfulness* with which we *live* and the *confidence* in which we *die*?

"If you confess with your lips that Jesus is Lord and believe in your heart that God raised him from the dead," Paul testified, "you will be saved" (Rom 10:9). With a slight change in wording, we can also imagine Paul saying, "You *demonstrate* your salvation if you confess with your lips that Jesus is Lord and believe in your heart that God raised him from the dead." *Confessing* Christ—*declaring* our belief that Jesus is Lord—is as truly necessary as *believing*, Paul said, and making public our belief is what *identifies* us as believers. It means demonstrating Christ's resurrection—that Jesus is alive and powerfully at work, ministering in the world even today. An intellectual assent to the resurrection isn't enough. It must be declared. And that means it must be acted *upon* and acted *out* in our daily lives. And *that* means participating actively in the life of the Christian community, the community in which Jesus is known as Lord. If we *believe* that *Jesus* is *Lord*, then our words and our deeds will be one continuous and unambiguous *declaration* of that truth. To *think* that it is true but not be willing to declare it to *others*, not be willing to *act* upon it in our daily activities, casts *doubt* upon our belief. Are we *embarrassed* by Christ, that we want to *hide* our identity as believers? Do we *distrust* his power and his commission? Do we think that the *world* doesn't need to know about him? Does each of us think that he died only for *me*, and for no one else? Are we in fact not sure that we really *want* him to be Lord of our lives, guiding our choices, stimulating our generosity, prompting our forgiveness, summoning our obedience?

The Christian faith *is* not and must never *become* some vague religious sentimentality, some unspecific belief that there is probably a God out there somewhere who kind of looks after things and sort of wants us to be good citizens and generally expects us to provide for our families. Frankly, that would be a pretty poor reason for Jesus to have died on the cross. A sacrifice like his should elicit from us *more* than a lukewarm, mushy, inarticulate faith that makes not much difference to us and no difference at all to the people around us. Do we believe that Jesus Christ is alive, risen from the tomb, the Son of God, the friend of sinners, the Prince of Peace, the center and pivot point of all of history, or do we *not*? Do we accept Jesus Christ as Lord, the authority from which our lives take their direction and the goal toward which our lives lead, or do we *not*? Are we willing to declare and live out our allegiance and our commitment, our hope and our trust, or are we *not*? Do we affirm that that makes us all members of the one body of Jesus Christ, answering a common calling and sharing a common destiny and finding God's blessing and seeing Christ's face in each other, or do we *not*? Do we stake our very lives on the identity we have been given in the waters of baptism and the vows solemnly made at the font—that we have died with Christ and have risen with Christ and now we belong to Christ in whom we have found our salvation—or do we *not*? Are we free from the world's assessments and liberated from the world's claims to be what God *created* us to be and Jesus died so that we *can* be and the Holy Spirit gives us the *power* to be, or are we still in the shackles of pride and doubt and uncertainty that tie our tongues and hobble our feet and paralyze our hands so that no one else would ever suspect that the life, death, and resurrection of Jesus Christ mean anything to us of any real importance? If we are afraid of being regarded like one of those street-corner preachers whom so many people find annoying and turn some passersby off from Christianity altogether, well, frankly, the chance of that for the average Christian is far less than the chance that we will die without even our closest friends and family members knowing whether the life, death, and resurrection of Jesus really had much effect on us.

The early Christian church perceived that the truth of the gospel was endangered by people who proclaimed errant beliefs. Probably the most dangerous heresy and the most persistent one was the teaching that theologians and church historians refer to as "Gnosticism." The term comes from the Greek word for "knowledge," *gnosis*, which we also see in our English words "diagnosis" and "prognosis" and "agnostic." It may well be that the Gospel of John was written to counter the teachings of the Gnostics. But Paul had already sensed the dangers inherent in the belief that salvation is a result of what a person "knows." Specifically, the Gnostics taught that people are saved by having a supernatural knowledge of God, a level of understanding not available to everybody but only to the spiritual elite, so that their salvation does not really depend upon the death of Jesus on the cross.

The practical effect of supposing that salvation is all about what a person *knows* is that salvation comes to be thought of by some people as a private affair, and one that has no real implications for the way one lives, certainly imposes no responsibility to give of oneself in any way for the benefit of others in thanksgiving for the divine love that led Jesus obediently to the cross and led God faithfully to raise Jesus from the tomb. Paul must have been aware of people in his own time who identified themselves as Christians but for whom the death and resurrection of Jesus prompted neither confession nor discipleship. How could *belief*, in such a case, qualify as *faith*? Faith, if it is *genuine*, is something that must be *declared*, and something that must be *acted upon*, and not just now and then, but *constantly*, as the motive of one's every word and every deed. "If you confess with your lips that Jesus is Lord and believe in your heart that God raised him from the dead, you will be saved" (10:9)—and, if *saved*, you will be a part of Christ's *community*, a member of Christ's *body*, bearing a *resemblance* to Christ, doing the *works* of Christ, speaking the *truth* of Christ, walking the *way* of

Christ. And, because they see Christ alive within you, all people will know that *you* believe Jesus is Lord.

Second Sunday in Lent

Grace Episcopal Church, Ponca City, Oklahoma
February 21, 2016

Genesis 15:1–12, 17–18
Philippians 3:17—4:1
Luke 13:31–35

"Practicing the Promise"

Things had not been going exactly the way Abram might have expected following God's choosing him to be the Lord's agent in forming a people for himself. In answer to God's promise to make of him a great nation, Abram had taken Sarai his wife and Lot his nephew and all his servants and had left the safe familiarity of Haran. And in answer to God's promise to give the land of Canaan to his descendants, Abram pitched his tent there and surveyed the length and breadth of the country and established his flocks and herds there. And they flourished to the point that it became crowded in Canaan—fertile though it was, the area Abram had settled in could not support both *his* family and that of *Lot*. And that led to strife between Lot's herdsmen and his own, which Abram settled by generously dividing the land between himself and Lot. But God reiterated to Abram the promise of land and offspring. And then neighboring kings took Lot captive, but Abram went to his aid with a small army and was successful in rescuing Lot and all the goods that his enemies had seized along with him.

The Lord prospered Abram in many ways; things always seemed to work out, except that he and Sarai still had no child—the key to the promise—and so all the land and all the possessions and all the success in dealing with his rivals seemed to Abram to be without purpose, as God's promise of offspring to inherit it all and constitute a great nation was going unfulfilled. Though God had been faithful in so many other ways, Abram's main focus was on the one rather important detail that God had seemed to overlook. "Do not be afraid, Abram," God assured the old man who had unquestioningly left his family home and gambled everything on the hope that God would fulfill God's promise, "I am your shield; your reward shall be very great" (Gen 15:1b).

But *talk*, even *God's* talk, was no substitute for *action*. Words were not enough to give a seventy-five-year-old patience in the matter of his wife, also well advanced in age, giving birth. The biological clock was not only ticking; it appeared to have wound all the way down. "Abram said, 'O Lord God, what will you give me, for I continue childless, and the heir of my house is Eliezer of Damascus?'" (15:2). Abram went on to explain, "'You have given me no offspring, and so a slave born in my house is to be my heir'" (15:3). Childless men of means *did* sometimes adopt their servants and make *them* their heirs, but Abram reckoned *that* to be a disappointing substitute for what God seemed to have promised Abram back before he started the journey to Canaan—his own seed multiplying in the land to become a great nation. Still, God stubbornly insisted on the truth of the promise that God had originally made. "'*This* man shall not be your heir; no one but your very own *issue* shall be your heir'" (15:4). And we can imagine that Abram looked around his tent, perhaps cast a glance over toward Sarai, beautiful but elderly, and put on a skeptical expression and muttered under his breath, "Yeah, right."

At that point, God "brought [Abram] outside and said, 'Look toward heaven and count the stars, if you are able to count them.' Then he said to him, 'So shall your descendants be'" (15:5). And then, the thing that made Abram a model of faith for hundreds of generations to come, including you and me—"he *believed* the Lord, and the Lord reckoned it to him as righteousness" (15:6). And then, reminding Abram that he had brought him safely all the way to Canaan, after all, God directed him to set up a ritual of sacrifice by which God sealed the covenant with Abram that, although the progeny of Abram would one day be enslaved in a foreign land, God would redeem them and they would inherit abundant blessings.

At any point, Abram could reasonably have decided that God's promise was bogus. He could have given up and gone back to Haran. He and Sarai could have quit trying for a child—in their circumstances, probably, most couples would have concluded that intercourse was a wearying exercise of futility rather than a pleasurable engagement in hope. But not only in the marriage bed but in everything *else* Abram did, he remained *faithful* to the belief that *God* would be faithful to the promise, despite the stubborn facts of biology and the hazards of setting up housekeeping in a dangerous neighborhood.

We learn later in Genesis that it was another twenty-five years or more before Abram, by then "Abraham," and Sarai, by then "Sarah," together had the child that God had promised—Isaac. Beyond all human reason, beyond the facts of life that everyone thought they knew, beyond the textbooks and the taunts, God brought to pass what God had said God would do—brought forth life from a womb that was as barren of life as a tomb. And what Abram, Abraham, did in the meantime—following God's direction, acting upon the covenant promises as if they were already accomplished fact—marked him as "righteous" and laid the foundation upon which a nation was built and a spiritual race was inaugurated—one that has lasted for thousands of years and that includes you and me within God's orbit of blessing that we, in turn, will be a blessing to others, *all* others, even as God swore to Abram way back before he started his journey to the future that God purposed for humankind and all of creation—the spiritual race that culminated in Jesus the Christ and his church.

On these Sundays of Lent, the Gospel readings are moving us from the glory and promise disclosed at the transfiguration of Jesus on the mountaintop ever closer to the gore and dismay played out on the hill called Calvary. Peter had wanted to enshrine the moment of splendor with monuments of some sort, and no doubt, over the course of the ensuing weeks, Peter had many occasions of wanting to go back to that bright, shining moment when it seemed that nothing could stand in Jesus' way of victory over whatever Jesus wanted to defeat—sickness, hunger, sin, death itself. "This is my Son, my Chosen" (Luke 9:35), God had declared on the mountain. And Jesus *acted* on that promise, daily, righteously doing the things of God—forgiveness and salvation, wholeness and life—fully trusting that God *meant* what God had *said*, that God's *promise* was his own *agenda*, that the eternal destiny of creation was the truth that made urgent every moment in which an illness could be cured or an empty stomach could be filled or a relationship, broken by sin, could be restored. The headlines might mock the hope, and popular wisdom might deny the covenant, but Jesus was tutoring his followers in the ways of the kingdom as he himself lived in righteousness, that is, fully in faith that God does not lie.

"Abandon your work," some Pharisees appealed to Jesus one day. "Get away from here, for Herod wants to kill you" (13:31). *His* vow is the one that you must heed, they warned—the vow to put an *end* to healing the sick and feeding the hungry and forgiving the sin-burdened and reuniting the estranged. *His* is the reality that the world must abide in—the rule of pride and cruelty and jealousy and fear. *His* ways of force and oppression are the standard to which every knee should bow and every heart should conform—*his* and *everyone's* who feels *threatened* by Jesus' proclamation that what God promises *for* and will bring about *in* the *future* should be the daily work and witness of God's people *now*. But in response to the tyrant's *threat*—the *corruption* of God's blueprint for the world, the assertion that faith in God's *future* has little or nothing to do with how people who are faithful to God must conduct their lives *today*—Jesus answered, "Go and tell that fox for me, 'Listen, I am casting out demons and performing cures'" (13:32a). The reputation of Jerusalem and the mocking judgment of Herod cast a shadow over the near future, but Jesus would not allow the eventuality of persecution and even his own death to turn him from being faithfully obedient to God in the present. The Easter resurrection had not yet happened when Jesus, certain of God's purpose of mercy and wholeness and life, spoke the words of truth and did the deeds of salvation that put him in the crosshairs of Herod's wrath and sealed his fate on Calvary.

Lent is the season of disciplining ourselves to be *citizens* of *heaven* by living the *certainty* of the *resurrection* in a world clinging to the habits of *despair*. It is the season of practicing the promises of God despite every assertion that God's purpose is no match for disease, for hunger, for sin, and for death. Had Jesus not had faith in God's faithfulness to all that God had declared in the law and the prophets and at his own baptism and at his transfiguration, Jesus would have left the sick unhealed, would have left the hungry starving, would have left the tax collectors and harlots and outcasts unforgiven and unbefriended, would have done everything he could to avoid the cross. He would have lived his life by *Herod's* rules, would have heeded popular prejudices and left worldly judgments unchallenged, and you and I would be left buried in our sins and estrangement and all of humankind with us. But, instead, Jesus, being righteous, journeyed to the cross by upsetting social convention and religious taboo, casting out demons and touching wounds and embracing those whom the world said were to be shunned and opening the gates of heaven to those whom the gatekeepers had declared to be unforgiveable. And he said that anyone who had faith to follow him must do the same.

Lent is the season of disciplining ourselves to be *citizens* of *heaven* by living the *certainty* of the *resurrection* in a world clinging to the habits of *despair*. It is the season of practicing the promises of God—of living at once in the shadow of the cross and in the light of the resurrection. And just as those who believe the promise that Jesus Christ is the Son of God must live their lives in testimony to the truth of the resurrection, we also live our lives in the sober knowledge that the world around us will continue to deny that Easter requires taking seriously the marks of Lenten discipleship. Are you praying this Lent? For what are you praying? Are you reading the scriptures this Lent with an openness to the Holy Spirit? How are you being led?

Whom will you touch with God's healing power this Lent? To whom will you offer bread for the stomach and sustenance for the spirit? What jealous and hateful powers of death and despair will you defy by faithfully testifying to God's promise of life and salvation in a world that scoffs at hope and dares to dictate who may and who may not receive mercy? What false wisdom will you unmask by championing the oppressed and confronting the oppressor? How will you live your life for the sake of others as you see that the cross of Jesus Christ is the very way that God has fulfilled the promise of eternal life?

Do not surrender to the world's ways of darkness and despair and death, but live righteously, serving others as a witness to light and hope and life, as God has promised. Practice this Lent God's promise, disciplining your thoughts and your words and your deeds to demonstrate the truth of the resurrection. Renew your faithful discipleship as a follower of Jesus Christ, who healed the sick, who fed the hungry, who freed those enslaved, who forgave the sinner, who embraced the stigmatized, who befriended the outcast, who gave hope and restored life to those in despair and whose spirits were dead. Practice this Lent the promise that brought joy to an elderly childless couple and brought forth the Lord Jesus Christ from the bleakness of the tomb and has given us life with God. And live righteously, as *Easter* people, all year round.

Third Sunday in Lent

Spanish Springs Presbyterian Church, Sparks, Nevada

March 7, 2010

Isaiah 55:1–9
1 Corinthians 10:1–13
Luke 13:1–9

"Invitation to Salvation"

An automobile traveling in a rainstorm along an interstate highway suddenly becomes airborne as it leaves the pavement at the point where a bridge has just washed out moments before, and the driver and passengers plunge to their deaths in floodwaters gushing through the normally dry streambed below. Gunshots from an assault weapon drown out the happy sound of children at play in a schoolyard, and parents are suddenly childless. A tornado rips apart a church building while the congregation is at prayer on a Palm Sunday morning, and the pastor's own daughter is killed in the building's collapse. Family members grieve and some ask, "Why?" Friends sigh and some say, "It was God's will." Strangers have a new topic for coffee-cup conversation and some declare, "Well, they must have done something to deserve it." You know what I am talking about. It is the normal set of responses to tragedy, and it has changed little over the centuries since biblical times.

There is a psychological need for an explanation whenever tragedy occurs, not only as a way of coping with the loss of a friend or family member or whomever, but also as a way of coping with our own mortality. What is keeping that same tragedy from befalling *us*, we wonder? And one of the psychologically satisfying answers is that such tragedy is a punishment for sin far more serious than any *we* have ever committed. Of course, that explanation overlooks the fact that *all* of us will one day die; some die as newborns, some quite advanced in years, most of us sometime in between, and there are plenty of *sinners* walking around in perfect *health*. It overlooks Jesus' announcement that God *favors* the poor and the maimed and the blind and the crippled, so that we must not automatically assume that poverty and disfigurement and infirmity and illness are in any sense punishments from God. Still, it is a seductively simple response to an age-old problem, and one day it was presented to Jesus.

It seems that Jesus did not care much for hypothetical questions—the kind that some congregation members ask of ministers as soon as the worship service is over (well, not here, of course, but in other churches), the kind that Presbyterian ministers are fond of confounding each other with on the floor of presbytery, the kind that seminary students use to bluff their way around the fact that they haven't read their lesson. "What if" and "Suppose" and "But, teacher"—those were the words used by Pharisees who were trying to justify themselves and by comfortable people who didn't want to examine their own motives for disobedience. Jesus realized that the human heart is a deceitful organ. It will prompt people to ask all sorts of things about other people's foibles in order to divert attention from its own perversity. On at least two occasions, Jesus repudiated theoretical questions based on the notion of retributive justice—if something bad has happened to someone, it must be because of some guilt. One of those, in the Gospel of John, was the case of the man born blind. When his disciples asked him, "Rabbi, who sinned, this man or his parents, that he was born blind?" (John 9:2), Jesus answered, "Neither this man nor his parents sinned; he was born blind so that God's works might be revealed in him. *We* must work the works of him who sent me while it is day; night is coming when no one can work" (9:3-4). And in our Gospel reading today, in Luke, some of the multitude told Jesus that Pontius Pilate had ordered killed some Galileans who, it seems, were in the act of making their sacrifices in the temple, and Jesus responded, "Do you think that because these Galileans suffered in this way they were worse sinners than all other Galileans? No, I tell you; but unless you repent you will all perish as they did. Or those eighteen who were killed when the tower of Siloam fell on them—do you think that they were worse offenders than all the others living in Jerusalem? No, I tell you; but unless you repent, you will all perish just as they did" (Luke 13:2-5).

Do you hear the disdain Jesus had for people's speculation about other people's sins? "No, it wasn't because they were particularly sinful that those Galileans were slain or that the tower fell and crushed those Jerusalemites. Pilate is a murderer. The tower was structurally unsound. Calamity is no respecter of persons. Sometimes the saints suffer. Sometimes the wicked prosper. Righteousness will not keep tragedy from your door. But if you're not careful, you will die in your sins. Take heed, and repent while you may." And did you hear what Jesus said about the man born blind? "It wasn't because of this man's sin or his parents' sin that this man was born blind. Why do you waste time speculating about that, when God has put before you this opportunity to show his healing power?" It is not for the disciple of Jesus to moralize about others' tragedy, but to be reminded how unexpectedly life can end and to be prepared for that, and to use the gifts with which the Spirit has endowed us to minister to those whose lives tragedy has touched. Let *non*-believers vainly speculate and idly gossip. The Christian should be much too busy turning away from sin and turning to the works of Christ to have time for such chatter. Certainly, Luke the evangelist considered such terrible events in this time before the second coming of Christ, whether they be the result of human guilt or rampaging nature, as an *invitation* to *salvation*—*our* salvation through faith based upon what we have heard and seen about *Christ*, and *others'* salvation through faith based upon what they hear and see in *us*. And that invitation to salvation is what we ought to be concerned with in this time of expectant waiting. We are mortals formed from dust, and to dust we shall return. Luke urgently appeals to us his readers to repent while we are able to do so, as the *prophet* had appealed to *his* readers centuries before:

> Seek the LORD while he may be found,
>   call upon him while he is near;
> let the wicked forsake their way,
>   and the unrighteous their thoughts. (Isa 55:6–7a)

It might occur to us that God has plenty of reason—based on those *other* people's sins, at least—to end it all right now. If disasters were a way for God to *punish* the *sinful*, the *real* question might not be why there are so *many* tragedies in the world, but why there are so *few*. Who, after all, is beyond the need for repentance? Who is guiltless before God? The assurance of God's *forgiveness* is never far from the call to *repentance* in Luke's Gospel, or in the rest of the Bible, for that matter. The sentence in Isaiah that begins,

> Seek the LORD while he may be found,
>   call upon him while he is near;
> let the wicked forsake their way,
>   and the unrighteous their thoughts (Isa 55:6–7a)

ends with *these* words:

> let them return to the LORD, that he may have mercy on them,
>   and to our God, for he will abundantly pardon. (55:7:b–c)

God's judgment and God's mercy may seem contradictions to us, but they are inextricably *linked* in scripture and certainly in the teachings of Christ. "'Unless you repent you will all soon perish'" (Luke 13:5), Jesus told the multitude. "Then he told this parable: 'A man had a fig tree planted in his vineyard; and he came looking for fruit on it and found none. So he said to the gardener, "See here! For three years I have come looking for fruit on this fig tree, and still I find none. Cut it down! Why should it be wasting the soil?" [The gardener] replied, "Sir, let it alone for one more year, until I dig around it and put manure on it." [Yes, that word is in the Bible.] "If it bears fruit next year, well and good; but if not, you can cut it down"'" (13:6–10).

Judgment hangs over Israel, judgment hangs over the church, judgment hangs over each of us like an axe poised to fall on a tree trunk. Why would anyone put off repentance—acknowledging our sin and turning ourselves around—with cars plunging into rivers and guns as common as licorice and tornado season under way? And yet the only reason that the world isn't dashed to bits this very instant is the restraining hand of God's mercy, ever hopeful that the tree he has planted in his garden will finally bear the fruit he intended, ever hopeful that each human being will lay aside disobedient selfishness and rebellious pride and turn to Jesus Christ in love and humility. God's judgment is certain. God's mercy is just as certain.

> For my thoughts are not your thoughts,
>   nor are your ways my ways, says the Lord. (Isa 55:8)

The more I read the Bible, the more it seems to me that gratitude to God for *God's* steadfast faithfulness is the purest motive for *our* steadfast faithfulness to God. A thankful heart carries us through many seeming contradictions or hard sayings of the Bible. I have never believed that anyone can be frightened into an abiding faith in God. I have certainly never believed that anyone can be frightened into *loving* God. I do not believe that Jesus spoke his words about the urgency of repentance in order to *terrify* people, but rather to point out an important lesson about the realities of tragedy and mortality. Planning to amend our lives *someday* is foolish. Thinking about starting to obey God *tomorrow* is a lie. The need for repentance, the absolute importance of acknowledging our failures and asking God's forgiveness and responding to God's forgiveness with a rededication to obeying God, is a matter of immediate urgency simply because tomorrow may never come, much less our vague "someday." Who knows but that the vinedresser has long been busy digging about our roots and piling manure around us, and we have been so preoccupied with romance or making money or taking the spiritual pulse of *other* people that we have failed to notice the smell? The same may be true of a nation. Or of a church.

I was astonished by an incident that occurred in law school. One of my classmates had organized a group of students for Bible study and had started a little newsletter about the group and various faith issues. While standing in the hallway outside the classroom one day, waiting for the class that met just before ours to be dismissed, our professor noticed a copy of the newsletter tacked up on the student bulletin board, and recognized the name of my classmate as the editor. "Now there's a waste of youth," said the professor. "Why would someone his age be interested in such stuff as that? Young men are supposed to sow wild oats, not brood about religion." I was not a part of the group—I did not agree with the theology my classmate espoused and I was put off by his presumption that no one had ever known about God until *he* discovered God—but I was amazed at the professor's attitude, as if repentance should be scheduled and response to the love of God in Jesus Christ could be turned on and off like a light switch. Faithfulness is not something that can be delayed to a more convenient time, like when we have nothing better to do.

If we are truly grateful to God for our blessings, how can the question of putting off faithful living ever come up? The need for repentance is now. God's merciful offer of forgiveness is now. Christ's invitation to salvation is now. And it is as urgent and as gracious *now* as ever it has been.

> Ho, everyone who thirsts,
>   come to the waters;
> and you that have no money,
>   come, buy and eat!
> Come, buy wine and milk
>   without money and without price.
> Why do you spend your money for that which is not bread,
>   and your labor for that which does not satisfy?
> Listen carefully to me, and eat what is good,
>   and delight yourselves in rich food. (Isa 55:1–3)

But doesn't simple gratitude for the invitation to salvation compel us to repent *now, daily*, and recommit ourselves to live in the way that is most pleasing to God? The news that God's *judgment* may come at *any time* moves the Christian to rejoice that God's *mercy* is operating *every moment*. The tragedies around us are nothing to be happy about. They should call us to sober remembrance that God's judgment is ever near, but they should call us to *joyful* remembrance that God's *salvation* is near as well.

Fourth Sunday in Lent

First Presbyterian Church, Dodge City, Kansas

March 22, 1998

Joshua 5:9–12
2 Corinthians 5:16–21
Luke 15:1–3, 11–32

"Learning to Say 'Brother'"

I may have to change morning television news programs. The show that I have watched for thirty-five years is getting too loud. Sometime during the past year, the producers must have decided that journalism should be more like mud wrestling, or maybe mud*slinging*, only a lot noisier. And ever since, at least one interview each morning, and usually more than that, turns into an unmannered argument between two people on opposite sides of an issue. No matter what the topic, they seem to end up shouting at each other, impugning each other's motives, repeatedly interrupting each other so that neither person is allowed to make a relevant point in a reasoned and intelligible manner. I wonder if they've been encouraged to *bait* each other. If they aren't needling *each other*, then the *host* quotes something unflattering they've said about each other. It must be good for ratings, which says something disappointing about the American television-watching public. Civility, respect for another person's opinion, appreciation for another person's experience, and simple courtesy are all thrown to the wind as people show their worst sides on national TV. This is informative? This is enlightening? I may have to change morning television news programs. *That's* no way to start the day.

In the 1960s, our nation was deeply divided over many public issues—race, war, sexism, the environment. The Presbyterian Church acknowledged those sharp divisions by adopting as part of its constitution the Confession of 1967. The Confession of 1967, with its emphasis on reconciliation, is based on our epistle reading for today.

Thirty-some years after the Confession was approved by the General Assembly meeting in Portland, Oregon, it seems that polarization has been raised to an art form. Those of us who lived through the decade remember the 1960s as a time of turmoil. But I'm not so sure that in society at large back in the 1960s, and certainly in the church, there wasn't in fact more of a *consensus* about what society should be like. In such widely diverse places as Haight-Ashbury and Wall Street, Peoria and Selma, there was still a sense of shared destiny, even if there were profoundly different opinions of how to get there.

Today, there is a much more radical individualism in our culture that denies responsibility for each other's welfare, that ignores each other's needs. When God said to Cain, "Where is your brother Abel?", Cain replied, "I do not know; am I my brother's keeper?" (Gen 4:9). In the 1960s, we instinctively knew the answer to that question, conditioned perhaps by folk singers and preachers and statesmen (there were not yet many states*women*): yes, we *are* responsible for the condition of our brother and our sister. Today, we would not be surprised to hear the reply, "What do you mean 'my brother'?" Watching some of the interviews on the *Today* show recently, I'm not sure that the antagonists would even acknowledge a shared *humanity*, much less any sense of *obligation* toward each other. Do they see in each other's face the image of a brother or sister? And the way that single-issue politics has come to dominate the political agenda, and even the agenda of religious denominations, the sad reality of "Me first" seems to have deteriorated into the even sadder "Why anybody else?"

If the Bible has any implication for the relationship between people—and it most certainly *does*,—it is fundamentally the ethic of how people who have been created to live in community with *God* should live in community with *each other*. God did not intend fellowship to have only a *vertical* dimension; we were created for *each other* as well as for *God*. "It is not good that the man should be alone," God said of the human being God created; "I will make him a helper as his partner" (2:18). From the very beginning, the importance of *community* has been a fact of human life—*and* mutuality, *and* living for the sake of one another. The most profound expression of that community is how people who have been forgiven by God forgive each other. That there will be disagreements, that there will be differences, that there will be difficulties, even, the Bible takes for granted. Scripture is no fairy tale. It is not blind to the human condition. It does not ignore human shortcomings. It's the most honest book ever written. The nastiness only *begins* with Cain killing Abel—over what? Jealousy? If we were made for community with God and with our fellow beings, and if we are constantly about the business of *disrupting* that fellowship, then *reconciliation* is our *greatest need*.

To the apostle Paul, the fundamental issue in ministry was the need for reconciliation—reconciliation with God, reconciliation with each other. In a world filled with always faithfully obedient people, servant-minded and generous in heart, it would not be so. But people yelling at each other on TV is only a symptom of a deep and pervasive spiritual disease. Even in the Christian church at Corinth, even among people Paul referred to as "saints," there were deep divisions, bitter and disruptive, detrimental to the cause of the kingdom of God, bringing disrepute upon what the apostles called "good news." To that quarrelsome, prideful, childish group of people, Paul declared that *all* Christians are called to be engaged in the ministry of reconciliation. And that means that *all* Christians are called to regard people not through the warped lenses of pride and fear and jealousy and envy and lust, but the way *Jesus Christ* regards people—as created in the image of God, and worth dying on a cross for. *All* Christians must learn to regard each other as sister and as brother. Just as *God* allows *nothing that anyone does* to stand in the way of his love and mercy for that one, so God wills that *nothing that anyone else does* may stand in the way of *our* love and mercy for that person.

Jesus felt at home with all sorts of people. The Son of God did not scruple to have conversation with the most wretched sinners, harlots, Gentiles, traitors, or to heal them, or to forgive them, or to bless them. Once, when Jesus was being criticized by the Pharisees and the scribes for not only *tolerating* sinners and tax collectors in his presence, but even *eating* with them—a very public sign of acceptance of a person into one's friendship,—Jesus responded by telling three stories about the joy of a person who found something that had been lost. Jesus told about the joy of a shepherd who had found a *sheep* that had been lost. Then Jesus told about the joy of a woman who had found a silver *coin* that had been lost. Finally, as a climax, Jesus told about the joy of a father who had found a *son* that had been lost.

Whether out of wanderlust or boredom, whether out of enterprise or contempt, the young man had left home with his share of his father's estate. By doing so, he broke all ties to his family and even to his religious heritage, going off to a distant country, to a Gentile land. He squandered his inheritance by spending it in all the wrong ways, and, if that were not bad enough, a famine struck the land. He gave himself up to the ultimate indignity for a Jew—feeding pigs—but still he did not make enough money to live on; even the pig fodder looked good to him. One day, he "came to himself." He swallowed his pride, admitted to himself his error, and resolved to return to his father and ask to be hired as a servant. He did not *deserve*, and could not *expect*, to be treated as a son any longer. We can imagine how he practiced his speech all the long way back home, but the young man had barely started his confession, and did not even have a chance to ask to be hired as a servant, when his father, who, having seen the young man, abandoned all of his pride and decorum and ran through the streets to greet him, embraced him and kissed him and shouted, "It's party time!" How deeply the father had grieved his son's absence most of us can only imagine, though some people in this sanctuary have experienced it. How many nights he spent in prayerful anguish he had surely lost count. His love was as constant as the candle burning in the window, and it burned so purely that it consumed any possibility of revenge or retribution.

But the man had another son, an older son, who, when he heard about the preparations for a party, was all resentment and disgust. He had probably long ceased to care about his brother, but now that the boy had dropped in out of the blue, he was consumed with hatred—but not so much toward the brother as toward the father's welcome. "What do you mean, throwing a party?," he demanded to know. He did not even acknowledge his relationship to his father by addressing him properly. Even less did he acknowledge his father's long grief. "I've been obedient all these years, never caused you any trouble, did just what I thought I was supposed to do, and you never threw even a tea party for me. But when this son of yours comes back—this son of yours who has devoured your property with prostitutes,—you kill the fatted calf for this son of yours!" He was enraged. What had his years of obedience earned *him*?

Ah, there is the point! He had been obedient not out of *love*, but because he thought obedience would *earn* him something. "Then the father said to him, 'Son, you are always with me, and *all that is mine is yours*. But we had to celebrate and rejoice because *this brother of yours* was dead and has come to life; he was lost and has been found'" (Luke 15:31). Now, the Pharisees and scribes could not have missed the point of Jesus' parable; they—the righteous, the scrupulously obedient, the super-critical—had demanded to know what Jesus was doing throwing a party, showering God's love, bestowing God's kisses, upon people who had lived much like the younger son. And the fact that this parable is in Luke's Gospel, written for the instruction of the church, must mean that there were people in Luke's congregation who were acting like the Pharisees of Jesus' day, like the older brother in the parable, criticizing those who would welcome into fellowship and minister to people who were different, people who were unsavory, people who were only just beginning to show the slightest glimmer of interest in things religious after long lives of inattention or outright hostility to God. Jesus, through Luke's Gospel, answers every critic: "He is your *brother*. She is your *sister*. You are *always* with me, and everything that is *mine* is *yours*. But we should celebrate and rejoice, because *this brother of yours, this sister of yours*, was *dead* and has come to *life*; *this brother of yours, this sister of yours*, was *lost* and has been *found*."

Did you notice the subtle use of language in the parable? In his complaint to his father, the older son speaks of the prodigal *not* as his "brother," but *distances* himself from the sinner by referring to him as "this son of yours." But the father reminds his older son of *his* close relationship to the younger boy by specifically saying, "this *brother* of *yours*." The first step in *repentance* is learning to say, "my sin," "my debt." The first step in *reconciliation* is learning to say, "my brother," "my sister." The older son in the parable cared nothing about either his father's grief at the separation, nor his brother's misery in the distant country. In angry rage, he would not even utter the word "brother," and so he *could not* say the word "father." Only if we recognize the most miserable human being as our brother, our sister, only if we can admit *responsibility* for him or her, only if we will rejoice with God and welcome that one at the table of reconciliation and then invite that one to our table of friendship, can we, with any conviction, call God "Father."

When we learn to say "brother," when we learn to say "sister," when we see the image of Jesus Christ even in the face of the person with whom we disagree the most, even in the face of someone we think has wronged us greatly, even in the face of a person who has spent a lifetime far away from God and distant from the church, we regard that person no longer from a human point of view, but from *God's* point of view. "All this is from God, who reconciled us to himself through Christ, and has given us the ministry of reconciliation; that is, in Christ God was reconciling the world to himself, not counting their trespasses against them, and entrusting the message of reconciliation to us" (2 Cor 5:18–19). Declaring the message of God's reconciliation in Christ requires doing the *deed* of reconciling *ourselves* to *others*, and that can happen only when we have learned to say "sister," only when we have learned to say "brother."

Fifth Sunday in Lent

Spanish Springs Presbyterian Church, Sparks, Nevada

March 28, 2004

Isaiah 43:16–21
Philippians 3:4b–14
John 12:1–8

"Through the Eyes of Faith"

A Presbyterian missionary stationed at Ganado, Arizona, and working among the Navajo people in the 1940s wrote about an encounter with a middle-aged Navajo man. The man could not understand what the missionary meant when he talked about "faith." So the missionary described it this way: it's like planting corn, and anticipating the harvest. It's like when you look at your young son, still an infant, and in your mind's eye you imagine him grown into manhood—what he will look like, what he will do—or like when you look at your young daughter, still a toddler, and in your mind's eye you imagine her grown into womanhood—what she will look like, what she will do. The missionary looked deep into the eyes of the man, wondering whether he had sparked any comprehension of what it means to have faith. The man reportedly smiled and nodded. He had begun to understand.

There is a difference, of course, between the missionary's explanation and the full reality of Christian faith. Christian faith is not just *imagining* what *might* be, *if* the weather cooperates, *if* the child survives infancy. Christian faith is *trusting* what *will* be, what *God* has *promised*, without qualifications and without conditions. It is not *wishful* thinking. It is not even *positive* thinking. And it is radically opposite from the way most of us are conditioned to go about life in a culture that tells us in a million ways that we make our *own* future, that we fashion our *own* destiny, that we must make *every* effort for success, should plan for *every* contingency. And we are much more eager to receive praise for *human achievement*—"My, hasn't he done well?" or "My, hasn't she done well?"—than to listen to praise for *divine faithfulness*—"My, hasn't God done well with him?" or "My, hasn't God done well with her?"

For a lot of us, certainly including ministers, faith is not always our most powerful motivator. If it *were*, surely we would *never* be content to allow *any* person to go *hungry*, citing the impracticalities of feeding everybody; we would *never* be satisfied to allow *any* person to go *homeless*, citing the expense of building housing for everybody; we would *never* be content to allow *any* person to go without *medical care*, citing the cost of curing everybody. If *faith* were always our most powerful motivator, rather than things like *fear* and *pride* and *greed*, we would not be working ourselves to exhaustion as a society; we would not make more than we need or use more than our share; we would never go to war. If *faith* were our most powerful motivator, we would live in true freedom, remembering God's liberating deeds in the past and trusting God's liberating purpose in the future.

It seems that the exiles in Babylon were having a hard time mustering the faith it would take to set out on a journey from their place of captivity to the promised land they had once inhabited and were told by prophets that they would inhabit yet again. They knew about the history of how God had dealt with Pharaoh in Egypt and opened a way of escape for their ancestors through the waters of the Red Sea—what a miracle it was. But, for the *life* of them, many could not begin to imagine that God was going to make a way for *them* to travel back to Judah, far across the hot, dry desert from the banks of the Euphrates. Talk of *freedom* must have seemed to many of them just *that*—*talk*. Their Babylonian overlords would *never* let them go. And if they *did*, how would they *ever* travel the many hundreds of miles by themselves to Palestine? It was foolish nonsense, impossible and cruel.

But then Cyrus the Persian conquered Babylon and, for reasons perhaps known only to God, decreed that the Israelites should be released to travel back home. And, so, the only remaining obstacle was the will to make the journey. Would the people accept the message of God's forgiveness of their past sins and the proclamation of God's promise of a prosperous future? Looking through the eyes of human logic, examining the map, scanning over the stock quotations, reading the political headlines of the day, there seemed to be *no way* that the prophets could be *right*. But God had made a *promise*. All *they* needed to do was to *act* upon that promise in *faith*, *despite* the map, *regardless* of the stock quotations, *irrespective* of the political headlines. After all, if their *ancestors* had allowed human logic to rule *their* actions, they would still all be slaves in Egypt. Miraculous as *that* exodus from bondage to freedom had been, an even *more* miraculous exodus was about to begin.

> Thus says the Lord,
>   who makes a way in the sea,
>   a path in the mighty waters,
> who brings out chariot and horse,
>   army and warrior;
> they lie down, they cannot rise,
>   they are extinguished, quenched like a wick:
> Do not remember the former things,
>   or consider the things of old.
> I am about to do a *new* thing;
>   now it springs forth, do you not perceive it?
> I will make a way in the wilderness
>   and rivers in the desert.
> The wild animals will honor me,
>   the jackals and the ostriches;
> for I give water in the wilderness,
>   rivers in the desert,
> to give drink to my chosen people,
>   the people whom I formed for myself
> so that they might declare my praise. (Isa 43:16–21)

Would the people have faith to do the same illogical thing that their ancestors had once done, and walk into God's freedom, right through the impossibility of natural and political and economic obstacles, right into God's promise? God was miraculously clearing away every barrier. All that was necessary now was for the people of God to see through the eyes of faith.

Most of us recognize the spiritual problem posed if people leave their morality behind in the sanctuary when they exit the church on Sunday and head out to their workplaces, to their places of amusement, to their homes, to the market, to the boardroom, to the classroom on Monday. But it is just as spiritually hypocritical, if you will, to leave our *faith* behind in the sanctuary when we go out to be God's people working in hospitals, working in the legislative hall, working in the embassy, and instead put our faith in charts and polls and statistics. It isn't that we *disregard* the promises of God, perhaps. It isn't that we *forget* the miracles. But as much as we *praise* them in the *sanctuary*, we seem not to *trust* the promises or *expect* the miracles *outside* the sanctuary. They're still valid, the promises are. They're still happening, the miracles are. But we don't seem to *see* them. It's like we have a different set of eyes when we're out in the world, dealing with everyday reality.

One of the most astonishing things about the story told in the Gospels is how people could *hear* the *words* of Jesus, could *witness* the *miracles* of Jesus, and then go on with life as if the words had never been *spoken* or the miracles had never *happened*. "What was *wrong* with those people?," students sometimes ask in Bible study groups. How could they *possibly* not *believe*? Well, the same thing can be said of us today, can't it? Why do we keep hedging our trust in God by stockpiling our money, by stockpiling our possessions? Why do we put so much effort, many of us, into trying to preserve our appearance of youth? Why do we go to war to solve problems? Why do we spoil the environment that is God's gift to his promised future generations? Why are we able to be scared by advertisers—and, more and more, instilling fear *is* the technique—into buying their line, and then buying their product? Why does the world not seem to change much, or the way that *we behave* in the world?

The disciples of Jesus had just recently witnessed the greatest miracle that Jesus had ever worked, a deed that clearly demonstrated that he had the power of God at his command: Jesus had raised from the tomb a man who had been dead for four days! If any event could instill life-changing faith in a person, world-changing faith in a society, surely this was *it*. And yet, so quickly, the chief priest and the Pharisees had decided that they had to *kill* Jesus to maintain their accustomed power and privileges, and even the disciples had just gone back to business as usual, had resumed their ordinary perspective on life—all of the disciples, that is, except one: Mary, one of the sisters of Lazarus, the man who had been raised from the dead. When Jesus returned to Bethany, where they lived, he attended a dinner, with Lazarus at the table with him, and Martha, Lazarus's other sister, busy serving the guests. In the midst of this gathering, Mary entered the house and went to Jesus and bathed his feet with a perfume made of nard, which came from India and was very expensive. The fragrance filled the entire house. Then, shamefully, totally violating the mores of the time, she wiped his feet with her hair. Mary's scandalous deed of devotion was no doubt motivated by thanksgiving for her brother's restoration to life, but also, doubtless, by her glimmering understanding of who Jesus was and what Jesus deserved. And so, her lavish gift was not wasteful, but wholly appropriate, and her sensual behavior was not brazenly erotic, but an innocent expression of the purest sort of love (not unlike the love that, less than a week later, prompted Jesus to wash his *disciples'* feet).

Judas, John reports, objected, because he was a thief at heart, and wanted access to the money Mary had spent on the ointment for his own purposes. In Matthew and Mark, *several* of the disciples objected to what the woman was doing, not just *Judas*. But they were looking at the deed through the eyes of the *world's* logic, not through the eyes of faith. Would *any* expense have been too great to lavish on the Son of God? Would *any* act of servant-like devotion have been too extreme? "Surely not!," we say. And then *we* turn around and *ration* what *we* give to Christ—how much time we devote to worship, how much time we devote to study, how much time we devote to prayer, how willing we are to forgive those who have wronged us, how much effort we put toward serving the hungry and the homeless and the sick and the bereaved and the oppressed, how much money we give to the church—ministers every bit as much as other Christians. And, worse yet, we defeat great works of faith before they are even launched, as individuals and congregations and denominations, by declaring a hundred reasons that they won't work, rather than trusting the *one* reason that they *will*—that they are being attempted in reliance upon the promises of God. So we really don't have any grounds on which to fault the people of *old*; *we* are *just* as likely to look at the world through the eyes of un-faith as *they* frequently did, and are thereby *just* as likely, perhaps, to *hinder* God's will of peace, to *deny* God's will of forgiveness, to *ignore* God's will of fullness, to *retard* God's will of wholeness, to *obstruct* God's will of life abundant and free and everlasting. Even our reasons for *failing* to act faithfully can be made to sound good and reasonable: "'Why was this perfume not sold for three hundred denarii and the money given to the poor?'" (John 12:5) "'You always have the poor with you'" (12:8a), Jesus responded, loosely quoting from the book of Deuteronomy, where the full sentence reads, "Since there will never cease to be some in need on the earth, I therefore command you, 'Open your hand to the poor and needy neighbor in your land'" (Deut 15:11). Anyone who has faith enough to give generously to Jesus will certainly have the faith that leads him or her to be generous with the poor.

"I am about to do a new thing," God declared to the exiles in Babylon; "now it springs forth, do you not perceive it?" (Isa 43:19a–b) Only through the eyes of *faith* could the *exiles* see *beyond* the bleakness of the desert wasteland and the bleakness of the daily headlines, past the customary attitudes of choking cynicism and dusty doubt, and set forth in *hope* toward the future that God had promised. Only through the eyes of *faith* could the *followers* of *Jesus* see *beyond* the grimness of death and the stubbornness of entrenched privilege and the tyranny of narrow expectations, to see in their friend Jesus the Christ, the Son of God, the Savior of the world, the giver of eternal life, and to trust him for the power and the courage and the grace to minister, selflessly and hopefully, in his name.

Palm/Passion Sunday

Spanish Springs Presbyterian Church, Sparks, Nevada

March 28, 2010

Isaiah 50:4–9a
Philippians 2:5–11
Luke 19:28–40

"What Was Jesus Thinking?"

"After he had said this, he went on ahead, going up to Jerusalem" (Luke 19:28). And so, Luke begins the story of Holy Week. The last words of the parable that Jesus was telling immediately before today's reading—the parable of the ten pounds that the man entrusted to his slaves while he went off to be crowned king, although some of the citizens of the place did not *want* him to be king—were the words of the man after he returned to his home country following his coronation: "But as for these enemies of mine who did not want me to be king over them—bring them here and slaughter them in my presence" (19:27). How ironic that Jesus was just then coming to the very place where *he* should have been hailed as king, but where, instead, he was slaughtered by *his* enemies!

"Jerusalem." The one word says it all—the city holy to God, built on Mount Zion, the site of the great temple where God was worshiped and where sacrifices were made for atonement; the city where God's Son rode in on a donkey and was saluted by the poor and the sick and the lame and the outcast with the words,

> "Blessed is the king
>   who comes in the name of the Lord!
> Peace in heaven,
>   and glory in the highest heaven!" (19:38);

the city where, within a matter of days, God's long-awaited Messiah was executed for the very reason that he was so faithful to his task.

Jesus' *first* journey to Jerusalem was with his *parents*, who brought him up to the city to dedicate him to God. Jesus' *final* journey to Jerusalem was with his *disciples*, who followed him as he carried out the *full measure* of his dedication to God. *Every* first-born male Jew was dedicated to God by his mother and father, but *no other* child so truly fulfilled what *real* dedication to God *means*.

And no other *Gospel* so regularly *reminds* us of Jesus' *destination*—what his dedication to God would *require* of him. Luke mentions Jerusalem about as many times as the other three Gospels together. Within days after Jesus was born, there was no doubt what his faithfulness to God would demand of him. It would demand of him his life.

Those of us who have grown up in the Christian faith, who have heard the familiar stories over and over until we can recite at least parts of them by heart, may have become so used to the passion story that we no longer recognize how wrong it all is. A comparative nobody, so far as the movers and shakers were concerned, parades into the capital as if returning victorious from some great battle, only this one rides not a majestic steed but a lowly donkey, is greeted not by patricians and dignitaries but hailed by beggars and harlots, is neither dressed in armor nor treads on brocade, but wears the common tunic of the poor and is honored with sweaty rags. And then murmuring and plotting, arrest and trial. He is ushered into the court not to judge and pronounce sentence but to *be* judged and have sentence passed on *him*. Then a *second* parade, not as a matter of *honor* but as a sign of *defeat*, to a place where the soil that has soaked up the blood of countless thieves and murderers will receive the blood of the only genuine innocent.

It was all so wrong, when you pause to consider the pieces. And yet, many centuries before it happened, the scenario had been described by the prophet Isaiah, pondering the mystery of obedient suffering, the strange ways of how God would work the redemption of the very people who insulted and wounded his faithful servant. "Maybe if I sent my beloved son," the owner of the vineyard said to himself in one of Jesus' last parables. But the tenants in the story "discussed it among themselves and said, 'This is the heir; let us kill him so that the inheritance may be ours.' So they threw him out of the vineyard and killed him" (20:14–15a). "I gave my back to those who struck me, and my cheeks to those who pulled out the beard," said the obedient servant in Isaiah; "I did not hide my face from insult and spitting" (Isa 50:6).

What was Jesus *thinking*? What kind of sincerity, what kind of purpose, what kind of faith allows a person, *compels* a person, to persist in the very life's commitment that invites others' insults, others' threats, others' slander, and, finally, the cross? Yes, Jesus was the Son of God. But that only begs the question: What was it, deep within him, that caused Jesus so utterly to abandon concern about what others—even religious leaders, even the most reputable members of society—thought about him, so utterly to give of himself at every turn, so utterly to disregard his own safety, that he "set his face like flint" (50:7) and journeyed up and into the very place where his enemies were most powerful and most likely to put him to death? Let us not dismiss the passion simply by saying that Jesus knew God would raise him from the dead three days after the crucifixion and enthrone him in glory. If Good Friday was merely an act, then the cross has no meaning. If Jesus made a deal with God to endure a few hours of pain in exchange for an eternity of glory, then the whole story is a sham erected on a gimmick. But if obedience to God was the primary—in fact only—motive for everything that Jesus said and did, culminating in his willing entrance into the city where his foes were sure to seize him and see that he was put to death, while God looked on and stayed his hand because the salvation of the world depended upon Jesus' faithfulness to the very end, then we are dealing with a mystery too deep for human explanation, one that deserves every ounce of gratitude we can raise, one that means every moment you and I suffer for obedience to God binds us closer to the one who now reigns forever at God's right hand.

There was a poignant reminder on the television screen this past week of the sort of scene that must have played out in the streets of Jerusalem that first Good Friday as some hurled insults and spat upon Jesus, when Congressman John Lewis, veteran of civil rights marches and now an elected member of the United States House of Representatives, who had been insulted and spat upon many times in the 1960s, endured again the same sort of shameful treatment in 2010 for being obedient to his conscience. What sort of commitment enables a person to bear such treatment? What sort of conviction keeps a person from returning like for like? What voice do people hear whispering in their ear each morning that they reject the temptation to answer threat and abuse with rebellion, that they don't simply turn back and away from the gauntlet of hatred and cruelty?

What was Jesus *thinking*? A lot of people can't imagine that *anyone* would have done what Jesus did without some prior assurance about the resurrection. Of course, the Gospels do, in places, quote Jesus as saying that the Son of Man would be raised on the third day. But whatever Jesus may or may not have anticipated in the way of resurrection, we mustn't suppose that that meant none of the suffering that Jesus endured—from insult as well as from whip and thorns and nails and sword—was irrelevant. Perhaps you and I can't conceive of saying and doing anything that would invite rejection and slander and an unjust conviction and a barbaric execution without promise of a reward—specifically, a guaranteed timetable for a first-class seat to heaven. But the testimony of the prophets is that such a guarantee is not what being God's obedient servant is about—that's not *obedience*; it's *barter*—and it's not what *Jesus* was about.

The *crucifixion* was the *only* guaranteed reward for absolute, selfless obedience to God. And absolute, selfless obedience to God, coupled with unconditional love for all whom God loves, was the sole and driving motive in Jesus' life from the time he was a young boy with the teachers in the temple until, abandoned even by God, as all thought, he was nailed to the cross. He did not cry out at the unfairness of it all, though it was the greatest injustice ever worked in a long and continuing history of injustice. He did not appeal to his impressive record of curing the sick and restoring sight and hearing and soundness of limbs. He raised not a single protest in his defense, nor did he utter a single malediction in condemnation of his opponents. And, even though it became apparent throughout that long afternoon of pain and shame that it was not just the will of his *enemies* that he should be put to death, but even the will of *God*, Jesus the servant remained steadfast in his obedience and did not abandon his commitment, but prayed to a God now agonizingly silent, "Father, into your hands I commend my spirit" (Luke 23:46). That, my friends, is faith.

Listening to God and speaking *faithfully* for God and doing the things that God would *have done* renders the servant *different* from other people. And it exposes the servant to criticism and antagonism, even by and among many who consider themselves godly and righteous. The temptation to rebel and turn back is almost overwhelming—*would be* overwhelming to anyone who did not have as their sole consideration being obedient to God, even though God allows such injustice, doesn't intervene to prevent it, remains disconcertingly silent while the servant is suffering abuse and disgrace, injury and death. But it is that very *obedience*, offered and performed without any expectation of reward, offered and performed without any expectation of notice, even, that redeems the world—the obedience of Jesus, and the obedience of those whose faith in him is absolute.

The very next verse in the prophecy of Isaiah reads,

> Who among you fears the LORD
>   and obeys the voice of his servant,
> who walks in darkness
>   and has no light,
> yet trusts in the name of the LORD
>   and relies upon his God? (Isa 50:10)

Who thinks that way? Is there anyone? That is the question for each person who vows to follow the servant, I think. That is the question for his church. Are we single-mindedly obedient to God, even if that obedience should take us all the way to the cross? Or do we value something else more, some idol of reputation or politics or financial security, perhaps, so that our sensitivity to abuse and injury is raised and we finally say, "I will turn back and go another direction toward some other destination"; "I will heed the insults and avoid the shame"; "God will have to bring salvation to perfection by some other means than by my being faithfully obedient"?

> [A]t the name of Jesus
> > every knee should bend,
> > > in heaven and on earth and under the earth,
> > and every tongue should confess
> > > that Jesus Christ is Lord. (Phil 2:10–11b)

So Paul declared to the Philippian Christians, who seem to have been asserting personal prerogatives and expecting perquisites for any instances of faithfulness. He was reminding them that, at the name of Jesus, the servant who

> humbled himself
> and became obedient to the point of death—
> even death on a cross (2:8),

every person should submit to Christ's authority, every person should follow Christ's example, every person should have the same mind that was in Christ, who was wholly set on obeying God, who was wholly set on going to Jerusalem regardless of the consequences. Christ acted in obedience to God on our behalf without any view of reward or gain. The one who by rights was entitled to every *honor* in fact became a *slave* and died at the hands of those who thought him of no account. And *that*, Paul observed, is *precisely* why God *exalted* him. In a world of pride and individualism and self-assertion and discord and self-serving behavior that infects even the church, the words of Paul intertwine with the words of Isaiah, calling us to single-minded obedience to God not because of what we hope to get out of it, but simply because it is *God* who has issued the call. "Let the same mind be in you that was in Christ Jesus" (2:5).

Maundy Thursday

Spanish Springs Presbyterian Church, Sparks, Nevada
April 8, 2004

Exodus 12:1–4, 11–14
1 Corinthians 11:23–26
John 13:1–17, 31b–35

"The Center of Life"

I was surprised, a few months ago, to hear a Presbyterian minister raise a question about a particular document that was under discussion in a presbytery-related meeting—a question that had to do with some wording in the document concerning the eucharist, the sacrament of the Lord's Supper—and finish his statement with the disclaimer, "It's not that I'm a *sacramentalist*." By the way that he ended his statement, it almost seemed that he wanted others to know he didn't spend much time thinking about the sacraments, or didn't regard them as all that important. He was almost being apologetic for suggesting that there might be something about the sacraments that calls for theological reflection.

If so, he is part of a growing trend in the modern church that regards baptism as something whose meaning is pretty much up to the individual, and that regards communion as something that is "nice" to add on to worship now and then. As sanctuaries are coming to be replaced by "worship centers" that are more like lecture halls or showrooms, as the chancel is coming to be spoken of as a "stage," one of the casualties of recasting Christian worship as lecture and entertainment is the loss of the historic insistence that worship involves both word and sacrament, both prophetic speech and symbolic act, so that what we *do* in worship, and even the way the sanctuary is designed, is an expression of our faith. And so, the most characteristic activity of Christian worshipers in the early church and ever since—the Lord's Supper—is seen by some as *dispensable* in the interest of outreach and relevance and brevity. It somehow doesn't seem to fit in with the fast-paced computerized gadgetry of modern communications, doesn't seem to jive with theater-style seating and preachers on JumboTron.

The Lord's Supper is remarkably primitive in its simplicity of bread and cup. Oh, over the centuries, people have sometimes pressed the bread into wafers and bejeweled and filigreed the cup. But, ultimately, communion remains stubbornly resistant to being modernized, mechanized, or miniaturized, despite the minimalist approach to the sacrament by some clergy and congregations. And, if I may venture to voice a generality, the *less frequently* people *receive* the sacrament of the Lord's Supper, the *more individualistic* their faith becomes. The very word "communion" speaks of doing something in concert with others, in the company of others, and draws attention to the fact that the sacrament is not just about "Jesus and me," but also about "me and others." Paul says that Jesus described it as the new covenant in his blood, and a *covenant* is a relationship that is defined by mutual obligations. The Lord's Supper is the act in which, physically, at least in those churches that come forward to receive the elements, Christ draws us to himself and, in the process, inevitably draws us toward each other.

When Paul heard that the Christians at Corinth were coming to the Lord's table in an individualistic manner, elbowing out their neighbor and shoving others aside, the idle rich getting there earlier in the day than the working poor and grabbing the choicest food at the dinner that preceded the bread and the cup, Paul took the congregation to task for not receiving the sacrament in a manner worthy of Christ. "Whoever, therefore, eats the bread or drinks the cup of the Lord in an unworthy manner will be answerable for the body and blood of the Lord. Examine yourselves, and only then eat of the bread and drink of the cup. For all who eat and drink without discerning the body, eat and drink judgment against themselves" (1 Cor 11:27–29). When that part of Paul's letter to the Corinthian Christians is read in isolation, it might seem that the apostle, when he talks about "discerning the body," is referring to the physical body of Jesus, which had been nailed to the cross and then had been buried and then had been raised from the tomb. But just a little later in the letter, Paul talks about "the body" as being the *church*, and each member of the church as having some important function necessary for the welfare of the body, which is the *whole* church. "Now you are the body of Christ and individually members of it" (12:27), Paul writes. So, their individualistic behavior—*deprecating* the value and contributions and gifts of *some* and *accentuating* the value and contributions and gifts of *others*, regarding some as less important while assigning others more privileges—was a disparagement of the body of Christ, which, ever since Christ's resurrection and Christ's ascension, is the *church*.

Why make such a big issue over what was happening during the eucharist, the Lord's Supper, the communion of Christ's followers with Christ himself and with each other? Because the Lord's Supper was the truth of Jesus Christ that cannot be spoken or intimated, but can only be done, and experienced. The sharing, the nourishing, at the hand of the risen Lord Jesus Christ was the very *center* of the Christian's life, and the life of Christians together. "For as often as you eat this bread and drink the cup," said Paul, "you proclaim the Lord's death until he comes" (11:26). To partake of the Lord's Supper together was, *is*, to proclaim the whole story of redemption in Christ, and to recall among believers the true scope and setting of the life Christians are called to share together. *No wonder* the early church could never conceive of Christian worship without the sacrament of the Lord's Supper. It is a tradition that is the center of life for the Christian. Over and over again, in every corner of the world, it is a vital and integral element of the faithful community's commitment to be with Christ and to be his body active in the world. It is an indispensable part of the church's message of the cross. By gathering at the Lord's table, remembering the story, repeating Jesus' actions with the first disciples—taking, blessing, breaking, and giving and receiving the bread, sharing the cup,—Christians proclaim Christ crucified and reveal the startling power and wisdom of God more eloquently than any sermon, more graphically than any audio-visual extravaganza, more graciously than any media blitz. And by gathering at the Lord's table, remembering the story, repeating Jesus' actions with his *first* disciples, *we* become *part* of the story; the self-giving of Christ for the world continues in our midst and, we can even dare to say, continues *through* us.

At the table, where the elements representing the incarnation of Christ and the crucifixion of Christ are generously offered to us by Christ himself, we are nourished by his body broken and his blood shed to *be* his body offering eternal life to the world. At the table of the Lord, everybody, whether weak or strong, man or woman, child or adult, rich or poor, Jew or Gentile, comes to join in commitment to the Lord Jesus and to one another in Christ. At the table of the Lord, we learn by doing together in *worship* what Christ has commissioned us to do out in the *world*: proclaiming by the gift of our own life in Christ, and Christ's life in us, the death of the Lord until he comes, announcing the gospel of life and salvation. Anything that points to distinctions among us makes the sacrament counterfeit. Any assertion that we can be faithful *without* such communion is a lie. Any suggestion that *knowing* about it is a substitute for *participating* in it ignores the command of Jesus, "Do this in remembrance of me" (11:24).

"The Center of Life"

It is not just a matter of knowledge. It is a matter of covenant. It is not just a matter of words. It is a matter of deeds. It is not just a dream or an ideal. It is how we are to live. Eating "this bread" and drinking "this cup" means taking bread, giving thanks, and breaking the bread as Jesus did. The command "Do this in remembrance of me" calls for something to be *done*, not just *said*, something to be *lived out*, not just *thought about*. The promise "This is my body that is for you" (11:24) is not just a *suggestion*; it is the whole truth of Jesus Christ. The eucharist, the Lord's Supper, is a living witness to Christ's presence—active, creative, effective, prophetic—by which his voice is heard through our lips, and through which his gestures find contemporary expression in the actions of *our* hands and *our* feet. The eucharist, the Lord's Supper, is where our common identity is enacted and sustained. It is the center of life.

So, we do not camouflage the Lord's table as a flower stand. We do not shove it to the side of the room, out of the way of our worship, but place it in a position of prominence and easy accessibility. And our liturgy of the Lord's Supper is not a nodding tokenism on Maundy Thursday or any other occasion, but the fullness of remembering and giving thanks for the mighty acts of God for our salvation, culminating in the greatest redeeming act of all—the life, death, and resurrection of Jesus Christ, who gave himself for all people, and for each of us, and for us together in the church, his body, and who, nourishing his followers with his own life, commissions and empowers *us* to give *ourselves* for others, too, in the company of all the faithful of every time and place, and emphatically in communion with each other in this congregation.

Is this meal a sentimental pastime that merely points to a hopeless ideal? Is it just an option for people who say they believe in Jesus Christ? The testimony of the church through the ages, commanded by its Lord and confirmed by its experience, is that this sacrament is the center of life, sealed in the blood of Christ's death, through which we are made part of him and he part of us, so that our words and actions today are his continuing teaching and ministry in the world, so that our forgiveness of sinners is a genuine expression of his mercy, so that our ministrations to the sick are miracles of his healing, so that our works of reconciliation are confirmation that he still reigns as the Prince of Peace, so that our giving others food to eat is his gracious multiplication of loaves for the hungry today, so that our befriending the lonely and the outcast is his powerful demonstration of the love of God for all people, as we are commanded to love one another. All of that has its root in what we do here tonight as we hear again how Jesus, the Son of God and the servant of all, gave himself for others, in the company of his disciples, taking, blessing, breaking, and giving the bread; taking, blessing, and sharing the cup: "[T]he Lord Jesus on the night when he was betrayed took a loaf of bread, and when he had given thanks, he broke it and said, 'This is my body that is for you. Do this in remembrance of me.' In the same way he took the cup also, after supper, saying, 'This cup is the new covenant in my blood. Do this, as often as you drink it, in remembrance of me.' For as often as you eat this bread and drink the cup, you proclaim the Lord's death until he comes" (11:23b–26). Very truly, this table is the center of life.

Good Friday

Spanish Springs Presbyterian Church, Sparks, Nevada
April 2, 2010

Isaiah 52:13—53:12
Hebrews 10:16-25
John 18:1—19:42

"One Particular Cross"

It was a more or less familiar sight, the cross. Crucifixion had been practiced in the Near and Middle East for centuries. It was a common symbol of empire long before the *Romans* adopted it as a gruesome method of torture and execution. The Persians had crucified their enemies and undesirables. The Assyrians had done the same, and the Scythians, and the Thracians. Alexander the Great is reported to have crucified thousands, grisly spectacles meant to intimidate besieged cities and punish conquered peoples, and his successors competed to match that figure. At one time, even the leaders of the Jews crucified their opponents, driving home the message that such people were accursed by God. On one occasion, a century before Christ, one of Israel's Jewish rulers crucified eight hundred Pharisees who had opposed him and allied themselves with a foreign enemy. The Dead Sea Scrolls include a description of this official as someone who "used to hang men alive."[1] But *most* of what we know about crucifixion is based on what the *Romans* did. They reserved this atrocity primarily for traitors and for murderous or rebellious slaves. Indeed, crucifixion was commonly referred to as the "slaves' punishment"—the penalty for those who were generally regarded as less than human, with no rights of their own.

The Romans carried out crucifixions in public places—along heavily traveled roads, often on the tops of hills, where the victims could be seen

---

1. Evans, "Crucifixion," 806.

from miles around, and at city gates, where people couldn't miss the point that this was what happened to those who dared to defy the Roman order. It was customary for the condemned man to carry the crossbeam to the place of execution, sometimes wearing a placard around his neck that declared his name and the charges against him. The placard would later be nailed to the upright post. The victim would already have been beaten, usually scourged with whips that had woven into them hooks or sharp pieces of metal. He would be stripped, and then his wrists or ankles would be nailed to the cross, and he would be left to die by asphyxiation, sometimes for days, if it took that long. In many places, the dead bodies were just left there in contempt, nailed to the cross, to rot or be picked apart by birds and rodents.

Most Roman authors who mention it regarded crucifixion as the worst form of death. The Latin words for "cross" and "cruelty" actually derive from the word for "torture"; the intention to cause pain and humiliation was obvious. The whole point, of course, was deterrence—the principal reason that torture still exists today, and one of the main arguments for capital punishment in our own country. As one Roman author explained, "Whenever we crucify the condemned, the most crowded roads are chosen, where the most people can see and be moved by this terror. For penalties relate not so much to retribution as to their exemplary effect."[2] At least, among the Jews, no bodies were left hanging after sundown. In order not to violate the laws of Moses about the treatment of corpses, the Jews who practiced crucifixion, and the Romans who crucified criminals in Jewish communities, removed the bodies and buried them.

On the first full day of Passover that one year, there were three crucifixions outside of Jerusalem's northwestern gate. Walking to or from the city, you or I would not have thought it an unusual scene, even if it still disgusted and revolted us, even if we felt pity and sympathy for those being so punished. Just three more criminals, like so many, being made an example of, though our attention might have been captured by the placard atop the middle cross, which read, "Jesus of Nazareth, the King of the Jews" (John 19:19). We might have been offended by that. Otherwise, there was nothing unusual or exceptional. Protestations of innocence. Maybe one or more of them *was* innocent of the *charges*, though *not* innocent of having done *something* to draw the officials' angry attention. And if one or more *was* innocent, what *difference* would it make in the larger scheme of things? It wouldn't be the *first* time *or* the *last* that an innocent person had been arrested and put to death and forgotten. A few friends and family members weeping and wailing. Well, that was to be expected, even for the most hardened criminal.

---

2. Quoted in Evans, "Crucifixion," 807.

"One Particular Cross" 139

Soldiers standing nearby or amusing themselves with ribald comments and crude behavior. That was usual enough. Three men on three crosses. All three were naked. All three were suffering. All three were dead by the end of the day. And the passersby were oblivious to the pivotal significance that the one in the middle, the one with the placard over his head that read, "Jesus of Nazareth, the King of the Jews" (19:19), was just that.

Why is it that the account of this particular crucifixion moves us to mourn—some of us, indeed, who, had *we* been there, passing by on the road, would most likely not have mourned the deaths of *any* of the three men? The Suffering Servant passage from Isaiah, which Christians have come to associate so closely with the passion of Jesus, says, after all,

> he had no form or majesty that we should look at him,
> nothing in his appearance that we should desire him.
> He was despised and rejected by others;
> a man of suffering and acquainted with infirmity;
> and as one from whom others hide their faces
> he was despised, and we held him of no account. (Isa 53:2b–3)

Try as I might to picture myself as an exception, I really can't flatter myself that *I* would have been any different from the average person walking along, perhaps glancing up, then going about my business.

But, reflecting on what happened, with the help of what the prophet wrote about the ways of God hundreds of years before Good Friday, you and I and all humanity must look back across two thousand years with all the gratitude we can muster and demonstrate by the way we live today our understanding that *that* crucifixion worked the salvation of the world. For in Jesus of Nazareth, who was indeed the promised and longed-for and only worthy king of the Jews, God took upon himself all the infirmities and diseases and transgressions and iniquities of the human race and bore the punishment that we all deserve. We, looking on, taking his guilt for granted, and, if we had known of him before, perhaps even offended by the way his behavior worked a judgment upon *our* behavior, "accounted him stricken, struck down by God, and afflicted" (53:4), as *every* person hung on a cross would be considered. But as the Jews of old thought they were piling upon a hapless goat all of the consequences of their wrongdoing and then cruelly sent him out into the wilderness to die, Jesus of Nazareth was in fact "wounded for our transgressions, crushed for our iniquities; upon him was the punishment that made us whole, and by his bruises we are healed" (53:5).

It may be that it was by "a perversion of justice" (53:8) that he was crucified, but it was necessary. Only God himself, in Christ, could do for humankind what humankind was incapable of achieving—salvation, even for those who put him to death. What? Even his executioners? Yes, thankfully. For *each* of us, at one time or another, has taken a turn at pounding the nails into his hands and feet, has tugged on the rope that hoisted him up on the cross, and then has passed by scarcely turning our head, as we so often pass by those suffering ones he loves with barely a glance. Jesus' punishment in place of ours. No one has ever satisfactorily explained it. We can only wonder at it, such a loving sacrifice, and respond in devotion, thankful and obedient. Apparently just another man dying on another cross, which, sadly, society has come to take in its stride. And yet, as it turns out, the one absolute necessity for life without end.

There are today in the world more crosses atop church buildings than ever there were alongside the crowded roads of ancient empires. What was long a symbol of cruelty and fear and agony and shame, we now see as a symbol of God's astounding and limitless love. But we must never overlook the truth that that astounding and limitless love *was* and still *is* at the cost of all those other things. Indeed, it must make us scrutinize our *own* lives and the ways of our own *society* to identify and root out the cruelty and fear and agony and shame that would again and so often put on the cross the Son of God, crucified for daring to heal, befriend, feed, forgive. For every time we reject those whom Jesus loves, we reject *him*. Every time we leave unfed those whom Jesus fed, we turn *him* from our door. Every time we ungratefully disobey his word and refuse to live by his example, we are walking along the road right past the Son of God, who is looking up and pleading, "Father, forgive them, for they do not know what they are doing" (Luke 23:34). God forbid that it would be because we thought *we* were rejecting someone, or leaving someone unfed, or withholding mercy or comfort of fellowship in the name of our religion, as did the Jews of old!—accounting him as having been in fact "struck down by God" (Isa 53:4), numbering him as an enemy of God, "although he had done no violence and there was no deceit in his mouth" (53:9b). But all these things took place "in order that the scripture might be fulfilled" (John 19:36)—that, as Isaiah prophesied, the sins of many might be borne, that intercession might be made for the transgressors, that he might be allotted a portion with the great. The death of Jesus on the cross was scripted before the foundation of the world. Such is the depth of human sin. Such is the depth of divine love. And Easter morning testifies to the deep significance of that one particular cross.

The Resurrection of the Lord
Spanish Springs Presbyterian Church, Sparks, Nevada
April 8, 2007

Acts 10:34–43
1 Corinthians 15:19–26
Luke 24:1–12

"The Great Easter Adventure"

Today is the nineteenth Easter Sunday on which I have preached a sermon. That means that this is the nineteenth Easter that I have been a solo or senior pastor, or, in the case of one church I served, the associate pastor who was asked to preach on Easter a few short weeks after the senior pastor had retired.

A lot of us have heard many more Easter sermons than *that*. The story of Christ's resurrection is a familiar one, though the various Gospels tell it in different ways, and there are still a lot more details that we might like to know. Even *non*-Christians are acquainted with it, in broad outline if not in its particulars. Muslims, Buddhists, Jews, even atheists know about the man from Nazareth in Galilee who taught about the kingdom of heaven, who healed the sick and cast out demons, sometimes on the sabbath, who befriended the outcast and forgave sins, often in defiance of popular opinion, who challenged the assumptions of just about everybody and refused to be co-opted as a mascot by anybody, and that he was plotted against by the religious authorities of his day, who had become jealous and fearful of him, and that he was arrested and tortured and executed in a barbaric way, was buried in a tomb, and then, on the morning of the third day, some of his followers discovered that the stone sealing the tomb had been rolled away and the body was gone, and that he then appeared alive again to his followers. And even non-Christians are aware that people who recognized him as the Messiah, the Christ, long promised by ancient prophets, and people who have faith *today* that he is the Messiah, the Christ, testify that God raised him from the dead as vindication of the truth and power of all the things that he had said and done, and proclaim that he is *still* alive, even present among them whenever they meet in his name and when they eat and drink the ritual meal he inaugurated, and that *they* will be *similarly* raised by God from the dead at some future time.

That much, as I say, even *non*-Christians can recount. And some *Christians* suppose that that's all there is to it, although it seems quite a lot. The novice Christians in ancient Corinth seem not to have believed even all of *that*—at least, the part about the promise of their *own* resurrection from the dead. To be fair, their culture had long held that material things, including the body, only hamper the soul's progress toward perfection and immortality, so they regarded Christian teaching about the raising of the body from the dead to be uncouth and undesirable. The apostle Paul, who had established the Corinthian church and had preached there about Christ's resurrection, wrote to say that if the Corinthians believed nobody could be raised from the dead, then, obviously, *Christ* hadn't been raised from the dead. And if *that* were the case, then they could not have been saved from their sins by Christ's death and resurrection. That, we may hope, got their attention. The promise of salvation from sin was the reason they had listened to Paul and had become Christians to *begin* with.

But Paul never suggested that the importance of Christ's resurrection stopped with our salvation from the death grip of sin, though some Christians even today continue to take that as the sum total of Easter's meaning. Paul, and the other apostles as well, insisted that the saviorhood of Christ, ratified by God in the resurrection, means that we are not only saved *from* our sin, but that we are saved *for* the very purpose for which God *created* us—in the words of the Westminster Shorter Catechism, to "glorify God and enjoy him forever."[1] And *that* happens by living a new, different, and fuller life of Christlike love, Christlike generosity, Christlike mercy, Christlike service. The resurrection of Christ means that, for those of us who have *faith* that he was *raised*, and that *God* did it, and that it was because God *approved* of everything that Christ had said and done, *we* can be raised from the dull sameness, the narrow horizons, and the dark holes we have been put in or have put ourselves in, to a new life, a great adventure of living trustfully, lovingly, and hopefully. That is what it means to "glorify God and enjoy him forever."

---

1. *Book of Confessions* 7.001.

"The Great Easter Adventure"

This past week, I received the monthly newsletter from the Presbyterian church in Lamoille, Nevada, and I am grateful to the editor for including in this issue a story first told by the Danish theologian and philosopher Søren Kierkegaard and recently retold by the church's pastor. I had never heard it before, though I understand it has been quoted by many pastors and commentators over the years. It's a parable, really, or even an allegory, and it goes like this:

There was a little town of ducks. Every Sunday the ducks waddled out of their houses and waddled down Main Street to their church. They would waddle into the sanctuary and squat in their proper pews. Then the duck choir would waddle in and the duck minister would come forward and open the duck Bible (the ducks had their own special version of the scriptures). The duck minister would preach to the duck congregation: "Ducks! God has given you wings! With wings you can fly! With wings you can mount up and soar like eagles. No walls can confine you! No fences can hold you! You have wings! God has given you wings and you can fly like birds!" And all the ducks in the congregation would quack, "Amen!" And then they would waddle back home.

Too many of us hear the scripture testimony to the resurrection read and preached every Easter, and then continue to live the way we were living before—even sincere Christians, even pastors,—content to waddle through our days and years like all the other people around us in the customary cautious way, watching our steps out of a habitual motive of self-preservation, risking nothing of importance, expecting nothing exceptional when we could, *should*, live life as people who have been saved for something better, more exciting, more significant, more adventurous—glorifying God and enjoying God forever. Too many of us leave the sanctuary each Easter comforted by what we have heard, certainly, congratulating ourselves, perhaps, for our renewed belief in what the *rest* of the world judges to be absurd or unimportant, but then we don't do anything about it. We never flex the wings God has provided us to soar beyond the confines of the walls we have built and the fences that society's expectations have erected.

The world and its politics and its economies want us to think that there is no truth but the one *they* promote, that there is no reality beyond what can be *seen* and *touched*, that there is no morality except power and wealth, that there is no judgment except fame and fortune. The powers and principalities declare that we are bound by the rules they have made and the limitations they have announced, which are the practices of greed and war, the motives of jealousy and fear, the habits of selfishness and hatred, the ways, as the Bible says, of sin and death. They thought *they* had won the battle on Good Friday, once again, like they *always* did—*this* time by putting to death on the cross the one person who was completely obedient to a voice they could not control, living out a goodness with which their decrees could not compete, calling people to a new standard of attitude and behavior that would raise people *above* the instincts of fear and greed and jealousy and hatred, and breaking the grip of old habits and false wisdoms. They couldn't stand that. And even Jesus' most devoted followers sadly assumed that love and peace and mercy and hope had been soundly defeated when the stone was rolled in place to seal the tomb. All the wonderful experiences they had had with Jesus—the miracles of healing they had witnessed, the miracles of feeding hungry crowds they had participated in, the miracles of eyes opened and hearts lightened and sins forgiven that Jesus had performed—the whole great adventure was over, they thought. But then God proved faithful.

It wasn't to celebrate the *resurrection* that the women went to the tomb early on Sunday morning, but to complete the ritual of *death*. "Why do you look for the living among the dead?" two men in dazzling clothes chided them. "He is not here, but has risen" (Luke 24:5). So, the adventure *wasn't* over. In fact, his followers soon found out, it had only just *begun*. Full understanding dawned upon them all *slowly*—in fact, it took Jesus actually appearing to them later that day in his resurrection body for them to be convinced. And then, fifty days later, as Jesus had promised, the Holy Spirit came upon them and unleashed among them a power that made their faith confident and bold and winsome enough to propel them on mission journeys to the far corners of the earth, preaching, teaching, baptizing, healing, changing hearts, and opening minds. They were convinced by their own contemporary experience that Jesus the Christ was still with them, was still their Master, was still their friend, was still the worker of miracles that dislodged old certainties and debunked old convictions and brought history to the threshold of the kingdom of God. It happened on a large scale, sometimes—hundreds converted here, an emperor and his entire court converted there,—but ultimately the adventure consisted of and depended upon individual believers taking the risk, daring to break taboos, and trusting the one who commissioned their witness.

Most likely, for instance, Peter had never been in the house of a Gentile before—that just wasn't *done* by a good Jew in those days. The Spirit had come to Peter in a vision, directing him to accompany three men who would come looking for him—messengers from a Roman centurion, the very epitome of what every good Jew was supposed to hate and fear. Peter had just had *another* vision, *this* one about setting aside the old Jewish taboo on eating certain kinds of foods, and a voice declaring that nothing that God has made should be considered unclean. Peter went with the messengers, entered the centurion's house, preached to him and his entire household and baptized them, and then remained under their roof, *eating* with them even, for several days. And the barrier between Jew and Gentile began to break down. And the love of God was shared. And the reconciliation of peoples with each other and with their Creator, for which Christ died on the cross, was finally being realized.

That is every bit as much the Easter story as the story that *most* people can recount about the discovery of the *empty tomb*. *That* is part of the great adventure that the women's report inaugurated. It is a story that you and I and all followers of Christ have been commissioned to be a part of daily, an adventure that can and should become more exciting each year as we return anew from the empty tomb and tell everyone that Christ is not there, but has risen. Have we heard that news? Do we believe it? Then how can we be content to waddle back home again? God has given us wings! God has done everything that is necessary for us to be part of a great Easter adventure of declaring the joyous news of God's victory over death in Jesus Christ to all people far and near, in words of truth and actions of hope, miracles that proclaim the nearness of the kingdom of God and the end of fear and jealousy and greed and hatred, the defeat of death, and the beginning of genuine life.

Second Sunday of Easter

First Presbyterian Church, Dodge City, Kansas

April 23, 1995

Acts 5:27–32
Revelation 1:4–8
John 20:19–31

"Closing Argument"

Ladies and gentlemen of the jury: For centuries now, my client, Thomas—known as Thomas the Twin among his friends—has stood accused in the public mind. "Doubting Thomas"—how many people have glibly been called that simply because they wanted some kind of proof before committing themselves to a plan, before agreeing to do something, before believing what on the face of it seemed too fantastic to believe? "Doubting Thomas"—how many people have congratulated themselves on their *own* faith because they happened to be born *after* the scriptures were written that tell of the several appearances of the risen Christ, because they happened to come along generations *after* scholars had first pointed out how Christ and his resurrection fulfilled the Old Testament prophets? Remember, ladies and gentlemen of the jury, that Thomas did not have the benefit of the Gospels and the epistles and theological textbooks. Thomas, when he voiced his doubt which has been immortalized in the Gospel of John, did not have the benefit of such long reflection on the teachings and actions of Jesus—only the word of a few frightened, unschooled fisherfolk and such who were desperate for some glimmer of hope in the aftermath of a shocking catastrophe, the brutal execution of their dear friend and teacher and companion. They could scarcely believe that the events of the previous Friday had actually happened, that things had gotten so out of control and had gone so wrong. Given their shock and dismay, was it not natural to take what they said with caution? Their nerves were frayed to breaking; their emotions were on the edge. Could not their joint *wish* have given rise to the common *thought* that it wasn't real, that it was just a horrible dream, that Jesus was still alive and that things would continue as they had been before?

My client was not present at the time they say it happened—when Jesus, who had been crucified, who had died on the cross, and been buried, as has been shown by testimony, was suddenly there in the room where they were huddled in fear, standing in the midst of them, speaking to them, his hands still bearing the gruesome marks of the nails, his side still showing the awful wound from the sword. By the time Thomas arrived, they say that Jesus had vanished. All *Thomas* saw in the room were the disciples themselves. They told Thomas that Jesus wished them peace and that then he breathed on them, saying that it was Holy Spirit they were to receive. They told Thomas that Jesus finally declared that those people whose sins *they forgave* would be *forgiven*, and those whose sins *they retained* would remain *un*forgiven. A fantastic story!—fantastic from start to finish. And because Thomas, upon hearing this fantastic tale, ventured that until he saw the nail marks himself and could touch the marks in Jesus' hands and the wound in Jesus' side, he simply could not believe their story, he has been branded ever since—unfairly singled out among those first disciples, unfairly ridiculed by the public for generations.

For two thousand years, over and over again, Thomas has been tried and judged and condemned and ridiculed, but really, ladies and gentlemen, is it *just* that *Thomas* should be put on trial before the court of historical opinion? You know the story. Put yourselves in his place. The unthinkable has happened—the kindest, most truthful, most caring person you have ever known, with whom you have spent the better part of three years traveling through the villages of Galilee and the streets and courtyards of Jerusalem, was betrayed by one of your comrades and within twenty-four hours was falsely accused and tried without a jury and sentenced by the rabble and whipped and spat upon and hoisted onto a cross with nails pounded into his hands and feet and thorns pressed onto his head and died and was put in a tomb. Frightened, you and the other companions of Jesus have shut yourselves up in a room without any idea what to do next. But, finally, you have to get away by yourself for a few hours to breathe, to move, to think. You risk going outside and being seen. You come back a while later and give the password, and the bolted door is suddenly flung open and it's like you've just landed on another planet, so *great* is the change in the mood and manner of your friends. And they quickly tumble out words and half-sentences about Jesus having been there with them and talking to them. What would *you* think? What would *you* say? What would *you* do? Would you be all-believing and convinced of the truth of it? Or would you suppose that they had all gone mad with being shut up in that stuffy room for three days and wonder whether the next knock on the door would be the soldiers or the temple guard come to drag *you* off to be executed?

Thomas, I think, has been made a convenient scapegoat by a lot of people who would have reacted with just the same cautious disbelief. Would it not, in fact, be more just to try his glib *accusers*, all the *armchair* disciples over the centuries—those who regard *him* as more stubborn than themselves, more slow-witted than themselves, more unfaithful than themselves, those who talk much about religion, but who never seem to put enough *stock* in their Christianity to mark them as much different from the people around them?

Ladies and gentlemen of the jury, the facts are before you. Let us review them to see what they tell us about the personality and character of Thomas. He had followed Jesus as his disciple for some time, and Jesus had thought well enough of him to call him specially as one of his apostles. Jesus had sent him out with authority over demons and to cure diseases, to proclaim the kingdom of God and to heal, and he had done so. He had made the same sacrifices as the others. He had endured the same hardships—greater sacrifices and greater hardships, I daresay, than any of *us* is likely to face for the sake of Jesus Christ. His mettle was tested in a hundred ways that you and I will never know in situations far more hostile than *we* are likely to face. True, as his critics point out, he was not *present* at the cross. In fact, only *one* of the apostles was present there, but none of the others has endured history's ridicule like Thomas has—not even *Peter*, who denied Jesus three times the night that he was arrested! *None* of them was particularly valiant that night and into the next day. But *Thomas had been* valiant in an hour of danger. Remember the testimony about when Jesus, having heard that his friend Lazarus was ill, announced his intention of returning from across the Jordan to Bethany in Judea, in spite of the hostility of the Jews. They had wanted to *stone* Jesus on his *last* visit. Many of the disciples tried to dissuade Jesus from going. But then, two days later, when Jesus told them that Lazarus had died, and *again* proposed that they should go to Bethany, it was *Thomas* who said to his fellow disciples, "Let *us* also go, that *we* may die *with* [Jesus]" (John 11:16 RSV). But history does not call him Thomas "the Valiant," Thomas "the Courageous," nor even Thomas "the Reckless," but Thomas "the Doubter."

History has regarded my client as a skeptic. But there, in the upper room, when Jesus said, "Let not your hearts be troubled. Believe in God, believe also in me. In my Father's house are many rooms. If it were not so, would I have told you that I go to prepare a place for you? And when I go and prepare a place for you, I will come again and will take you to myself, that where *I* am *you* may be *also*. And you know the way where I am going" (14:1–4 RSV), surely Thomas only voiced what all the *others* were thinking: "Lord, we do not know where you are going; how can we know the way?" (14:5 RSV). Clearly, *Philip* misunderstood what Jesus was saying that night, too—Jesus chided *him* for not understanding after all that time they had been together. Which of *us* would have understood what Jesus was telling them? And which of the disciples—which of *us*—wouldn't have *doubted* if he or she had not been present when Jesus first appeared that Sunday night after the crucifixion? If *Thomas* is guilty of doubt, ladies and gentlemen, then we are *all* guilty of doubt.

But then the question becomes: which of those guilty of doubt has rebounded to replace disbelief with faith, to deserve *not* the title of "Doubter" any longer, but "True Believer"? Recall that, on the *next* Sunday, the disciples were *again* in the house, and Thomas was *with* them this time. He knew that the doors were *shut*. Suddenly, Jesus appeared *again* and stood among them, greeting them again with words of peace. He spoke directly to my awestruck client, inviting him to touch the wounds in his hands and his side as, we admit, Thomas had insisted just a week earlier. Apparently, no one recalls Thomas actually doing that—touching the wounds,—but he immediately confessed a faith absolute and personal as not even Peter, it seems, had done: "My Lord and my God!" (20:28 RSV). "Have you believed because you have seen me?" (20:29a RSV), asked Jesus. "Blessed are those who have not seen and yet believe" (20:29b RSV). But he *did* believe.

Should Thomas have believed the testimony of those who said that they had seen for themselves Jesus risen and alive—improbable but, after all, exactly what Jesus had told them would happen—that he would rise from the grave? Should Thomas have grasped the significance of their testimony, given his previous relationship with Jesus? John has not told us the story of Thomas in order for history to *condemn* him for *not* believing what he had not *seen*. John has told us the story of Thomas in order for us to learn the importance of belief based upon the testimony of those who *have* seen. And though Thomas was slow in starting, yet, when he *did* see the risen Christ, at a single bound he leaped far ahead in grasping the full truth and significance of the resurrection. Of all the disciples, Thomas was the first to understand who Jesus really *is* when he exclaimed, "My Lord and my God!" (20:28 RSV)—Christ, the very Son of God. And even though he at first *failed* to believe, Christ chose and trusted him, just as Christ has chosen and trusts *us* many generations later, to carry on his ministry in his name and with his authority. And there is evidence that points to Thomas carrying the gospel farther than any of the other apostles, to India, bringing the good news of salvation to people in that distant land, where, finally, he was martyred for his faith. Who would have been able to do that? Thomas "the Doubter," whose uncertainty would lead him to do nothing at all with the teachings of Jesus, or Thomas "the Faith-full," whose faith, when it came, propelled him with courage and energy beyond all the others, right to the head of the class? *Doubting* Thomas, who never quite got the point? Or *Believing* Thomas, who grasped the tremendous truth that *nothing* would be impossible with the God who had raised Jesus from the grave—not even the building of a church that Thomas could not yet see with his own eyes, a church composed of millions of believers who, without having *seen* him *themselves*, nevertheless know and trust Jesus Christ as Lord?

Ladies and gentlemen of the jury, before perpetuating history's harsh judgment on Thomas, search your own hearts, and ask yourselves how willing *you* have been to *believe*, really believe and *act* upon that belief, without having seen with your own eyes, but trusting the reports of the witnesses, and trusting the character of God. *Then* decide whether you are not perhaps rather like *Thomas*—cautious, tentative, reserved, slow to commit. But then remember the words of Jesus, "Blessed are those who have not seen and yet believe" (20:29b RSV)—words that John intended for you and for me. Then, finally, do not condemn Thomas for *dis*belief, but give thanks to God for his *belief*, which gives us testimony of the identity and power and importance of the risen Lord Jesus Christ.

Third Sunday of Easter

Spanish Springs Presbyterian Church, Sparks, Nevada

April 25, 2004

Acts 9:1–20
Revelation 5:11–14
John 21:1–19

"Godparents All"

I think that you can tell a lot about a church by looking at its sanctuary. The use of space, the placement of furnishings, *should* be and generally *are* a clue as to what the church regards as important, how it spends its time, what its focus is. From the beginning of *this* congregation, even when we were meeting up at the elementary school, our worship space has been centered on font and table—the theological axis around which our worship revolves and our life, as Christians, revolves as well—our entrance into Christ, our continuing fellowship *with* Christ. Many churches have the *table* in the front of the sanctuary, though sometimes its meaning is obscured by flowers or offering plates or other things. Not so many have the *baptismal font* front and center. But it is a reminder to us every time we enter *this* place that we are *baptized* people, and that means people who have been chosen, received, forgiven, accepted, reborn, and commissioned.

Every time we baptize someone, we hear the familiar command of Jesus from the Gospel of Matthew that his followers should go out and "make disciples of all nations, baptizing them in the name of the Father and of the Son and of the Holy Spirit" (Matt 28:19). Every time we baptize someone, we are reminded of the Bible's testimony to God's saving actions through the medium of water. Every time we baptize someone, we hear a new member of the household of God renounce evil and embrace Christ. Every time we baptize someone, we hear and see the cleansing and refreshing water poured. Every time we baptize someone, we see and smell the new identity of being *Christ's own* sealed with fragrant oil. Every time we baptize someone, we pray for the person *being* baptized.

Whether the candidate for baptism is younger or older, an infant or a child or a youth or an adult, the words and actions are the same, for the meaning is the same. Even the *question* asked of the *congregation* is the same, and although it is not itself a part of the *act* of baptism, it is as important to understanding the *meaning* of baptism as anything else that happens when we baptize—and, I hope, our placement of the baptismal font front and center in the midst of all of us helps us all feel that *we* have been a part in the *act* of baptism whenever the sacrament is administered. "Do you, as members of the church of Jesus Christ, promise to guide and nurture this person by word and deed, with love and prayer, encouraging him or her to know and follow Christ and to be a faithful member of his church?"[1] And the congregation is expected to respond, "We do"—not just with their *words* on that *particular* Sunday, of course, but with their *actions* all the rest of their days.

Sometimes, especially in the case of infants and children, I am asked about naming godparents for those who are being baptized. In the Episcopal and Roman Catholic tradition, godparents are particular individuals—not necessarily members of that congregation—who agree to take on themselves special responsibilities for the Christian upbringing of the newly baptized. But in *Reformed* theology, which informs our Presbyterian understanding of *baptism*, the *entire congregation* constitutes the "godparents"—those people who, in addition to the *parents* or *guardians* of the child, *promise* to be and are charged with *being* responsible for the spiritual upbringing of the child to the day when she or he *confirms* the vows of belief and practice that were made on her or his behalf at baptism. In the Episcopal Church, the godparents are to answer many questions, including these: "Will you be responsible for seeing that the child you present [at baptism] is brought up in the Christian faith and life?" And, "Will you by your prayers and witness help this child to grow into the full stature of Christ?"[2] Those are very close to the question that we *Presbyterians* ask of the entire *congregation*.

Perhaps it would help us Presbyterians to understand that we are *all* godparents of *each* person baptized here if the minister were to ask *each* of us *individually* those questions at *every* baptism. How many of us are daily conscious that we have taken on the responsibility for bringing all of the children here up in the faith, and for nurturing the faith of those who are

---

1. *Book of Common Worship*, 406.
2. *Book of Common Prayer*, 302.

baptized as *adults*, too—for modeling the love and justice and compassion and righteousness of Jesus Christ, for praying *for* the baptized and *with* the baptized, for praying for the *parents* of our children, for teaching the children and the adults who are *new* to the church of Jesus Christ the heritage of faith that is ours as people who call ourselves "Christian," for exercising the *same* patience with children and with new believers that *Christ* did and offering ourselves humbly, sacrificially, selflessly, and personally for their Christian nurture? It is not the job of someone *else* in the church; it is *our* commitment, each one of us, a commitment that we never outgrow, a commitment that we shoulder *obediently* because of Christ's *command* to baptize and teach, a commitment that we shoulder *cheerfully* because *we* remember how some minister or teacher or choir director or other saint in some congregation showed *us*, in *their* words and *their* attitudes and *their* actions, what it is to be a disciple of Jesus Christ.

Our reading from Acts tells how *Saul* the *persecutor* of the Christians became *Paul* the greatest of Christian *missionaries*. It is but one of several stories of conversion in the book of Acts. We find it between the reports of Philip's baptism of a eunuch, a minister of Candace, queen of the Ethiopians, and Peter's baptism of Cornelius, the Roman centurion at Caesarea. None of these stories of blossoming to faith is exactly the same as another, but they all have several points in common, one of which is that, according to each of them, God made use of one of Christ's *disciples* to help bring the new believer to the point of useful and obedient servanthood as a follower of Jesus Christ—in the case of the Ethiopian eunuch, it was Philip; in the case of Saul, it was Ananias; in the case of Cornelius, it was Peter. In each case, too, the disciple was not expecting to be *called* to such a duty, and in fact might have regarded the person to be shepherded as an unlikely prospect for Christianity. We see this dramatically in Ananias, who reminded the Lord in some dismay and bewilderment, "Lord, I have heard from many about this man, how much evil he has done to your saints in Jerusalem; and here he has authority from the chief priests to bind all who invoke your name" (Acts 9:13–14). Nevertheless, Ananias acquiesced dutifully when the Lord said to him, "Go, for [Saul] is an instrument whom I have chosen to bring my name before Gentiles and kings and before the people of Israel; I myself will show him how much *he* must suffer for the *sake* of my name" (9:15–16). Ananias was an instrument, fulfilling a function; he was not the boastful "soul-winner," but a humble servant taking the risk of answering the Master's call to minister to a person whom Christ had *already* encountered on a public highway.

Contemporary evangelists should notice that Ananias was careful to put credit for Saul's coming to faith in the right place—it was not *he*,

Ananias, who had brought Saul to Christ, but the risen Christ himself: "'Brother Saul, the Lord Jesus, who appeared to you on your way here, has sent me so that you may regain your sight and be filled with the Holy Spirit.' And immediately something like scales fell from his eyes, and his sight was restored. Then he got up and was baptized, and after taking some food, he regained his strength" (9:17b–19a). And in the process of taking responsibility for nurturing the zealous persecutor of Christians to become one of the most devoted of all servants of Jesus Christ, Ananias embraced Paul with his own heart. Did you notice in the text how Ananias first answers the Lord's command by referring to Paul abstractly and coolly as "this man," and then later addresses Paul endearingly as "Brother Saul"?—not unlike how Luke contrasts the two references to the prodigal son who wandered from home and then returned: "this son of yours," in the words of the disgusted older brother, and "your brother," in the words of the merciful father. So, from the story in Acts, we learn that no one—child or adult—who is baptized in response to Christ's command can remain an *abstraction* to us who profess membership in Christ's body. We *must speak of* and *act toward each* baptized person as a brother or sister entrusted to our care and worthy of our every effort to bind them lovingly and securely into the household of God.

What does it mean, in practical terms, that each of us is the godparent of every child, every youth, every adult who has been baptized in the name of the Father, the Son, and the Holy Spirit? It means, first of all, that we take the time to know that person, including the children of our congregation—and to know them by name, greeting them, visiting them and their parents or guardians in their homes. It means praying for the members of our congregation, and for the children of our congregation, that they will grow up knowing and loving Jesus Christ, but also praying that they will be healthy and well fed and well educated and treated with dignity and respect all their days, and that their experience in the church will be such that they will always regard the church as their true home, wherever they may be. It means giving sacrificially to support the church budget so that they will have an inviting place for worship and fellowship and church school and so that they will have an authentic encounter with God through word and sacrament and quality educational materials in the classroom and faith-building experiences in discussion sessions and retreat settings. It means actively supporting our teachers and youth group leaders and offering *ourselves* to be teachers and youth group leaders and vacation church school volunteers, personally devoting the time and energy to give *substance* to our prayers. It means personally encouraging them to be a part of worship and church school and youth group activities and the fellowship events of the whole congregation. With regard to children, it means that we *bear with* their childlike ways in the sanctuary and the classroom even as we encourage them to Christian maturity, and that we rejoice in their youthful spontaneity and enthusiasm and exuberance, by which *God* is certainly not offended. It means being patient enough to be content with sowing *seeds* rather than laying claim to the *harvest*, and remembering that we pray, we smile, we pledge, we teach, we preach because that is what it means to be obedient to Jesus Christ, not because of any satisfaction or acclaim that we incidentally receive for only doing what is our duty. It means recalling that *others* were once stubborn and patient and generous and faithful enough to give *their* dollars and *their* time and perhaps occasionally their *tears* that *we* might hear the good news of the gospel, and know all that Christ commands, and have strong family ties with the household of God, and grow into the fullness of the stature of Christ.

One morning long ago, a little band of discouraged men decided to give up their three-year adventure of following a teacher and preacher and healer after he was executed as a criminal, and they returned to their accustomed occupation of fishing. As they were out in their boat, a man called out to them from the beach, but, through the morning haze and the fog of their own frustrations and discouragements, they could not distinguish who it was. Finally, one of them said, "'It is the Lord!'" (John 21:7), and Peter jumped into the water and splashed his way to shore. They all had a meal together, as was their custom. Then Jesus, perhaps remembering Peter's pledge of loyalty that even if all his *other* followers proved *un*faithful, *he* would *not*, but remembering also that Peter had then *denied* him three times, said,

> "Simon son of John, do you love me more than these?" [Peter] said to him, "Yes, Lord; you know that I love you." [Jesus] said to him, "*Feed my lambs.*" A second time [Jesus] said to him, "Simon son of John, do you love me?" [Peter] said to him, "Yes, Lord; you know that I love you." [Jesus] said to him, "*Tend my sheep.*" [Jesus] said to him the third time, 'Simon son of John, do you love me?" Peter felt hurt because [Jesus] said to him the third time, "Do you love me?" And [Peter] said to him, "Lord, you know everything; you know that I love you." Jesus said to him, "*Feed my sheep.*" (21:15–17)

If we profess to love Christ, we *must* care for those he has entrusted to us, young and old and in between—praying for them, nurturing them, sacrificing for them our time, our money, our interest. In the church of Jesus Christ, we are godparents all. Our Lord Jesus Christ ordered us to *teach* those who are *baptized*. Do we, as members of the church of Jesus Christ, promise to guide and nurture those we baptize by word and deed, with love and prayer, encouraging them to know and follow Christ and to be faithful members of his church? Do we?

Fourth Sunday of Easter

Spanish Springs Presbyterian Church, Sparks, Nevada

April 25, 2010

Acts 9:36–43
Revelation 7:9–17
John 10:22–30

"The Subversive Gospel"

In the year 410, an event occurred that shook Western civilization to its core. Rome, the center of the greatest empire that history has ever known; Rome, the home of the Caesars; Rome, the eternal city; Rome, the center of Western Christianity, fell to Alaric, chief of the Goths. He and his forces had already besieged the city in 408 and again in 409. Each time, Rome had successfully resisted. But on August 24, 410, the army of the Visigoths entered Rome and conquered it. Think of the psychological impact of the September 11 attacks, and multiply it by a hundredfold, and perhaps you can come close to what people felt from Spain to Armenia and from Britain to Libya.

Rome had been so dominant for so long, its economy a well-oiled machine, its military invincible, its infrastructure the marvel of the ancient world. It had long boasted the ability to keep its citizens safe and well fed and content. But the image of power that it projected obviously did not match the reality of a creaking foundation under the vaunted architecture and communications and legal administration. And when the city that had become a nation and then an empire was overrun by a barbarian tribe from the hinterland, everything that Rome had claimed for itself suddenly came into question. Pride and certainty were replaced by dismay and doubt; the accustomed sense of security and stability yielded to fear and panic. And some sought to find quick and easy culprits on whom to fix the blame. And quite a few decided to point the finger at the Christian faith, which had turned people away from the ancient gods that were worshiped in Rome's golden days.

The greatest theological mind of the age, Augustine, responded to the charges by writing his monumental book *The City of God*, which dealt with the fundamental difference between Christianity and the world, between the ways and virtues of God and those who honor and obey God, and the values and customs of the world and those who live according to them. Augustine acknowledged that worldly government and administration have a role to play, but he explained that the only lasting peace, security, and blessedness are to be found in the realm where God is acknowledged as ruler, and people live in faith and obedience. The values and customs of the *world* can only bring about *temporary* good and *transitory* contentment. The things of *God* are *eternal* and lead to *salvation*. And that includes the *church*. In the words of the nineteenth-century hymn by Arthur Cleveland Cox,

> O where are kings and empires now, Of old that went and came?
> But, Lord, thy Church is praying yet, A thousand years the same.[1]

Empires were not just a curiosity of ancient history. Just then, the Union Jack was flying over countries and colonies on every continent, and the United States was beginning to have imperialist ambitions and exercise imperialist ways. Was the hymn meant, in part, as a warning? Another nineteenth-century hymn writer, Englishman John Ellerton, put it this way:

> So be it, Lord; Thy throne shall never,
> Like earth's proud empires, pass away;
> Thy kingdom stands, and grows forever
> Till all Thy creatures own Thy sway.[2]

And yet, from ancient times to modern, it is the nature of empires to put *themselves* in the place of *God*, whether they *call* themselves "empires" or not, and to make claims that one way or another demand idolatrous allegiance and vesting one's trust in *earthly* achievements and *human* assurances.

The fact that by the time of Augustine Christianity had for many years been the official religion of the Roman Empire made no real difference in the fact that *every* government tends to assert authority that rightly belongs only to God, tends, in the name of good order and securing the peace, to restrict even the times and manner in which God may be honored. Take, for instance, the announcement last week that one American city is considering

---

1. Coxe, "O Where Are Kings and Empires Now."
2. Ellerton, "The Day Thou Gavest, Lord, Is Ended."

an ordinance that would make giving money to beggars a crime, and other cities are considering following suit. At the very time that jobs are not to be had and people are losing their homes, city councils are considering criminalizing obedience to the biblical instruction to give to the poor! But long before Augustine tackled the subject in a Rome that regarded itself as the *guardian* of the Christian faith, another Christian theologian tackled the subject of a Rome that was out to *destroy* the Christian faith. John, the writer of Revelation, reported his vision concerning an empire that had become drunk on the blood of Christian martyrs, using the rationale of peace and security to justify *persecuting* the *followers* of the *Prince of Peace*, God's faithful ones whom the apostles had instructed to *pray* for their earthly rulers.

Those who argue that politics and religion should always be kept separate apparently have never considered the witness of the Old Testament prophets, which makes up about a quarter of the Bible, nor have they understood the implications of the book of Revelation.

> After this I looked, and there was a great multitude that no one could count, from every nation, from all tribes and peoples and languages, standing before the throne and before the Lamb, robed in white, with palm branches in their hands. They cried out in a loud voice, saying,
> "Salvation belongs to our God who is seated on the throne, and to the Lamb!" (Rev 7:9–10)

We may understand that as a straightforward *spiritual* claim about being saved from *sin*. But Christians were not being persecuted because of their beliefs about *spiritual* matters. They were being persecuted because their beliefs threatened the *secular* power and authority of the Roman government. The Roman emperor and his governors were not concerned with whether someone believed he or she would go to *heaven* when they died. The Roman emperor and his governors were concerned with whether people would obey their *decrees* and pay their *taxes* and not disrupt the way things *were* by saying that God demanded something *different*. Rome had for centuries declared that *it* was the supreme reality in the universe, that what *it* decreed was right and that what *it* said was so and that only *it* could guarantee human safety and well-being and that safety and well-being could only be secured if everyone did as the emperor required. Rome, in sum, declared that *it* was the source of salvation to whom every knee should bend. The emperor had even declared *himself* to be a god, and the Roman Senate had agreed. The city of Pergamum in Asia Minor—one of the churches to which the Revelation is addressed, in which, as John says, "Satan's throne is" (2:13)—was the center of emperor worship in the region. The message of the book of Revelation is a direct contradiction of Rome's claims, and an encouragement to the believers who, in the face of persecution, were bravely trying to *resist* Rome's threats and seductions.

> And all the angels stood around the throne and around the elders and the four living creatures, and they fell on their faces before the throne and worshiped God, singing,
> "Amen! Blessing and glory and wisdom
> and thanksgiving and honor
> and power and might
> be to our God forever and ever!"

—*not* the emperor, *not* the empire.

> "Amen." (7:11–12)

The Bible is a supremely political book, and no part of it is more so than Revelation. The Bible is a supremely subversive book, and no part of it is more so than Revelation. "Then one of the elders addressed me, saying, 'Who are these, robed in white'"—the color of the garment worn at baptism,—"'and where have they come from?' I said to him, 'Sir, you are the one that knows.' Then he said to me, 'These are they who have come out of the great ordeal; they have washed their robes and made them white in the blood of the Lamb'" (7:13–14)—by the afflictions they have faced, the persecution they have endured, they have participated in the suffering of Christ that won him eternal glory.

> "For this reason they are before the throne of God,
> and worship him day and night within his temple,"

—not the *emperor* day and night within *his* temple—

> "and the one who is seated on the throne will shelter them'"

—will protect them, will keep them safe, not the *emperor* and *his* legions.

> "'They will hunger no more, and thirst no more'"

—they can be assured that they are fed by the bounty of God's hand, not dependent upon the emperor's bread and circuses;

> "the sun will not strike them,
> nor any scorching heat;
> for the Lamb at the center of the throne will be their shepherd,
> and he will guide them to springs of the water of life,
> and God will wipe away every tear from their eyes." (7:15–17)

What *Rome* offers as salvation and punishment in order to maintain the status quo is transitory; it is not entitled to the social, religious, and economic allegiance it demands. Rome does not really care whether people are sheltered and fed, except insofar as the economic machine keeps running and the elite remain at the top and the multitude stays at the bottom. *God's* salvation and judgment are *eternal*, and so it is *God* who deserves all praise and honor—the God who sacrificed even his own Son on the cross for the sake of the least, that creation might be restored to be what God intended—not an empire built on force and ruled by fear and rewarding greed, but a kingdom on whose throne sits the one who offered his life for the salvation of all and whose hallmark is *God's* justice and *God's* peace and *God's* mercy, where flow not rivers of *blood* but springs of the water of *life*, "and God will wipe away every tear from their eyes" (7:17c).

The good news of Jesus Christ—of his life, death, and resurrection—is explosive. It blows apart all earthly pretensions. It blasts to bits all worldly excuses. It destroys all human claims to privilege or exclusion, all theories that defend rationing the things that are needful for life and philosophies that justify withholding the mercy that Jesus commands. The good news of Jesus Christ—of his life, death, and resurrection—is subversive of any human being or human scheme that makes *itself* judge of who will be fed, who will be healed, who will be sheltered, who will be forgiven. The good news of Jesus Christ—of his life, death, and resurrection—is the promise of God, who is eternal, who created everything that *is* from the motive of sheer love and who desires all creation to live in fellowship with him and at peace with itself, that no power or principality that threatens and oppresses and injures and thinks it has silenced the Word of God will have the final say. *God* will. And God's own appointed Shepherd will tend those who suffer, will keep them from ultimate harm, will feed them with heavenly food that cannot perish or be taken away. And every earthly authority must eventually bow to him, must finally yield to his rule of generosity and kindness and humility and mercy.

The good news of Jesus Christ—of his life, death, and resurrection—is explosive—and it will *still* be good news, it will *still* be God's firm and faithful promise, when the claims of every earthly king and every earthly empire shall have faded from history. Jesus Christ, the Lamb whom Caesar and his governor thought they had slaughtered, will still be on the throne, inviting people of every condition, of every class, of every race, of every nationality, to the springs of the water of life, and God will still be reversing the fortunes of all those who suffered for their allegiance to the one who rules not with force but with love, wiping every tear from their eyes.

Fifth Sunday of Easter
First Presbyterian Church, Dodge City, Kansas
May 17, 1992

Acts 14:8–18
Revelation 21:1–6
John 13:31–35

"The Miracle People"

Paul and Barnabas had been traveling through central Asia Minor, preaching wherever people would listen. At Antioch in Pisidia, they had spoken to Jews and to Greeks who were friendly toward Judaism, but the Jews eventually stirred up the citizenry against the apostles, and they were driven out of that area. At Iconium, some Jews and Gentiles banded together and made plans to stone Paul and Barnabas, but, learning of the plot, the two apostles went on to the town of Lystra. And there, apparently near the city gate, a man who was crippled from birth, and who had never been able to walk, listened to Paul's words of good news, and those words sparked faith in the man. Paul looked at him and recognized the glimmer of hope in his eyes, and he said to him in a loud voice, "Stand upright on your feet" (Acts 14:10). And the man jumped up and was able to walk.

This was not the first miracle of healing after the resurrection of Jesus. *Peter* had *also* told a lame man to rise and walk, and he had done so. But it is the first record that we have in Acts of *Paul's* being an instrument of healing. And what makes it *especially* interesting is the reaction of the people who saw that a person known to have been lame since *birth* was up and walking around. In their astonishment, they said to one another, "'The gods have come down to us in human form!'" (14:11)—an event not uncommon in Greek mythology, which told of such a divine visitation once before in that very neighborhood. Barnabas they supposed to be Zeus in human form.

Paul, the one who had been preaching, they called "Hermes" after the Greek god of oratory. Lesser men might have seized the advantage that such a situation had offered for *personal* benefit, but Paul and Barnabas, being followers of Christ and proclaiming the truth that there is but *one* real God, could not allow their audience to misconstrue what had taken place. When the priest of Zeus brought sacrifices to them, the apostles tore their garments to demonstrate their disgust at the blasphemous notion that anyone should offer worship to mere human beings. "'Friends, why are you doing this?'" they cried out to the crowd. "'We are mortals just like you, and we bring you good news, that you should turn from these *worthless* things to the *living* God, who made the heaven and the earth and the sea and all that is in them'" (14:15). Paul went on to tell the crowd about the God of Israel, who is the God of all creation, and draw their attention to the footprints of God's providence, which are detectable everywhere in nature. "Even with these words, they scarcely restrained the crowds from offering sacrifice to them. But Jews came there from Antioch and Iconium and won over the crowds. Then they stoned Paul and dragged him out of the city, supposing that he was dead. But when the disciples surrounded him, he got up and went into the city. The next day he went on with Barnabas to Derbe" (14:18–20).

Wherever the gospel went in those early days of Christianity, there were similar signs of God's power to restore the minds and bodies and spirits of the people who heard the good news. Of course, it was not everywhere that those who witnessed such miracles of healing supposed the apostles to be *gods* and offered sacrifices to them. Still, most people realized that only a *divine power* could bring about such a miracle. The apostles themselves invariably made it clear that the *source* of the miracle was nothing lying within their own ability; rather, it was *God's* power in the *risen Christ* at work *through* them. It may strike us as rather comical, this picture of the citizens of Lystra, their minds clouded with pagan superstitions, scurrying about to make a sacrificial offering to Paul and Barnabas as gods, but it was distressing to the apostles, who were so intent on preaching the good news of the gospel that they could tolerate no misinterpretation of their deeds nor any misunderstanding of their words. What Paul had displayed in the streets of Lystra was the power of the compassion and healing of Christ himself, at work through the apostle, but only as a mere instrument of God's blessing.

But, then, believers *too* sometimes mistake the gospel as being something *magical*, and approach it with something *less* than faith, clinging superstitiously to its form and distorting its substance, enshrining its prohibitions while warping its spirit, so that it becomes anything *but* good news. And, as scandals in various churches have made clear in recent years, even believers sometimes ascribe to the human *representatives* of Christ a loyalty and devotion that really belongs to *Christ alone*. So, we occasionally witness curious confusions of the message and the messengers, as when billboards sprang up all over Dallas a few years ago advertising a nondenominational megachurch in one of the city's suburbs, showing the church's pastor, looming over the freeways with arms outstretched in a way reminiscent of our Lord on the cross, the caption reading, "Larry Lea presents Jesus." The risen Christ does not need photogenic salesmen with television smiles to *market* his salvation; Christians are not called to be gods or demigods, and should be offended at the very notion. The risen Christ *does* ask for humble and obedient *servants* to be his instruments in the compassionate task of redeeming creation. We can excuse the pagan citizens of Lystra for supposing that they were entertaining gods in human form, even as we breathe a sigh of relief that Paul and Barnabas quickly set the record straight. The apostles were not gods; they were bringers of good news. They did not draw the curtains back and command Christ to perform on cue; they were prompted by the Spirit of the risen Christ to testify to the powerful truth that *they* had come to know through *his* grace at work in *their* lives and in the life of his church. *They* did not *possess* the power of Christ; *it* possessed *them*—they were blessed to be chosen as dutiful stewards of it. Luke wants us to be clear about that distinction; disciples of Jesus Christ do not become God, but they are to *proclaim* God. We do not follow the Son of God in order to be regarded as magicians or celebrated stars in our own right, but in order to make manifest to all people the compassion and wholeness of which Christ himself is the very definition. We are not sorcerers conjuring up amazing and entertaining spectacles, but people grateful for our redemption, praying that Christ will perform deeds of love through us.

The personality and outlook of Jesus were very different from the personality and outlook of many of his modern followers, including many of his more vocal representatives. Jesus always used the power of God to *help* people and to bring people to *faith*, and in the process of *doing* so, he always pointed beyond *himself* to *God*, the *only* source of all *true* miracles. Jesus' motive was always pure—it was the motive of *love*. His healings were always an *encouragement* to faith or a *consequence* of faith, not a *proof* of faith. His first disciples witnessed many miracles he did while he was with them. He called on *them* to do the same sorts of things that *he* had done, and not only *these*, but things even *greater*. And on the night before he died, when he knew that the time had grown very short before he would be raised up on the cross, he provided his followers with the key to being miracle people themselves. It was in the form of a commandment—a *new* commandment, no less binding on the faithful than the commandments that God had given to his people through Moses long ago—"that you love one another. Just as I have loved you, you also should love one another" (John 13:34). By doing so, *they* would be like Christ himself.

John includes this new commandment, "Thou shalt love," in his Gospel. John doesn't just report what Jesus said to his *first* disciples, but reminds Christians of his own church and Christians of all subsequent ages that Jesus commands *them* to love. In the face of disputes as to doctrine, and threats of persecution by the authorities, and exclusion from their families and their old social circles, the members of the Christian congregation of which John was a part *needed* the blessings of harmony and the discipline of humble obedience and the courage to sacrifice for one another if they were to be faithful and if the church was to survive. They needed to be Christlike in every way, and especially they needed to be tangible expressions of Christlike humility and Christlike love. They needed to witness to Christ's humble love by telling the truth, by faithfully sharing the Word of God, by selflessly giving themselves even for people who were unresponsive to their witness, by being ready to surrender life itself if that should be required. Such love was not just a feeling, not merely a sentiment, but an active engagement with one another and with the world, by which blessings flowed abundantly and miracles became commonplace—the very sort of thing that Christ did all during his ministry. This love was a way of speaking and doing and being for one another unselfish, generous, forgiving. *Without* such love, the church would surely be a mere footnote in the monotonous history of the world's greed and war and lust and oppression. But *through* such love, God would be able to work every sort of miracle and transform all the former things into a new heaven and a new earth—a resurrected creation without any of the pain or sorrow or evil that have hung like a pall over the original goodness of God's world.

The miracle that so amazed the people of Lystra was a work of Christlike and Christ-empowered compassion and love on the part of Paul, a disciple of the risen Christ. Paul—not a god, not superhuman in any way, just an obedient, selfless servant of Jesus Christ who saw someone in need, someone in whom the words of life and truth and blessing that Paul was declaring had struck a responsive chord and sparked faith and hope and trust. And a man lame from birth sprang to his feet and walked. The wholeness that God had intended from the beginning and had designed by giving him legs to walk on, the wholeness that had been frustrated all those years by crippling disease, was finally *realized* as Christ's apostle looked intently at the man and saw that he had faith to be made well. The point of Acts is that you and I can be God's instruments of bringing wholeness to people in distress if *we* look intently at them, look compassionately at them, look imaginatively at them, look lovingly at them, at their condition and at the hope in their eyes, and if we offer *ourselves* as a channel for the working of a miracle of God.

Doesn't it make you wonder what *your* words and deeds of love and compassion and generosity and faith might contribute to God's raising the world from the clutches of death and decay and disappointment to *resurrection* as a *new* heaven and a *new* earth, crowned by a *new* Jerusalem, in which God will be in intimate fellowship with all who walk through the gates, which are never closed, and where God will wipe away every tear, and death shall be no more, and neither shall there be mourning nor crying nor pain any more, for the former things of selfishness and pride and fear and despair will have passed away? Paul and Barnabas, you and I, and Christians everywhere are the miracle people—people who have been called by Jesus Christ to be willing and humble and selfless instruments of his love and grace, which heals, which restores, which forgives, which empowers. If miracles are to happen in this world, they *must* happen through the faithful ministry of people who have heard and experienced the love and blessing of Jesus Christ in their own lives, the salvation of God to wholeness and new life as they have abandoned selfishness and pride and hatred and fear. And all the miracles begin to happen when Christ's disciples obey the new commandment that we love one another.

Sixth Sunday of Easter

Spanish Springs Presbyterian Church, Sparks, Nevada

May 20, 2001

Acts 15:1–2, 22–29
Revelation 21:10, 22–27
John 14:23–29

"Open Gates for the Spirit"

It is sometime in the mid-first century. A council of church leaders assembles at Jerusalem to determine whether those who reject a portion of the scriptural law may still be admitted to the Christian fellowship. It is 325. Bishops from everywhere in Christendom convene at a great meeting at Nicaea to unite the church by settling the critical and controversial issue of Christ's divinity, and they fashion a creed that expresses the mystery of the incarnation. It is 1529. Representatives of the Reformed and Lutheran faiths gather at Marburg, Germany, hoping to unite these two great Protestant movements, but in the end they disband, unable to reconcile their respective doctrines of the Lord's Supper. It is 1947. Representatives from the Presbyterian, Congregational, Methodist, and Episcopal mission churches in India vote on the manner of ordination, the only remaining obstacle to union as the Church of South India. It is 2001. The General Assembly of the Presbyterian Church (U.S.A.) is preparing to meet to grapple with the question of how inclusive the church should be.

All of these issues are related. Throughout its history, the church has struggled to balance its mission of proclaiming the good news of redemption with preserving the purity of its doctrine and practice, while demonstrating in its process the peace of Jesus Christ. The church is ever facing the questions of how broad is God's grace, how closely should sacred things be safeguarded from the world's contamination, how far is the Holy Spirit at work to bring about God's purpose of redemption in new and contemporary circumstances, how inclusive is the kingdom of God.

It is a curious twist of history that what began as perhaps the world's most radical crusade, welcoming into its fold people of every condition and background, challenging in unprecedented fashion the popular assumptions and religious authorities of the time, so quickly became one of the world's most conservative institutions. I think that our familiarity with the gospel story prevents us from appreciating just how fundamentally Jesus rocked the faith of many good and morally conscious people of his day—people who worshiped God regularly and observed the law rigorously. What the scriptures said to do, they did. What the scriptures said not to do, they avoided. They were careful to be morally correct in their own lives, and they encouraged others to do the same.

Then came Jesus. His followers explain that he *fulfilled* the law of Moses. But that is a theological assessment made years later. To many people of his *own* day, it must have seemed that scripture clearly *prohibited* some of the things he did on the sabbath. He made claims that seemed blasphemy to any righteous Jew. He socialized with those whom the righteous judged most harshly as sinners according to scripture, and invited them into his company and pronounced their forgiveness. And all of these things he claimed to do on God's own authority. Scandalous! How much more could anyone compromise the *purity* of the faith? And yet, who has ever so truthfully shown us the *essence* of the faith?

It soon became clear that Christ's followers, inspired and empowered by the Holy Spirit, would push the limits of the law even further. The Jews were the chosen people, bound to God in covenant and in their observance of the law according to the scriptures. But the apostles took the gospel beyond the Jews, to the Gentiles—people ritually unclean, and strangers to the covenant. Peter received a vision directing him to eat food that was forbidden by the law. He answered a summons to the house of Cornelius, a Roman centurion, even though it was unlawful for a Jew to associate with anyone of another nation. "'God has shown me,'" he declared, "'that I should not call *anyone* profane or unclean'" (Acts 10:28). Peter's visit to that household opened the way for the Spirit to be poured out on the Gentiles gathered there. And Peter commanded them to be baptized in the name of Jesus Christ. "'"John baptized with water,"'" he said, "'"but you will be baptized with the Holy Spirit." If then God gave them the same gift that he gave to *us* when *we* believed in the Lord Jesus Christ, who was I that I could hinder God?' When [the apostles] heard this, they were silenced. And they praised God, saying, 'Then God has given even the Gentiles the repentance that leads to life'" (10:16–18).

"Open Gates for the Spirit"

The apostles at Jerusalem had set apart Paul and Barnabas and sent them to Cyprus and Asia Minor. There, as they preached to Gentiles, they were attacked by Jews zealous to safeguard the purity of the faith. But Paul and Barnabas reminded them of the Lord's command to his chosen people:

> "'I have set you to be a light for the Gentiles,
> so that you may bring salvation to the ends of the earth.'"
> (13:47)

They carried the message of salvation far from Israel and far from the church at Jerusalem. But very soon there arose a dispute about this new inclusiveness of the gospel, and the freedom with which Paul and Barnabas were admitting to the church of Jesus Christ those who did not keep the full law of the Jewish scriptures. Rapidly the church had grown beyond its place and culture of origin. Now it faced a serious internal conflict that had to be resolved before it could begin the next stage of expansion—to western Asia Minor and to Greece, paving the way to Rome itself.

It seems that at Antioch, those who had come into the church from Judaism were insisting that Gentile converts must first be circumcised. They denied that Christian baptism was sufficient substitute for the ancient ritual of the covenant. In other words, they demanded that *Gentiles* become *Jews* in order to be admitted to the Christian church. Could there be such a thing as a *Gentile* Christian? There had also been trouble about Gentiles and Jews eating together around a common table—the most profound expression of religious fellowship. Were there to be two *separate* groups, dissolving the one universal church?

The deeper issue of circumcision was whether God was merely the God of Israel. Would Christianity be a closed, national religion as Judaism had been, or would it be an open, universal faith? The deeper issue of eating unclean food was whether there could be social relations between Jewish and Gentile Christians. Were there to be *grades* of Christianity? Were there to be *distinctions* of persons in the body of Christ? We know Paul's teaching that in Christ Jesus there is neither Jew nor Greek, slave nor free, male nor female. But, addressing the issue from the other side, the law of Moses had established a spiritual and moral pattern for the Jewish people. It had kept them intact through centuries of assault from the outside and apostasy from within. Was it now to be cast aside with liberal abandon, with nothing to replace it as a dependable framework for belief and action? If the dietary laws were abandoned, where would it end? If the faithful need not be circumcised, where was the bond of the covenant God first made with Abraham? All of this talk of love and grace and forgiveness and freedom—it was new and untried; it seemed undisciplined and dangerous. The law was there in bold letters in the scriptures, for everyone to see. And whatever *else* he might have said and done, even *Jesus* quoted the *scriptures*. Even *Jesus* was *circumcised*.

It is ironic that the gospel of *grace* has been entrusted to creatures who have a penchant for passing *judgment*. We like to know where we stand, what the rules of the game are and who is and isn't playing by them. We like to draw boundaries. We like to determine who and what are on our side of the line and who and what are outside. We like to erect fences. Peter, who at first had eaten freely with the Gentile converts, later came to fear the judgment of the conservatives, and so he *separated* himself from the Gentiles. On occasion, even so grace-conscious a person as *Paul* found it difficult to resist drawing lines of exclusion. But the gospel could not be the exclusive property of the Jews, as it was never the exclusive property of the righteous.

The Jewish Christians wanted to argue the issue on the basis of *principle*. But the Council of Jerusalem was ultimately more impressed with *experience*—the report of Paul and Barnabas about what happened as they preached the gospel among the Gentiles. The leaders who gathered at Jerusalem could either impede the work of the Holy Spirit by maintaining walls of exclusion, or they could recognize that God was already at work among the Gentiles *in spite of* the law. After hearing from Peter and Barnabas and Paul and James, the Council wisely chose not to ignore the activity of the Holy Spirit. They would not sacrifice a beautiful picture for want of a proper frame; circumcision, they decided, was not of the essence of the gospel, and so it could not be a barrier to the Gentiles. The gates would be opened to the Holy Spirit.

Many times since, the lesson has been resisted. Frequently, in spite of its heritage of bold initiative and its affirmation that God is at work everywhere, the church has tenaciously resisted the discoveries of both natural and social science, somehow convinced that they are hostile to the faith. The church has often labeled cultural custom—usually, the customs of non-European cultures—as irreligious and incompatible with Christianity. Likewise, many Christians of the first century feared exceptions to the law of circumcision. But had they prevailed, the church would likely have remained a small Jewish sect in Palestine.

It was James who stepped forward at the Council of Jerusalem to propose a compromise: the Gentiles need not be circumcised, but neither should they flaunt the law; they must observe a minimum of legal requirements, avoiding unchastity, and, out of respect for the Jews in their midst, they must avoid certain foods—inclusive freedom, brotherly respect, and trust in the Holy Spirit, whom God had sent as teacher and guide for the church. And with that compromise, we have a pattern for deciding issues of

"Open Gates for the Spirit"

inclusiveness (indeed, any controversies of legalism vs. innovation) in our own time. For now, twenty centuries after the Council of Jerusalem, we can look back and see that nothing of essence was lost, and something of great importance was gained—the joy and truth of the gospel were now open to millions who hungered for it.

Notice the central importance of the Holy Spirit in all of this. It was the Holy Spirit that led Peter to the house of Cornelius after his vision of the unclean food; it was the Holy Spirit that fell upon the Gentiles who heard Peter preach; it was the Holy Spirit directing that Barnabas and Paul be set aside and sent out among the Gentiles; it was the Holy Spirit that moved the Council of Jerusalem to a compromise permitting the spread of the gospel and the expansion of the church. This was no mere human decision, but one influenced by the Spirit. It was the Spirit that was the guiding force in the early church, not only in the work of theology and mission, but also in the practical issues of its life together.

Jesus had promised his disciples that after his departure the Spirit of truth would come from the Father to continue the work of the Son. The Spirit would be with the church, calling to mind the truths that Jesus had spoken, and interpreting them according to contemporary need. The Spirit would confirm and expound the teaching of Jesus throughout the ages as the church, seeking to be faithful to its risen and living Lord, faced new situations. For there is much more to the gospel than we have yet experienced. It did not end with the Bible. It was not complete at Nicaea. It was not exhausted in the Reformation. It is still being unfolded in all of its richness in the world today, and the Spirit is even now seeking to guide us deeper into the truth—deeper than the law of Moses, deeper than the Gospels, deeper than Paul.

The Spirit is abroad in the world as advocate, as counselor, as encourager, as peacemaker. The Spirit is a gift. Scripture tells us that the Spirit is not something we "get." The Spirit is bestowed, freely, upon those who believe in the risen Christ. We can never have that gift in the fullest measure, but neither should we attempt to hoard it, nor erect barriers to its work. For the Spirit is none other than God, and God is all-sovereign, all-loving. And God will achieve the divine purpose *through* Christ's disciples or *in spite of* Christ's disciples. We can open or shut the gates to the work of the Holy Spirit, but God's will of redemption shall be accomplished.

Is the gospel a welcome mat to the kingdom of God, or a locked door to a private club? There were those in the early days of Christianity whose zeal for the law would have prevented the church from being the Spirit's instrument of salvation to the uttermost parts of the earth. As the church of Jesus Christ in the world, we need always to be asking where we may be shutting gates to the Holy Spirit today. From whom is the grace of the gospel being withheld in our time? Who is being denied the full love of Christ in the fellowship of his church? Does the exclusion of some rest on principles that have more to do with prejudice than purity, more to do with manners than mercy, more to do with human judgment than divine redemption? Are we promoting distinctions, or are we coming closer to the insight of Peter, whom God showed that *no one* should be judged "unclean"? Are we building walls through whom none but the very righteous may enter, or are we making real John's revelation of a new Jerusalem—a city whose lamp is the Lamb, by whose light all the nations shall walk, a city in which no creature is called "unclean," a city whose gates shall never be shut?

Ascension of the Lord

Spanish Springs Presbyterian Church, Sparks, Nevada

May 20, 2004

Acts 1:1–11
Ephesians 1:15–23
Luke 24:46–53

"Ours Is the Power"

Like Moses on the mountain, for forty days, according to the book of Acts, the resurrected Jesus taught his disciples about the kingdom of God—that God's sovereign reign over all the universe was upon them, and that a new day of hope was dawning for the poor, the captive, the sick, and the oppressed. Jesus had always spoken with authority, but *now* his authority was unquestioned. No longer could anyone regard his words as simply a polite suggestion, a mere proposal for the way people should live with each other and with God. The resurrection had demonstrated that Jesus was not just another teacher or philosopher or healer or prophet. He was and is the Messiah, the Son of God, Lord of all, and his word was and is *God's* word, and his action was and is *God's* action, and his judgment was and is *God's* judgment.

The disciples still had not fully comprehended the teachings of Jesus; they yet thought in terms of Israel's glory days, when great kings like David and Solomon ruled the nation, and foreign princes bowed down to them and brought them riches, and the nation was respected throughout the known world. "Lord, is this the time when you will restore the kingdom to Israel?" (Acts 1:6), they asked him one day. Even now, they did not comprehend that God's kingdom makes meaningless political boundaries and transcends historical circumstance. Even now, they did not perceive that the kingdom is something that requires us to be more than mere spectators, but demands the activity and commitment of everyone who has genuine faith in God. "It is not for you to know the times or periods that the Father has set by his own authority," Jesus said to them.

> "But you will receive power when the Holy Spirit has come upon you; and you will be my witnesses in Jerusalem, in all Judea and Samaria, and to the ends of the earth." When he had said this, as they were watching, he was lifted up, and a cloud took him out of their sight. While he was going and they were gazing up toward heaven, suddenly two men in white robes stood by them. They said, "Men of Galilee, why do you stand looking up toward heaven? This Jesus, who has been taken up from you into heaven, will come in the same way as you saw him go into heaven." (1:7–11)

And ten days later, as they were all assembled in one place, the Holy Spirit came and filled them, giving them the power that Jesus had promised.

Ascension Day has not been much celebrated in the American church, but it is one of the most important days on the Christian calendar, and it is recognized in Europe, as it was recognized in the early centuries of Christianity, as having tremendous theological and practical significance for contemporary disciples of Jesus Christ. It celebrates and draws our attention to a reality that we confess in a few words in the Apostles' Creed, but perhaps too frequently voice without thinking much about them or taking them very seriously—that God not only raised Jesus Christ from the dead, but set him in the position of power and glory above all others. As Ephesians expressed it, "[God] has put all things under his feet and has made him the head over all things for the church, which is his body, the fullness of him who fills all in all" (Eph 1:22). Jesus' word is universal law. All things are subject to him. The old values and the old attitudes and the old methods are no more. There is a new standard of righteousness in the world. There is a new motivation. There is a new reality. It is Jesus Christ, and his Lordship requires a new way of looking at the world and at each other, a new way of relating to God and to each other. And there is a new hope abroad and in the heart of each believer that the kingdom of God is nigh. The powers of sin and death have been broken; they are still formidable, but God in Christ has demonstrated that they are not the ultimate facts of life. The habits of pride and greed and lust and self-sufficiency are discredited; they may still seduce us, they may still masquerade as the truth, but the Lordship of Christ means that they are a lie, and anyone who governs his or her life by *them* is wasting time. Jesus Christ is the way and the truth and the life, and anything else is aimlessness and emptiness and self-deception.

Vindicated by God's raising him from the tomb, having appeared to his disciples and having explained to them how his death and resurrection fulfilled scripture, and having taught them about the coming kingdom of God, Christ's physical presence among his little band of followers in Jerusalem came to an end. But then, something incomparably more wonderful happened—they sensed his presence with them wherever they were, directing them, encouraging them, empowering them, and they recognized that Christ was still with them through the working of the Holy Spirit in their hearts and in their minds, in their fellowship and in their worship, in their trials and in their triumphs. And they came to know and understand the truth that *Jesus Christ is Lord.*

The crucifixion had been like a *nightmare* for the disciples—to have seen their Master on the cross—he who had worked such wonders of healing, saving others from every sort of brokenness,—to have laid his body in the tomb—he who had been so loving to them and so patient with them and whose words seemed so wise and so true. At first, the *resurrection* was no *less* a crisis. What could it *mean* that the tomb was *empty*? Who had taken the body, and why? Would the officials be coming after the disciples next? Then as Jesus appeared to them and they recognized him, their hearts were glad again, their minds were at ease again, life seemed worth living again. But toward the end of the forty days, he spoke once more in strange phrases—"You will receive power when the Holy Spirit has come upon you" (Acts 1:8a). He spoke once more of enormous and dangerous undertakings—"You will be my witnesses in Jerusalem, in all Judea and Samaria, and to the ends of the earth" (1:8b). And then he was gone, and they saw him no more. But this time, a new spark of faith emboldened the disciples and gave them trust in Jesus' promise. Immediately, they began to organize themselves for the mission that Jesus had set before them. They assembled together and prayed and chose Matthias to replace Judas in the apostolic vanguard. And then, at the day of Pentecost, the Holy Spirit came as Jesus had told them and empowered them for their task of being Christ's witnesses to the ends of the earth.

The experience of children going away to camp is almost proverbial in our society. It has become a rite of passage, marking the point in a child's development to mature adulthood when one is first given the opportunity to learn to live apart from parental surveillance, to risk that there is a providence at work outside of the family circle, to discover that one can function even hundreds of miles from mother and father. Such experiences are important in a child's life in order to build confidence and prepare him or her for the time when the bonds of immediate closeness must be untied. It is when we are *away* from home that we first appreciate the significance, even the wisdom, of lessons *taught* at home. *Without* such experiences fairly early in life, the ability to function successfully as a grown-up, to assume the full responsibilities of adulthood, is in jeopardy.

In a similar manner, it seems that it required Jesus' *absence* for his disciples finally to perceive what Jesus had been teaching them all that time, and to perceive also that when he had called them to follow him, it was a preparation for their *own* ministry—a ministry that would take them from the familiar territory of the Jews into all the world. Now they were on their *own*. But not really. Raised to a station of glory and power that transcends the limitations of space and time, location and hour, Christ could be with his disciples *wherever* they were—present through the Holy Spirit. It was time for the disciples to translate their *memories* into *ministry*, to live in faith that the same power of God that raised Christ from the *dead* is available to *each* believer and at work in the church to do the same sorts of things that *Jesus* did when he was physically present at bedside, and people long ill became strong and whole again; on the hillside, and hungry people were fed to fullness; in the crowded streets, and the blind and the lame opened their eyes and saw, and stood up and walked. And the record of Acts tells us that the disciples rose to the occasion; filled with the Holy Spirit, the followers of Jesus began the adventure of taking the gospel from Jerusalem out into Judea and Samaria, then to Syria and Asia Minor and Europe and Africa, eventually to Asia and the Americas and the islands of the Pacific— into every corner of the globe. And wherever they have gone, inspired and empowered by Christ through the Holy Spirit, they have worked miracles as they have translated the scriptures and built schools and established hospitals and dug wells and planted crops, as they have restored dignity to the outcasts of society and confronted oppressors and exposed tyrants and called the privileged to account and the smug to repentance. What other explanation could there *be* for such miracles as timid people turned bold, selfish people turned generous, spiteful people turned loving, but that Jesus Christ is Lord of all?—not Satan, not his imps, not the planets, not hormones, not greed, not apathy, but Jesus Christ! *He* sits on the throne, and directs that through the church—his hands and feet and eyes and ears and tongue still present in the world to proclaim the good news and to identify those in need and minister to them—through the *church*, God's purpose of redemption is proceeding according to God's eternal plan, unlimited and unencumbered by anything except his disciples' own occasional failure to believe that they *have* the power, through the Spirit, to help bring to fruition the kingdom of God.

Even now, the church—including this congregation—has the power to turn the world upside down, if the church will but *act* upon its faith and *exercise* that power. Do we decry the rule of greed and violence and promiscuity in our time? Then, with the help of the Holy Spirit, let us commit ourselves to living in simplicity and peace and chastity, not seeing how much we can *make* from others, but how well we can *serve* others; not returning evil for evil, but meeting words of threat with prayers for patience; risking on the side of peace and setting aside all desire for revenge as individuals and as a nation; not just glibly preaching to our youth about sexual standards that we then mock in our entertainment and our jokes, but living out the mutual respect and dignity and forbearance and kindness that are at the foundation of every truly Christian union.

What an impact our example will have, if we dare genuinely to live it out! Do we believe that Christ is Lord of all? Then let us be willing to venture out in that faith, offering the full range of our talents, and a generous percentage of our material wealth, to the work of Christ's church, rather than throwing in with the world and imposing limits on our abilities and parceling the time that we will donate or excusing parsimony with every sort of rationalization. What wonders God will do with our gifts! Do we believe that the kingdom is something real, not just a fantasy or wishful thinking? Then there is nothing to keep us from imaginatively meeting more adequately the needs of the homeless and the hungry of our community, regardless of the language that they speak or the customs that they follow, and there is nothing to keep us from being involved personally in the mission of the whole church, that the full flowering of the kingdom of God may be that much nearer. Let us, in other words, be about the work that Christ's own life and witness have set before us as faithful disciples who believe, truly *believe*, that he is enthroned at the right hand of God, and who trust, really *trust*, that Christ is powerfully present with us in the Holy Spirit.

Now, Christ is physically gone out of the world to live with God and reign in power and glory. The world can no longer experience his power, can no longer see his glory, except through the witnesses whom he has commissioned to speak and act in his name. That includes you and me, proclaiming his promises, working his miracles, radiating his personality in each of our relationships, in each of our tasks, in each of our expenditures, in each of our dreams. We are the church, the body of Christ still present in the world. He has given us a commission. And Christ has promised that we have available to us through the Holy Spirit the power of God. We only need the faith to use it.

Seventh Sunday of Easter

Spanish Springs Presbyterian Church, Sparks, Nevada

May 20, 2007

Acts 16:16–34
Revelation 22:12–14, 16–17, 20–21
John 17:20–26

"'As We Are One'"

Today is Presbyterian Heritage Sunday, the day designated on our denomination's calendar to celebrate who we are as one branch of the historic Christian faith. We are the followers of Christ whose roots are in the Swiss Reformation that spread to the Low Countries and the British Isles and, from there, to North America, and eventually to Africa, and to southern and eastern Asia. Recognizing that God's purpose of salvation is worked out within history, we are *proud* of our heritage—most of it, anyway; we are or should be *repentant* for some of it, too. We try to be honest about our past. No other denomination in this country maintains so fine an archive as the Presbyterian Historical Society in Philadelphia. We are children, women, and men who know that we are privileged to have been preceded by a great parade of faithful people of God, and that we would not *be* here, our denomination and even our congregation would not *exist*, without *their* witness and *their* sacrifice, *their* bold proclamation and *their* whispered prayers.

Some of us were born into Presbyterian families. Some of us never set foot in a Presbyterian sanctuary until we first attended worship in *this* place. Most of us are somewhere in between those two extremes. *All* of us have made some conscious choice to pursue our Christian calling within the context and from the perspective of the Presbyterian way of worshiping, of learning, of doing mission, of speaking about God, of being the church of Jesus Christ. There is nothing peculiar about Presbyterians when it comes to beliefs and practices; we just emphasize certain things that distinguish us from denominations that emphasize *other* things. We don't see ourselves as the *only* route to God—indeed, no one can claim that but Jesus. But we *do* regard ourselves as an authentic and significant *expression* and *part* of the whole church of Jesus Christ. In previous generations, we have wanted to draw the distinctions more sharply, have wanted to state our emphases more forcefully. But over the past 100 or 150 years, words like "cooperation" and "ecumenical" have become more important to us, and we have seen the damage that can be done, especially in the mission field, when the witness that churches make is one of division and contention. Twenty-four years ago, nearly a quarter century now, we healed a particularly embarrassing breach when the United Presbyterian Church in the United States of America and the Presbyterian Church in the United States, known respectively as the "northern" church and the "southern" church, finally reunited. That event was more than a century in coming after the end of the American Civil War during which the Presbyterian Church had split. More recently, the Presbyterian and Lutheran Churches entered into an agreement of cooperation, acknowledging our mutual failing for having remained apart all these many centuries since the Protestant Reformation. The sad, war-torn history of Europe would have been much different had these two main Protestant branches united or at least begun a habit of close cooperation way back in the 1500s.

Some Christians scoff at such developments as church unions, mergers, and agreements, saying that they are pitiful attempts by mainline denominations to shift attention away from their decreasing membership. Still other critics, often from within the denomination, say that mergers and reunions and agreements dilute our theological integrity by compromising points of doctrine for which our ancestors fought and sometimes died. Others of us, though, while taking fine points of doctrine seriously, take *just* as seriously the words of Jesus in this morning's Gospel reading, spoken to God in prayer and overheard by the disciples on the occasion of that last meal together before Jesus was put to death on the cross. Jesus prayed,

> "I ask not only on behalf of these, but also on behalf of those who will believe in me through their word, that they may all be one. As you, Father, are in me and I am in you, may they also be in us, so that the world may believe that you have sent me. The glory that you have given me I have given them, so that they may be one, as we are one, I in them and you in me, that they may become completely one, so that the world may know that you have sent me and have loved them even as you have loved me." (John 17:20–23)

The divisions between those who believe in Jesus Christ are not just a matter of purity of doctrine or administrative inefficiencies, or about jokes that begin, "A Baptist, a Methodist, and a Presbyterian were in a boat." The divisions between those who believe in Jesus Christ are a matter of whether, in fact, we *do* believe in Jesus Christ, and have faith in *him* above faith in our *own* ways and wiles, and whether the *witness* that we give to Jesus Christ is such that the world has a *true* picture of who Christ is or a *false* one, whether people around us are *attracted* to Christ or decide they want nothing to *do* with him. How dare *any* Christian ridicule any *other* Christian's efforts at reconciliation, at cooperation, at unity? For by doing so, they are ridiculing the very hopes of their Lord and Savior!

The Task Force on the Peace, Unity, and Purity of the Church, reporting to last year's General Assembly, in essence reaffirmed the declaration of the Presbyterian ordination vows that no one of those three things—peace, unity, or purity—has *priority* over any of the others, nor is any *subordinate* to the others; one Presbyterian's notion of purity cannot trump the necessity of peace and unity in the church, for, indeed, the church is only *pure* when it is also at *peace* and is *united*. The Task Force, appointed in response to contentious issues facing the denomination specifically in the areas of biblical interpretation, human sexuality, and ordination to the offices of minister, elder, and deacon, included clergy and laity who are of very different opinions on those particular issues. The Task Force was not charged with providing answers to the divisive questions, but rather with recommending to the church how it proceed to deal with them, and how it proceed in *being* the church while the issues are under discussion. Still, there are some congregations that are threatening to leave the denomination because the General Assembly—which is the whole group of commissioners elected by the various presbyteries around the country to meet and discuss and vote on matters facing the whole denomination—voted to approve the Task Force's report and its various recommendations. I gather that those congregations, or their ministers, think the report compromises their conception of purity.

Its specific recommendations aside, I was impressed—very impressed—that the Task Force, from the very beginning of its work, insisted that it worship together regularly, and receive the sacrament of the Lord's Supper together regularly. This group of men and women of such diverse opinions recognized that, above everything else, they are brothers and sisters in the Lord, and they accepted Christ's own invitation to dine regularly at the table of reconciliation, observing the sacrament instituted by Christ for the very purpose of overcoming and healing enmity and estrangement, the sacrament instituted by Christ to show the world what it means to believe in him and to have life in him, the sacrament instituted by Christ for the very purpose of proclaiming his sacrificial death as a servant until he comes again. And it was *at* that *Last* Supper with his disciples before his death that Jesus prayed that his followers would all be one—not just the disciples who were in the upper room that night, but all who would come to believe *through* them, just as he and God were, *are*, one. *That*, Jesus said, is how the world will come to believe that God sent him.

The unity of God and Christ in the Trinity is a mystery. It cannot be explained. But Jesus, in his prayer, said that the unity of Christians is to be like it. And, so, we can turn the analogy around: the unity of Christians (when they *are* united) is the way that we and the world to whom we are giving witness will come to understand what the unity between God and Christ is like—the unity of the Trinity. But there is a difference. The unity of God and Christ, and the Holy Spirit with them, is intrinsic. It is fundamental. It existed before creation ever was, and it will exist after creation has passed away. The unity to which you and I and all Christians should aspire *derives* from the unity that is *already* present between God and Christ. For the church to be "one" means that we mirror the mutuality and reciprocity that exists between God and Christ. But the *blessing*, for those who dwell in such unity, is that we are not merely *mirroring* that relationship; we are *sharing* in it. We do not *create* it; we need not try to *invent* it. Rather, we are to *participate* in it, and to *enjoy* it.

But, ultimately, our unity is not something that we, as Christians, may choose to adopt or ignore, and still be faithful. Our oneness is mandatory, if we are truly to be obedient to Christ, if we truly recognize and honor him as Lord, if we genuinely value him as Savior. Do we accept the disciples' commission of exhibiting Christ to the world, of showing to the world the identity and character of God revealed through the life and death and resurrection of his Son? A prime aspect of that witness is the oneness of God and Christ. What sort of a witness to what *God* is like do we offer to the world when we are at each other's throats, when we disparage each other's faith, when we impugn each other's motives, when we deny each other's salvation? According to Jesus' prayer, what will lead the unbelieving world to faith in Jesus as the one sent by God is the unity of those who believe in him. The more powerfully the reality of God's love is present in those who believe in Christ, the more fully unity is achieved among them. If the world does *not* believe in Christ, one prime culprit must be the disunity, the discord and the distrust, of those who say they *do* believe in Christ. Is it appropriate to wreck the effective witness to Christ by argument and contention over human formulations of doctrine about which Jesus never spoke? If we're going to die in the ditch, so to speak, wouldn't it be far better to do so as advocates for the very thing for which Jesus *prayed*, rather than practitioners of the very thing that Christ prayed *against*? The church is called to be pure—actually, the Bible's word would be "holy." But the very *measure* of its purity, or holiness, according to *Jesus*, is the degree of its *unity*.

Have you looked at the mission statement of Spanish Springs Presbyterian Church lately? Among other things, it says that we have pledged ourselves to exhibit the kingdom of heaven to the world. Surely, the kingdom of heaven is a place of unity and peace, as well as purity. That is why, for instance, we celebrate the Week of Prayer for Christian Unity each January, and I sincerely hope that those of you who haven't yet taken part in those worship experiences will do so, and regularly make that witness to the oneness among Christians for which Christ prays. It is why we are part of the World Council of Churches, and the National Council of Churches, and the World Alliance of Reformed Churches. It is also why we participate in ecumenical mission, cooperating with Christians of many different denominations in the effort to feed the hungry and house the homeless and present a united voice in raising faith concerns in halls of government. It is why I have asked our Presbyterian Women to consider participating in the World Day of Prayer. Our mission statement recognizes that the ministry of redemption in which we participate is a church-wide ministry that involves treating others with respect and extending hospitality and fellowship to *all*, not just *some*. And our mission statement obligates us, in recognition of our calling to make Christ known, to be his ambassadors of reconciliation, his agents of wholeness, and his messengers of peace. "The glory that you have given me," Jesus prayed, "I have given them, so that they may be one, as we are one, I in them and you in me, that they may become completely one, so that the world may know that *you* have *sent* me and have *loved them* even as you have *loved me*" (17:22–23).

Faithful Christians, believers who seek to fulfill Christ's will, are people for whom Christian unity becomes a conviction, not merely a sentiment, and not just an option. And the finest heritage of the Presbyterian Church, and of this or any congregation, will be its witness, in what it says *of* others and how it acts *toward* others, that the Father is in the Son, and the Son is in the Father. It really is not an option. It is so that the world may believe that Jesus Christ was, indeed, sent by God.

Appendix

Of the five sermons in this appendix, only two are based on the readings assigned in the Common Lectionary (Revised), but all were preached during Year C of the three-year lectionary cycle and perhaps bear some indication of the Lucan environment surrounding them. The first was preached at an early-evening family-oriented Christmas Eve service, featuring two youth in a donkey costume (one the front end, one the rear) moving about appropriately in the chancel as I voiced the sermon from the gallery at the rear of the sanctuary, with the congregation singing designated verses from Christmas carols and hymns. The "sermon" found itself employed in several of the churches in which I served over the years, sometimes using a modified horse outfit in communities whose costume shops had a more limited range of livestock available.

The second sermon was preached at the baccalaureate service for the graduating seniors from the three high schools in Sparks, Nevada, the year that my daughter, Bethany, completed her experience at Reed High School. I had left Spanish Springs Presbyterian Church at the end of 2011, but was accorded the privilege of addressing the gathering on this occasion, special to me, by the baccalaureate committee on which I had served throughout my thirteen years in the community.

The third and fourth sermons were delivered for the Week of Prayer for Christian Unity joint worship service attended by members and clergy from the congregations of several different Christian communities in Sparks. Both of the services, in different years, happened to be hosted by Spanish Springs Presbyterian Church. The Graymoor Ecumenical and Interreligious Institute, which prepares and distributes the liturgical materials for the annual observance, recommends that the preacher at the event be from one of the non-hosting churches, but on these two occasions I was happy to accept the preaching role for what I regarded as a prime opportunity to give witness to Christ's intention for his church.

The fifth sermon is included, frankly, because of my inability to choose between two possibilities to represent the Fifth Sunday in Ordinary Time. The sermon in the primary text and the one in the appendix are very different in content, expressing the frequent breadth of truth awaiting discovery in each set of lectionary readings.

Christmas Eve (early)
Grace Presbyterian Church, Plano, Texas
December 24, 1988

Isaiah 9:2–7
Titus 2:11–14
Luke 2:1–20

"Mary's Donkey"

Hee-haw. Hee-haw. Hee-haw. Hee-haw. Hee-haw. Hee—oh, excuse me. I was just practicing my braying. I get a little rusty now and then—not as young as I used to be, after all. Hee-haw. Hee-haw. There, now wasn't that pretty good? Yes, it has been a lot of ears—I mean, *years*—since I first learned to bray up in the hills of Galilee. And I've had a good life as donkey lives go. I've been a lot of places and seen a lot of things. . . . What? . . . What have I seen? Well, there was one series of events that was pretty extraordinary several years ago, yessirree, pretty extraordinary. . . . What's that? . . . You'd like to hear about it? Hee-haw. Hee-haw. Sure, I'd be happy to tell you. Just settle back, and get ready to hear of a wonderful event that began 'way up in Galilee at a place called Nazareth.

I was just a young fellow then, a cute little guy, when a woman named Anna came and bought me from my owner. At first, I was very unhappy to be taken away from my family, but I soon learned to like my new home. I especially liked my new mistress, a young woman named Mary. She was engaged to marry a carpenter named Joseph.

You see, Anna, Mary's mother, had bought me because Mary was going on a journey down to Judah to see her cousin, Elizabeth. Anna bought me so that Mary wouldn't have to walk all the way, but could ride on my back. See, you humans only have two feet, so you have a harder time walking long distances than those of us who are blessed with *four* feet. Hee-haw.

Well, one morning we started out on our journey to Judah, Mary on my back and a hired servant leading me. Mary kept repeating something to herself, like she was pondering what it meant. I didn't understand the meaning of it all at the time, but I can still remember the words: "Greetings, favored one! The Lord is with you. . . . Do not be afraid, Mary, for you have found favor with God. And now, you will conceive in your womb and bear a son, and you will name him Jesus. He will be great, and will be called the Son of the Most High, and the Lord God will give to him the throne of his ancestor David. He will reign over the house of Jacob forever, and of his kingdom there will be no end" (Luke 1:28, 30–33).

"To a Maid Engaged to Joseph" (stanzas 1 and 2)

It was as if she understood the words, but was uncertain of what the message meant. She was happy, I think, but she was also rather uneasy about it.

When we came to Elizabeth's house, Mary slid down from my back and knocked at the door, and Elizabeth came to greet her. "Blessed are you among women!" (1:42) she said. And Mary answered with beautiful words.

> "My soul magnifies the Lord,
>   and my spirit rejoices in God my Savior,
> for he has looked with favor on the lowliness of his servant.
>   Surely, from now on all generations will call me blessed;
> for the Mighty One has done great things for me,
>   and holy is his name." (1:46–49)

And Mary and Elizabeth hugged each other, and seemed to be weeping for joy.

So, we stayed at that place for about three months—wonderful months for me. All the servants of the house petted me and fed me. And finally, a wonderful thing happened—Elizabeth had a baby—John was his name—and there was great excitement in the household, and I even heard the neighbors talking about it as they passed my stable.

Well, it was just a little after that that we went back to Nazareth. Mary seemed to have changed—she seemed to tire more easily, and the servant seemed to have me stop more often in shady places to rest.

A little while after we got back to Nazareth, I found out why Mary needed more rest—she was going to have a baby, too!

"Lo, How a Rose E'er Blooming" (stanza 1)

As the day for the baby to be born got closer and closer, the people of the household got more and more excited. But one night, I heard Joseph get

Christmas Eve (early)—"Mary's Donkey"

real angry, and he stomped around inside the house. "Taxes! Taxes! Taxes!" he said. "And you in your condition. How can we go to Bethlehem with you ready to deliver at any time?" I had never heard Joseph get so excited and upset. Then I heard Mary talking to him in a soothing voice, and the house got quiet. But the next morning, the house was busy again with preparations for another journey—a journey to a place called Bethlehem. And with Mary seated again on my back (and weighing a few extra pounds, let me tell you), and Joseph leading, we set off on the road toward Jerusalem.

It took us several days to get to Bethlehem, having to stop frequently for Mary to rest—she really didn't look so good—and having to pass through Jerusalem. The traffic in that city was awful! We arrived just at the rush hour. Some of those city donkeys are so rude!—cutting in and out, forgetting to signal, double-parking. You have to understand that Nazareth is a quiet little country town, so I wasn't used to the big city. Well, anyway, we finally got out of Jerusalem and, just as night was falling, we came to Bethlehem.

"O Little Town of Bethlehem" (stanza 1)

Bethlehem was crowded, too, and we went from one place to another trying to find a place for Mary to spend the night. Poor Joseph. He tried so hard, but everybody kept slamming their doors in his face. Finally, a woman directed us to some caves where some cattle and other donkeys were kept. They weren't very friendly to me at first, but then we discovered that my third cousin on my mother's side grew up on the same farm as one of their best friend's aunt's neighbor. But I was really too tired for socializing. Boy, was I bushed! But poor Mary—it had been such a hard trip for her. But neither of us would have any sleep that night, because that's when it happened—the most wonderful thing I've ever seen.

"Bring a Torch, Jeannette, Isabella" (stanza 1)

Right there, in the cattle stall where I was standing, Mary gave birth to her baby, a beautiful baby boy. And because there was no other place for him, Joseph laid him in the manger, right where I had been eating, and where we could all see him asleep on the hay.

"Good Christian Friends, Rejoice" (stanza 1)

I had never seen a baby human before. Still, it seemed that there was something very special about this baby—so tiny, so beautiful, so . . . special.

Well, it wasn't very long before we had visitors.

"While Shepherds Watched Their Flocks" (stanza 1)

The shepherds who came told Mary and Joseph of a marvelous sight. About the time that Mary's baby was born, they said that they had been out on the hillsides tending their sheep. All of a sudden, an angel appeared to them.

"Hark! The Herald Angels Sing" (stanza 1)

The angel told them of the marvelous thing that had happened, and they had said to each other, "Let us go now to Bethlehem and see this thing that has taken place, which the Lord has made known to us" (2:15). And when they came into where Mary and the baby were, they knelt down and looked with wonder at the baby.

I think it was that same night that the star first appeared—not an ordinary star, but a very bright star that I had never seen before, and that all the people were talking about. It was the brightest star that I have ever seen, and it was right over Bethlehem. In fact, it seemed to be directly over the baby's manger, making the night almost as bright as day.

"What Star Is This, with Beams So Bright" (stanzas 1 and 4)

I think the star had something to do with our next visitors—three men in fine, royal robes who came riding on camels (smelly beasts!) and bringing some special gifts to the baby. They said that they had come a very long way.

"We Three Kings of Orient Are" (stanza 1)

They seemed very happy to have found the baby, and they immediately fell on their knees and bowed to him. Imagine that! Three such important men, worshiping a little baby they had never even seen before, and giving him gold, frankincense, and myrrh! I was standing right beside the manger, and I could smell the frankincense and see the baby's beautiful face.

So there we all were—Mary and Joseph and the baby, the shepherds, then later the three men, and me, and, of course, the other donkeys and cattle.

"The First Nowell" (stanza 1)

What a wonderful night that was when Mary's baby was born.

Pretty soon, though, we were all astir again, this time preparing for a very long journey, but we weren't going back to Nazareth yet. Instead, we set out for Egypt, because someone named Herod was angry with Mary's baby. Can you imagine anyone being angry at a dear little baby? But it must have been serious, because I mean we high-tailed it out of there. It's a good thing

I'd thought to bring my passport with me. And we had to stay in Egypt a long time before we could return to Nazareth.

Well, now you've heard my story about those marvelous things that happened so long ago. What do *you* think about it?

"O Come, All Ye Faithful" (stanza 1)

Sparks High Schools Baccalaureate

John Ascuaga's Nugget, Sparks, Nevada

May 20, 2012

Ezekiel 37:1–14
Hebrews 11:1–3

My children are probably tired of hearing me talk about the way things used to be. In a lot of families, that's almost a cliché. I never thought that, as a parent, I would fall into that habit. But I have told Christi, Jesse, and Beth from time to time how being a passenger on an airplane *used to mean* being pampered, even in coach class, and how sitting down at the same time at the same table to eat the same food and having a conversation with each other as a family *used to be* the rule rather than the exception, and how it *used to be* that when you made a telephone call to some business or other, a live person answered your call and acted as if he or she was there to serve *you* rather than the other way around. If your parents or aunts or uncles or whoever want to tell you about the good old days, please be patient. It might be, as in my case, that they want you to know how much they regret that you may never experience such things, may never realize that things could be different—more personal, more gracious, more humane—than the way they are. And they may be regretting that *they* have had a role in permitting things to become *less* personal, *less* gracious, *less* humane.

Some things, on the other hand, don't change that much from generation to generation. Most of you, I suspect, don't really remember a time when this country was not at war in the Middle East. Some of your friends or family members may be serving in Iraq or Afghanistan even now, or may be about to enter the military and find themselves in war zones, or perhaps you yourself. When I attended my baccalaureate service at Littleton High School in Colorado back in 1969, our nation was deeply mired in *another* war far away, fought for reasons not always clear and increasingly unpopular. All through your high school years, our nation and much of the world has been in deep economic recession, and, as you graduate, you are painfully aware that job prospects in many parts of our country, including

Nevada, remain bleak, while those of you who are going on to college and university have become aware that tuition costs are rising even as course offerings and faculty are being reduced. Historically speaking, this is not the best time to be coming out from under your parents' wings. *My* generation *also* faced recessions that made it difficult to find a job, sometimes combined with runaway inflation, though not nearly as long or nearly as stubborn as *this* recession has proved to be. But, robust economy or poor, *no one* has *ever* been *guaranteed* of quickly finding a job or receiving a scholarship or anything else.

As we grow older, we come to realize, often by painful experience, that there are a lot of things in life that we simply can't count on. And if we put our trust in people and institutions, or in economic theories or political doctrines, chances are we will be disappointed at some time in life—people will fail us, institutions will fail us, and neither capitalism nor socialism nor anything in between is perfect, and politics, no matter how politicians may pledge to work for the common good, is nearly always fueled by self-interest.

Graduation is a time when you will hear and see a lot of optimistic messages—in your commencement address, perhaps in cards that friends and relatives send you. Compared with that, the things I have been saying to you may seem pessimistic. I don't intend for them to be negative—just realistic. As people of faith in God—and I certainly assume that it's because each of you *is* a person of faith that you have decided to be here tonight,—we recognize that the hope that we have for the future does not ultimately lie in a particular degree or a particular job, not in a political election or an economic forecast, not in a romantic relationship or a financial investment. Marketers and candidates will try to persuade you otherwise, and even religious traditions sometimes adopt the strategies and vocabulary of the marketplace, essentially selling faith like a product, and of the political realm, clothing God in their own partisan opinions. The world around us confuses *hope* with *wishful thinking*, confuses *hope* with *positive thinking*, bases *hope* on *political polls* and *stock averages*. But for people who have faith in *God*—not just belief that there *is* a God, but *trust* that God is loving and just and merciful, and that this loving and just and merciful God is the highest and final authority in the design and function of the universe and the highest and final authority in our lives and all of human history—hope is something that is unshakable and true even though friends desert us, even though jobs are scarce and insecure, even though nations and corporations do abominable things.

The prophet Ezekiel was part of a group of Israelites who were carried off into exile in Babylon when the Babylonian empire conquered Judah and destroyed Jerusalem in ancient times. The people had every earthly reason to be demoralized—they lost their homes, they lost their livelihoods, they lost the temple that had been the center of their religious life. And many of them despaired. So many of the nation's youth had been killed in the wars that led up to the fall of Jerusalem. So many of the nation's older people must have died of illness and starvation during long months during which Jerusalem was under siege.

But Ezekiel, apparently one of those people who was taken away from the land that God had given the Israelites, was blessed with a vision from God. The Lord, Ezekiel wrote, set him in the middle of a valley, and the valley was full of bones. Perhaps it had been an actual battleground where Judah's army had been defeated by the army of Babylon. Perhaps it symbolized the destruction of Judah's society and way of life, its economy and customs as well as its government and its buildings. To all appearances—to every measure of sight and sound and touch—the scene was one of total hopelessness. And the Lord said to Ezekiel, "Mortal, can these bones live?" (Ezek 37:4) Then the Lord told Ezekiel to prophesy to the bones, which is a way of saying that Ezekiel was supposed to speak to the bones about the power and purpose of God, to interpret the situation as God saw it—the God who brought all life into being, the God who took the initiative to enter into a covenant with a people and promised to care and provide for them and befriend them for all time, the God who has demonstrated love and justice and mercy over and over again, the God who has never abandoned the faithful to despair, not even, as in the *Christian* testimony, to death.

We can wish for this or that in life—a certain girlfriend or boyfriend or spouse, a certain career, a certain car, a certain house, a certain physique, freedom from disease, freedom from financial worries, freedom from conflict. And we can work to try to bring those things about. But *wishing* is an exercise that has no *certainty* to it, often no basis in reality. To put our hopes in things or in people is, no matter how sincere we are, ultimately just a wish. Things can't respond to us, don't care about us, and people are fickle and fallible. True hope, genuine hope, is not something that an object or a theory or another human being can ever satisfy. Strangely, we can't ultimately rely on anything that is tangible, on anything that is visible. We can't touch hope. We can't manufacture it. We can't take it to the bank. Sadly, we can't ultimately rely on any other person, anything that he or she says or does, no matter how well-intentioned they are. True hope, genuine hope, rests not on what other people will or won't do. It doesn't depend upon whether the stock market goes up or down. It isn't tied to jobs or elections. It rests solely and squarely on the promises of God. And as our response to what God has done and is doing, what God declares and what God promises to do, our hope is the only solid ground for our confidence, for our joyfulness, for our endurance through hardship, for our freedom from threats, for a sense of peace even though chaos may be all around us.

The story of Abraham is fundamental to Judaism and to Christianity and to Islam. In the time in which Abraham and Sarah, his wife, lived, having children was perhaps the most convincing evidence of God's blessing. When Abraham was quite old and childless, God promised him that he would be the father of a whole multitude of peoples, and directed him to go to a place God would show him, taking along Sarah and all their servants and many of their relatives. Abraham and Sarah did so, trusting God's promise and pinning their hope on God's faithfulness. Surely you know the story of how, for many years, they still failed to have a child, well beyond the normal age of a man and a woman being able to conceive. They tried to take things into their own hands, Sarah offering her handmaiden to be the mother of Abraham's child. But the Bible testifies that the son born from that liaison was not the child to carry the promise that God had proclaimed—a son was still to be born to Abraham and Sarah, though it seemed biologically impossible. Finally, one was born—Isaac—and God then, paradoxically, ordered Abraham to sacrifice Isaac, his son. Still trusting God despite every earthly instinct, Abraham did so, and was just about to kill the boy on the altar, when God stayed Abraham's hand and provided another sacrifice instead—a ram caught nearby in a thicket. God proved faithful to God's promise. Abraham's and Sarah's hope was fulfilled. And the lineage was established that led to a great nation, a multitude of descendants, as God had said. Despite appearances, God's will was supreme, God's purpose was being carried out. Hope in God did not disappoint.

"Now faith," said a preacher whose words have been cherished as true and preserved for centuries in the New Testament, "is the assurance of things hoped for, the conviction of things not seen" (Heb 11:1). Faith in God is what gives us hope in God's promise—the promise of God's everlasting care, of God's everlasting friendship, of God's everlasting love. It does not require having a perfect romance, a perfect education, a perfect job, a perfect home, a perfect checkup. But it is what carries us through disappointing romances and flawed education and frustrating jobs and family difficulties and illness, even the loss of a loved one.

So, I encourage you to hope for the future, not because tomorrow's headlines will be better than today's, but because tomorrow belongs to God. And when you find yourself in some valley of dry bones in your life, as is likely to happen at some point, when everything looks impossibly bleak and forbidding, allow your faith in God to overcome your disappointment in the world. Because your life, the way you live it, the values by which you conduct yourself, the way you treat others, and the way your respect yourself are an expression of your hope in God, who brought you into being, who calls you into the full humanity for which you were created, who loves you beyond human imagining, and who has promised to be faithful to you for all eternity.

Week of Prayer for Christian Unity

Spanish Springs Presbyterian Church, Sparks, Nevada

January 23, 2004

Isaiah 57:19–21; 60:17–22
Ephesians 2:13–18
John 14:23–31

"The Peace of Christ"

A few days ago, a man came into our church building, asking me to look in on his elderly mother, who is ill and nearing the end of her life. She is a Presbyterian, he explained, and would like to have a Presbyterian minister to speak with before she dies. I readily agreed to contact her, and earlier this week made my first visit to her, and expect to see her again this next week. The man mentioned that he had grown up as a Presbyterian, and would like his daughter to become involved in our church. I expressed my pleasure at that, and then asked why *he* hadn't been in the church during his adulthood. "I was in 'Nam," he said, as if that were a full explanation. I didn't press him any further at that point, and have been wondering, since, whether he was angry with the church because of its *criticism* of the Viet Nam War, or angry with the church because it *didn't* speak out *more strongly against* the Viet Nam War, or angry with *God* because of the waste of life and landscape that he had witnessed in Viet Nam.

I would suppose that this last is the most likely reason, based on my conversations with other people who, having been through the war, dropped out of involvement in the church. They may have heard the choirs singing the angel's tidings of "Peace and good will," church members exchanging Jesus' greeting to the disciples of "Peace be with you," the minister or priest repeating the apostle's opening line to his fellow Christian, "Grace, mercy, and peace from God the Father and Christ Jesus our Lord" (1 Tim 1:2b), and then witnessed how the tides of war seem to crash upon and obliterate the promises of scripture and the hope of faith. And, so, they have been moved to cynicism, based on the cold, hard facts of human arrogance and pride and lust and greed. How can anyone, minister or politician, talk of "peace" while missiles are being lobbed and bombs are being dropped and landmines are being planted and men, women, and children—especially children—are being maimed and killed and orphaned?

For that matter, one might wonder how someone sitting unjustly in a prison cell could possibly write about peace and the end of hostility and division and the need for reconciliation and unity, or how someone on the night of his unjust arrest and before his unjust execution could possibly bestow a legacy of peace upon his followers. Paul, writing to the Christians at Ephesus, did the one; Jesus, dining with his disciples, did the other. The absurdity of *promising peace* in the midst of insanity did not start on any of the battlefields of the twentieth or twenty-first centuries. It is as old as the Christian church, it is as persistent as Jesus Christ, it is as ancient even as the prophets.

> I will appoint Peace as your overseer
> and Righteousness as your taskmaster, (Isa 60:17b)

God promised in the words of the prophet Isaiah—a promise to his people who had been long in exile and had returned home to find their cities ruined and their fields devastated by warfare:

> Violence shall no more be heard in your land,
> devastation or destruction within your borders;
> you shall call your walls Salvation,
> and your gates Praise. (60:18)

A far cry from the rulers of the world who proclaim that peace depends upon lobbing more missiles and dropping more bombs and planting more landmines.

God did not promise, Christ did not offer, the apostle did not testify to a magical end to missiles and bombs and landmines, or suffering and discord and injustice. The promise, the offer, the testimony are not about a headline moment in history. One day, when history is no more, neither will there be war, nor cruelty, nor oppression, but all things will be as God intends for them to be. The kingdom of this world will have become the kingdom of our Lord and of his Christ, and his reign will be acknowledged in every corner of every land and in every corner of every heart. But the promise of peace, the offer of peace, the testimony to peace is fully real even now, just as it was in Paul's grungy prison cell, just as it was in the kangaroo trial before the Sanhedrin and the pompous courts of Herod and the reptilian precincts inhabited by Pontius Pilate. For, in truth, the peace to which we are privileged as people of faith is not a doctrine, not a philosophy; it is not an absence of war or a quelling of weapons. The peace to which we are privileged as people of faith is a *person*. The *peace* of Christ is the gift of Christ *himself*. The *wholeness* of Christ is the single-minded obedience of Christ *himself*. The *unity* of Christ is the merciful love of Christ *himself*.

On the night of his arrest, Jesus spoke to his disciples of loving him, which meant obeying the words that he had taught, which were the very words of God. On the night of his arrest, Jesus spoke to his disciples about being untroubled and being unafraid. On the night of his arrest, Jesus spoke to his disciples about having a home with him because he and the Father were coming to make *their* home with *them*. And the Holy Spirit would come to the disciples and bring to mind all that Jesus had taught and would guide them in every new situation and need. "Peace I leave with you; my peace I give to you," promised Jesus. "I do not give to you as the world gives" (John 14:23). And then he said to them, "Rise, let us be on our way" (14:31). And after Jesus' promise of *peace*, they went out into the night and across the Kidron Valley to the place where Judas betrayed him, and he was arrested, and Peter tried to resist by drawing a sword and cutting off the ear of the high priest's servant, and Jesus told him to put his sword away, and the next day Jesus was tried and tortured and put to death on a cross. Indeed, it was *not* peace as the *world* understands it. It was *not* peace as the *world* would *give* it. But it *was* the peace that worked our salvation and still *judges today every* act of *violence, every* word of *threat, every* emotion of *hatred, every* thought of *revenge*.

To the leaders of the nations, as to most people, "peace" seems to depend upon other people agreeing with what we want, agreeing with our view of the world, agreeing with our aspirations. Obviously, *that* interpretation of peace will *never* mean an end of warfare, short of world domination— economic, political, or military. Obviously, *that* interpretation of peace will *never* mean an end of fear; indeed, it will only *increase* fear. Obviously, *that* interpretation of peace will *never* mean an end of cynicism and anger and doubt. It is making an idol of some human ideology, of some human philosophy, of some human vision of the future—emphatically *ours*, not *theirs*; *mine*, not *yours*. Peace that has anything to do with *Christ* finds its unshakable foundation in trust that *genuine* peace and the only peace worthy of the *name* is found in Christ himself alone—the *incarnation* of God's love, of God's justice, of God's mercy.

The same Caesar Augustus who issued a decree that all the world should be registered and sent Joseph to his hometown of Bethlehem and others to their hometowns all around his empire also inaugurated the Pax Romana, the "Roman Peace," assuring that commerce could flow and taxes would be collected and everybody would bow in the same direction, which was to Rome, the nation, and to him, its ruler. It was peace imposed and enforced. It depended upon bluster and fear. It was a system that tolerated no dissent, no question. And it reacted swiftly and decisively and, as *it* thought, conclusively, to stamp out even such a minor threat to its security as someone who healed outside the lines and forgave outside the borders and in whom a few peasants dared to see their hope for dignity and meaning. We know how that sort of thing happens—it was echoed thirty-six years ago on the balcony of the Lorraine Motel in Memphis, Tennessee. But imposing behavior, regulating thought, even banning certain weapons, is not peace, either among nations or among individuals or, for that matter, among Christians.

I suspect that those of us who are gathered here tonight, though we be from several different Christian traditions, on many things would find ourselves more in agreement with each other than with others in our particular religious communions. We are here, whether Presbyterian or Roman Catholic or United Methodist or Lutheran or whatever, because we realize that there is something scandalous about *naming* ourselves "Presbyterian" or "Roman Catholic" or "United Methodist" or "Lutheran," or even calling ourselves "Christian" if we do it in order to distinguish us from anyone *else* who professes faith in Jesus Christ. We are here because we recognize that we are incomplete, partial, and impoverished, even unfaithful, if we do not seek to *learn* from each other, if we are *distrusting* of each other, if we refuse to *pray* with each other. We are here because we confess, penitently, that we do nothing in the name of Jesus Christ unless we do it with love for all and mercy without condition and generosity that holds nothing back. We are here because we admit that we, and the churches to which we belong, have too often been what stands in the *way* of the world knowing the peace of Christ rather than being *instruments* of the peace of Christ. We are here to *lament* as well as to *praise*, to ask each *other's* forgiveness as well as to celebrate *God's* forgiveness. We are here because we know that there is nothing *we* can do to bring about peace and unity—that is something that only *God* can do, but, in truth, it is something that God has *already* done in the person of *Jesus Christ*. *We* can only give *witness* to it. But give *witness* to it we *must*. For our peace is to be found in a person—the one who *is* the love with which *we* are to love, the mercy with which *we* are to be merciful, the justice with which *we* are to be just, the food upon which *we* are to feed and to feed *others*, the sacrifice in whose name *we* are to sacrifice *ourselves* for the sake of the kingdom of God, in which there is no war, no suffering, no hatred, no fear, but a city whose walls are Salvation and whose gates are Praise. And not one person walks its streets because of his or her *doctrine*, nor religious *pedigree*, and certainly not because of his or her *politics* or economic *theories*, but solely because of Jesus Christ, his life and his death and his resurrection.

I guess I can understand why someone who has experienced the hell that is war might be suspicious of any place where people would venture to speak up on behalf of the God in whose world missiles are lobbed and bombs are dropped and landmines are planted. And I can understand why someone who yearns for peace might even avoid a place where people through much of the past two thousand years have been at war with others who don't think exactly like they do, and represent a heritage often characterized by ridiculing, slandering, smashing, drowning, burning, digging up and burning again those with whom they disagreed. But the peace of *Christ* is not the peace of the *world*. And the ways of the *world* are not the ways of the kingdom of *God*. And you and I are called to live *now* in the promised kingdom that is yet to *be*, and to live daily in the peace of *Christ* that has little to do with *speeches* and *strategies* but with a *person*, bathed in his life and death and resurrection through the waters of baptism, nourished by the fullness of his incarnation in the bread and wine of the eucharist, bound as *one* through the Holy Spirit's bringing to memory his life given for all in his servanthood, in his sacrifice, in his constant hopeful prayer for us even now, that we may abide together in the gift of his peace.

Week of Prayer for Christian Unity
Spanish Springs Presbyterian Church, Sparks, Nevada
January 22, 2010

Isaiah 61:1–4
Acts 10:34–48a
Luke 24:44–49a

"To What Do We Witness?"

As some of you know, I was an attorney before I attended seminary and was ordained to the ministry of word and sacrament. In fact, I am *still* an attorney, at least as far as the Supreme Court of the State of Colorado is concerned, although my practice has been quite limited since going into the ministry. So I still pay my annual attorney registration fee, I still pay my Colorado Bar Association dues, I still take at least forty-five hours of continuing legal education every three years, and presbyteries still nominate and elect me to committees that they think are a logical fit for someone with a legal background.

Naturally, after three years of law school and thirty-some years of listening and reading and observing out of a legal mindset, I have noticed that the Bible often draws on legal concepts and uses legal terms and interprets God's will and activity in legal analogy. So, parts of Job and the prophets pose the words spoken *to* God or the words spoken *by* God as arguments in a courtroom. Paul writes about "justification" and being "justified," borrowing from the legal lexicon to explain the redemptive power of faith in Jesus' crucifixion. And the Gospel quotation that gives us the theme for this year's Week of Prayer for Christian Unity is but one of many places where the Bible employs the word "witness" or "witnesses"—a very direct use of a legal term that you don't have to be a lawyer to recognize the meaning of. The actual word in the original Greek New Testament is "martyr"—our mind may take us back to the memory of some cop show on television where an important witness in a trial is killed to prevent the truth from being spoken, or as revenge after testimony has been given or someone has served time in prison. So, the term "witness" includes the suggestion that there may well be a cost, a risk, or at least an inconvenience involved in testifying truthfully to what one has seen and heard.

The earliest followers of Christ soon experienced the full range of inconvenience, risk, and cost involved. Some of them, beginning with Stephen, were killed for their testimony to Christ; that is the sort of consequence of being a witness to the truth of God that gave the word "martyr" its common meaning. Many of the earliest followers of Christ discovered that their livelihood was incompatible with being a Christian, and had to give up their occupations, either voluntarily or not. Old friendships were disrupted, unbelieving family members became critical, tension arose with spouses who grew jealous of time spent with new Christian friends and money donated to Christian causes. But the nature of the gospel left the early Christians with no choice—to know about the life, death, and resurrection of Jesus but not to tell anyone else, not undergo a transformation of habit and outlook, was inconceivable. "You are witnesses of these things" (Luke 24:48), the risen Lord Jesus proclaimed before leading the disciples out to Bethany, where they saw him carried up into heaven.

In its simplest use, the word "witness," as a verb, can refer to *observing* something, or, as a noun, it can refer to anyone who *has* observed something. In *that* meaning of the word, I am a witness of a countless number of things every day. But in the more technical legal sense, I am a witness only if I disclose what I have seen or heard when I am under oath in a setting in which an important decision is going to be made that affects people's lives and relationships and destiny. Had Jesus, when he said, "You are witnesses of these things" (24:48), meant the word only in its *simplest* sense, not one of us sitting here this evening would ever have heard of Jesus Christ. If the people who heard Jesus teach and watched Jesus heal and had their sins forgiven by him not *shared* with *others* what they had seen and heard and experienced, there would *be* no Christians and there would *be* no Christian church. The knowledge of Jesus Christ would have *died* with the first generation who had seen with their own eyes and heard with their own ears. Just so, the story of God's dealing with God's people would have died long before the time of *Jesus* had it not been for the Old Testament scriptures that evidence the testimony given by witnesses throughout the history of Israel, and the habits of worship and festival that served as a continuing testimony to God's grace and God's intention for Israel, that by being a witness to God, *all* peoples would be blessed. Now, Jesus "opened their minds to understand the scriptures, and he said to them, 'Thus it is written, that the Messiah is to suffer and to rise from the dead on the third day, and that repentance and forgiveness of sins is to be proclaimed in his name to all nations'" (24:45–47). The blessings of God were *still* for *all* people. And the *witnesses* still needed to *give* witness, not keep the knowledge of God's faithfulness in the life, death, and resurrection of Jesus to themselves. Soon, they would be given the power to do so—and, of course, the book of Acts tells not only about the coming of the Holy Spirit upon the followers of Christ, but about the *results* of their *witness*—a story that *continues*, or *should* continue, among the followers of Christ today, empowered by the Holy Spirit to be witnesses.

Somehow, in some places and among some people, there has been a tendency to treat the idea of being a witness to the life, death, and resurrection of Jesus in that *non*-legal sense of the word—of simply being an *observer* and not being a *reporter*, taking the attitude that the gospel is *private*, even *privileged* information that, once an individual has it, is a personal possession, or, at best, something to which his or her specific little group *alone* is entitled; if God wants others to know about it, God will have to drop it in their lap.

But how far that is from the meaning of Jesus' words in Luke's Gospel! "Repentance and forgiveness of sins is to be proclaimed in [the Messiah's] name to all nations" (24:47), Jesus instructed. "You are witnesses of these things" (24:48). There was to be no limit to the audience to whom the followers of Christ were to bear witness. And that surely meant that the witness itself must be unified; there must be no barriers or divisions or slander among the witnesses that would cause doubt or confusion or suggest unreliability or falsehood of the words and deeds of Jesus—the crucifixion and the resurrection, and the obedient life of humble and faithful servanthood upon which God's miracle at the tomb was the guarantee of God's approval of all that Jesus said and did that he was *indeed* God's beloved Son, in whom he was well pleased. It was just to *start* in Jerusalem, not to *end* there—the witness first came to those near to home, but it was not to be confined to them. And if the witness was for *all* nations, *all* peoples, *equally* and without *distinction*, then *all* nations, *all* peoples, *equally* and without *distinction*, were in fact included in the promises of God of which Jesus' resurrection was the assurance. The instruction that Jesus gave his followers to be witnesses in that active, reporting sense was no *less* a command than anything *else* he told his followers, and each of them, to do. The breadth of audience they were to reach—the number of jurors to whom they were to present their testimony, so to speak—was to be without limit. And if no one was to be left out—if no one was undeserving of the good news of Jesus Christ,—then all who responded were to be welcomed into Christ's church and included without distinction and without qualification—not of race, not of class, not of language, not of gender. And if *Christ* could not tolerate the thought that anyone should be excluded from his church on such grounds as those, how could the *church* allow *itself* to be balkanized into exclusive camps at war with each other over creeds and formulas, or who is entitled to partake of the bread and the cup that represent Christ's body and blood broken and shed for *all*?

To what do Christ's followers witness when they *dogmatize*, when they *exclude*, when, having issued the invitation inherent in the proclamation of Christ's death and resurrection, they compass the sanctuary with signs that read "Keep Out"? Luke reports that Jesus did not simply say, "Go and give witness." He said, "You are witnesses of these things" (24:48)—of the death and resurrection of the one who befriended, who embraced, who welcomed, who fed, who healed, who forgave. Their own *lives* were to be an accurate and convincing witness, and their own life *together*. Their very relationship with each other was to testify to what Jesus had said and done, to everything that Jesus was about and *continued* to be, for they were *not* just describing something that they had *once* seen or heard, but were demonstrating what they knew to be an *ongoing* truth and one that was becoming more thorough and amazing day by day as they experienced life together in him by the power of the Spirit that had come upon them when they were gathered waiting for the gift that he had promised. *They* were the story every bit as much as the events of Good Friday and Easter morning. The miracles happening among *them* were every bit as wondrous as what they told of Jesus healing lepers and restoring sight to the blind. The kingdom of God was approaching near by way of *their* sharing of possessions and acceptance of outcasts as much as through *Jesus'* call to repentance and proclamation of forgiveness. And Christ was as present and at work in the world through *their* words and deeds as if they had come from *his* lips and been worked by *his* hands. Not only had they seen and heard—now *they* spoke and showed forth.

There is something tragic about the fact that we even have to *have* a Week of Prayer for Christian Unity, that we even have to *have* ecumenical organizations and interchurch agencies, that it feels like something *groundbreaking* has been accomplished when Orthodox sit down with Roman Catholics, when Lutherans negotiate accords with Presbyterians and United Methodists, when *this* group of believers agrees not to anathematize *that* group of believers, when worshipers in *this* Christian tradition finally decide that they can eat at the same table as worshipers in *that* Christian tradition. It shouldn't be *news*. It should be *habit*. Denominationalism is an anomaly from Christ's vision. It should never be accepted as the norm of

Christian reality. How can any witness of the things of Jesus Christ consider the divisiveness of exclusivity of Christ's followers to be a *virtue*? Surely anything that corrupts the integrity of the testimony is a sin. "You are witnesses of these things" (24:48). Think about those words. What is it that we have witnessed in the teachings and actions of the Lord Jesus Christ? Is it to the teachings and actions of the Lord Jesus Christ that we are *giving* witness? Was Jesus about *erecting* walls between people, and between people and God? Or was Jesus about *demolishing* walls between people, and between people and God? Was a curtain *hung* in the temple when Jesus died, or was it *ripped in two*? Did his resurrection demonstrate God's *rejection* of those who had been considered beyond salvation, or did it guarantee the *opposite*? Did the gift of the Spirit ensure that the good news would travel *no farther*, or was it just the beginning of a travelogue of faithfulness that continues to this very day? If we are faithful in our witness, and if our witness is a genuine response to the obedience and love and mercy of Christ, the number of witnesses will grow, and the people to whom we declare the cross and the empty tomb will be numbered among the very people to whom Jesus once said, "You are witnesses of these things," because *they* will have seen and heard the truth of the crucified and risen Christ in what *you* and *I* do and say.

Fifth Sunday in Ordinary Time

Spanish Springs Presbyterian Church, Sparks, Nevada

February 4, 2001

Isaiah 6:1–8
1 Corinthians 15:1–11
Luke 5:1–11

"Salvation Doesn't End with Me"

Powerful fault lines are shaking and dividing the Christian church and our own Presbyterian denomination today. Some of them are at least as old as Christianity itself. The theological picture within the Presbyterian Church (U.S.A.) and other mainline churches is complicated by the admixture of *variant* traditions that have found their way into our faith family. After all, we are proud of our democratic tendencies and our well-meaning insistence on not only *tolerance* of, but, in fact, intentional *inclusion* of different voices and viewpoints, though some of those voices and viewpoints themselves are not at all tolerant. A few of these voices and viewpoints are novel, but many of them have been around for a long, long time.

At least one issue facing us is so fundamental and persistent that it impacts the church's proclamation and mission, teaching and program, in every age and in every land—the question, "What is salvation?" Is it a reward of holiness to be safeguarded, or a call to reach out and transform what is unholy? One theological stream has conditioned us to think of that question in individualistic or personal terms. In fact, the follow-up question that Jesus' own listeners commonly asked was, "What must I do to be saved?" Medieval paintings and plays graphically depicted salvation in terms of escaping the unquenchable flames. The emphasis of this way of thinking is on my own benefit, my own welfare, my own avoidance of an eternity of punishment. The bumper stickers read, "Jesus and me for all eternity"—suggesting, by implication, to hell with everyone else.

But throughout the Old Testament, and in the New Testament Gospels and the book of Acts, and, I would argue, in the epistles as well, salvation is never *just* or even *primarily* a matter of *individual* benefit or welfare. The Bible indicates that salvation is such a very important matter because it affects *more* than just the individual. It involves God's purpose for the *whole* creation. It's *not* just "Jesus and me." And that is why *biblically* based evangelism is never just a matter of the soul of the *individual* believer. Preaching and hymnody that suggests otherwise, frankly, is not faithful to the gospel of Jesus Christ.

I've mentioned before that the word "you" in the Hebrew and Greek scriptures seldom appears in the singular. Unless it is addressed to a specific person identified in the biblical text, the word "you" is almost always plural. The good news of the gospel, the commandments of God, the promises and the commissions are for the whole community *as* the whole community. And, by the way, that is one reason to be very cautious about drawing lines between ourselves and others concerning exactly who is "saved" and who isn't, or who is *going* to be "saved" and who isn't. Before *God*, *individuals* stand as representatives of *communities*. The authors of the Bible were well aware that we all live within a society that has an intricate network of connections and mutualities. To some degree, we are *all* responsible whenever anything that *shouldn't* happen within a community *does*, and we are *all* responsible whenever anything *doesn't* happen within a community that *should*. While no one should shirk his or her *individual* responsibility, *none* of us can shirk our *mutual* responsibility. As the prophet Isaiah confessed in this morning's Old Testament reading, we are not only *individuals* of unclean lips, but we live in the midst of a *people* of unclean lips.

And if that was true in ancient times, when everyone in a village might be related to each other, it is still true in our modern world, which is growing more interdependent daily. Whether it is a matter of benefiting from cheap shoes and clothing made in Southeast Asia by children forced to work long hours for little money, or benefiting from reduced federal income taxes because of United States weapons sales to warring countries, or benefiting from not having to pay Nevada income tax because of state revenues from legalized gambling, or benefiting from driving on Storey County roads that have been paid for by sales tax revenues from legalized prostitution, to name a few of the more notorious cases, *none* of us in a modern society is *unaffected* by the conduct of *any* of us.

But, of course, the question of who is or isn't saved is secondary to the question of what salvation *is*, and why God offers us salvation in the

Fifth Sunday in Ordinary Time—"Salvation Doesn't End with Me" 207

first place. Everyone who is a member of Spanish Springs Presbyterian Church has completed a new member class in which, among other things, we looked at our Old Testament reading for this morning, Isaiah chapter 6, verses 1–8. This passage is the pattern for our order of worship, which is the order of worship that every Presbyterian church is urged to follow, unless there are compelling circumstances that require doing otherwise. Isaiah the prophet was in the temple for the new year's festival of enthroning the king of Judah on the autumnal equinox, the first day of Tishri, the first month of the year according to Israel's civil calendar, corresponding to our September 21 or 22. It was harvesttime, a season for taking stock of God's goodness toward God's people—giving thanks to the *eternal* king, who is above all *earthly* kings. And there, as he was overcome by a sense of the presence of God in the temple, suggested powerfully by the translucence and odors of the clouds of incense and billows of smoke rising from the altar and the singing back and forth of the choirs and the carefully choreographed ceremonies of the priests, Isaiah was overcome *also* with a profound sense of his utter sinfulness. There, amidst all the reminders of the supreme holiness of God, his guilt came home to him in a moment of keen self-awareness. "Woe is me!" he cried. "I am lost, for I am a man of unclean lips, and I live among a people of unclean lips; yet my eyes have seen the King, the LORD of hosts!" (Isa 6:5) And immediately, it seems, his sinful lips were cauterized by a seraph—a heavenly being whose job it was to announce and to shield God's holiness—with a live coal from the altar—sharing the *cleansing effect* of the altar, so to speak—and the seraph announced that Isaiah was free from guilt and his sin was blotted out. No sooner was Isaiah forgiven of his sin than he heard the voice of the Lord saying, "Whom shall I send, and who will go for us?" (6:8b) And Isaiah said, "Here am I; send me!" (6:8c). And at that moment, God gave Isaiah a job to do—to go and deliver God's message to the people of Judah, the people of unclean lips among whom Isaiah lived.

Not all of us are called to be prophets, of course. But over and over again in the Bible, God's salvation is related to, and has the effect of, directing people *into* community and for the *benefit of* community. In fact, they stand before God on *behalf* of the community, on behalf of *others*, whether it is a Noah or a Jacob or a Moses, or a Peter or a John or a Paul. Salvation always involves restoration of relationships, repairing the ties of responsible community, not only with God, but with other human beings and the natural order as well. Whenever Jesus healed some individual of illness or blindness or lameness, or exorcised some individual of demons, or forgave some individual's sin, the effect was to restore the person's social relationships. They had been outcast from the community, they had been estranged from their family, they had been reckoned untouchable by society, and Jesus' cure or release or pardon was not only their ticket to eternal life with *God*, but their ticket back into the daily life of the *community* as well.

When Isaiah was purified by the merciful act of the seraph, it had the immediate effect of allowing Isaiah to hear God's call to go and serve others and to respond to that call. Isaiah's cleansing contact with the holy gave him the capacity to hear God's voice and to respond without calculation or reservation. Only someone who has recognized her or his own sin and has been set *free* from it can *knowingly* do the will of God, which is to *obey* God by serving *others* with genuine love and real sacrifice. Salvation is not a reservation at the Heavenly Hilton. Salvation is readiness to serve as God commands. Salvation is not a certificate of sinlessness. Salvation is being so grateful for God's merciful love in one's *own* life that we eagerly place everything we are and everything we have at God's disposal for the spiritual and *physical* redemption of humankind and all creation. Salvation doesn't *end* with "me"; God's forgiveness of me at the cost of his Son on the cross is the necessary but preliminary *first* step in dedicating my life to God by wholehearted and single-minded service to *others* in the name of Jesus Christ.

Simon Peter must have been a rough-and-tumble sort of fellow, living day to day, not concerned with much more than his fishing business and his family—a "me and mine" kind of guy who never thought much about other people's needs and welfare. Capernaum, after all, wasn't a very large place, and he had probably in all of his life not been farther than he could see from his front door. What he didn't *know* about, he didn't *care* about. What he didn't *care* about, he didn't *think* about. He was vaguely aware that he was a sinner; after all, everybody is. But he didn't brood over things that he couldn't seem to help. He probably attended the synagogue occasionally, kept the major feasts and festivals, especially the parts with food and wine. And then Jesus came to town—a teacher and a healer who spoke in the synagogue on the sabbath and impressed people with his authority, and even cured a man who was possessed by a demon, and then, more miraculous yet, cured Simon's own mother-in-law of her fever. He stayed around town, and people kept talking about him.

One day, as Simon and his partners were washing their nets after a disappointing night on the lake, Jesus came along the shore and got into Simon's boat and asked Simon to push it out a little way into the lake, which, though he was tired, Simon did. No harm, he thought. Jesus sat in the boat and preached to the crowd that had formed on the shore. And then, when he had finished, he asked Simon to take him fishing, way out in the deepest part of the lake. Simon must have been a little irritated at that request—it would almost have been amusing had he not been so tired from his long and frustrating night. "Master, we have worked all night long but have caught nothing" (Luke 5:5a). No sign that this changed Jesus' mind in the slightest. "Yet if you say so, I will let down the nets" (5:5b), Simon said, undoubtedly with a heavy sigh. And, so, they loaded the nets again and went back out onto the lake, and they caught so many fish that the nets were strained to the breaking point. The fishermen in the other boat rowed over to help; they hauled so many fish on board that both boats were in danger of sinking. And when Simon Peter saw what was happening—the miracle of fish by the ton that hadn't been there just a few hours before,—he recognized, as Isaiah had recognized in the temple many centuries before, that he was in the presence of the holy, and his sinfulness all came home to him. He fell down at Jesus' knees and begged him, "Go away from me, Lord, for I am a sinful man!" (5:8b). And in that moment of desperate confession and saving forgiveness, Jesus did not *condemn* Simon, but gave him a *job* for which he was *now ready*: "Do not be afraid," Jesus told him; "from now on you will be catching people" (5:10b). And when they had brought their boats to shore, Simon and his companions "left everything and followed him" (5:11b).

Saved *from sin*, Simon was saved *for discipleship*—speaking and doing the good news of Jesus Christ for the benefit of others. His sin was overcome by Jesus' call to discipleship and his own immediate response. His spontaneous willingness to serve others according to the direction of God in Jesus Christ brought him into the living, breathing, obedient relationship to God that he had not had before, had not even thought about. Simon discovered that salvation involves fulfilling God's will to reach out to all people—the people whom Jesus would direct him to "catch" in the tender web of God's merciful love.

Salvation is not an achievement. It is a commission. Salvation is not a private or an individual matter. We are saved for the sake of the physical and spiritual welfare of all humankind, indeed, all creation. And, so, true evangelism must always lead to social witness; living to Christ will always cause us to live with and for others; acknowledging our salvation must always mean bearing and confessing the sins of the society around us; being grateful to *God* for God's *mercy* will always mean showing love toward all people, because salvation doesn't end with "me."

List of Sources Cited

The Book of Common Prayer. New York: Church Hymnal Corporation, 1979.

Book of Common Worship. Louisville: Westminster John Knox, 1993.

The Constitution of the Presbyterian Church (U.S.A.). Part 1: "Book of Confessions." Louisville: Office of the General Assembly, 1999.

Coxe, Arthur Cleveland. "O Where Are Kings and Empires Now." In *The Hymnbook*, no. 431. Richmond: Presbyterian Church in the United States, 1955.

Dillard, Annie. *Teaching a Stone to Talk.* New York: Harper Perennial, 2008.

Ellerton, John. "The Day Thou Gavest, Lord, Is Ended." In *The Presbyterian Hymnal: Hymns, Psalms, and Spiritual Songs*, no. 546. Louisville: Westminster/John Knox, 1990.

Evans. Craig A. "Crucifixion." In *The New Interpreter's Dictionary of the Bible*, edited by Katharine Doob Sakenfeld, 1:806–7. Nashville: Abingdon, 2006.

Gealy, Fred D., Austin C. Lovelace, and Carlton R. Young. *Companion to the Hymnal.* Nashville: Abingdon, 1979.

Hays, Richard B. *First Corinthians.* Interpretation: A Bible Commentary for Teaching and Preaching. Louisville: John Knox, 1997.

Johnson, Luke Timothy. *The Gospel of Luke.* Sacra pagina 3. Collegeville, MN: Liturgical, 1991.

Sampley, J. Paul. "The First Letter of Paul to the Corinthians." In *The New Interpreter's Bible*, edited by Leander E. Keck, 10:773–1003. Nashville: Abingdon, 2002.

Schweizer, Eduard. *The Good News According to Luke.* Translated by David E. Green. Atlanta: John Knox, 1984.

Sterne, Colin (anagram for H. Ernest Nichol). "We've a Story to Tell to the Nations." In *The Hymnbook*, no. 504. Richmond: Presbyterian Church in the United States, 1955.

Wedel, Theodore O. "The Epistle to the Ephesians." In *The Interpreter's Bible*, edited by Nolan B. Harmon, 10:597–749. Nashville: Abingdon, 1953.

www.ingramcontent.com/pod-product-compliance
Lightning Source LLC
Chambersburg PA
CBHW071436150426
43191CB00008B/1150